Psychology: A Christian Perspective.
High School Edition.

by Dr. Tim
(Timothy S. Rice, D. Min., LPC)

Psychology: A Christian Perspective. High School Edition.

Published by
Rocking R Ventures, Inc.
104 Goss Street
Epworth, GA 30541
www.rockingrventures.com
www.homeschoolpsych.com

ISBN: 978-0-9815587-2-1

Cover Photo © Tina Rice

Contents

Acknowledgements. All photos and illustrations are believed to be from the public domain or used by permission. Thank you Dawn Burnette, DJ Jensen, and Valerie A. Smith, MA for your editorial and content suggestions. Thank you Daniel for getting me coffee. Thank you Tina. Though many helped, you persevered. Thank you God.

Introduction

Whatever you think about psychology and its effect on Christian students, the time to deal with it is now.

Do you think the study of psychology is tantamount to declaring the Bible inadequate? Do you believe that God created psychology when He created Mankind in His own image? Have you ever given it much thought?

Some Christians think that psychology is an important discipline, that it is consistent with a Christian worldview, and that it is an acceptable field of study and career choice. Other Christians see psychology as an idolatrous and ungodly rival religion. Some Christians think that God created psychology when He created Mankind. Others describe psychology as psychobabble, psycho-heresy, and the most deadly form of modernism to ever confront the Church.

Whatever you think about psychology, the time to deal with it is now because many Christian students go to college to become psychologists, counselors, or social workers. Most colleges (including Christian colleges) require students to at least take an introductory psychology class. Although there are many Christian professors, psychology departments are home to some of the more anti-Christian intellectuals on college campuses. In fact, psychology professors tend to have high levels of agnosticism and atheism and may attack the Christian worldview as unscientific, irrational, prudish, exploitative, controlling, inhibitive, oppressive, and naïve. Many psychology professors also believe that Christianity is incompatible with sound mental health, that it contributes to human suffering, and that the intelligent believer will eventually abandon their faith.

The material taught in any introductory psychology course will challenge a student's beliefs. Christian students are not usually well-prepared to recognize and refute modern psychology's core philosophical assumptions: naturalism, behaviorism, humanism, evolutionism, empiricism, moral relativism, and reductionism. Those core assumptions are embedded, sometimes very subtly, in modern psychology's theories and schools of thought, and they are presented under the banner of "science." Assumptions that are wholly inconsistent with a Christian worldview are thoroughly embedded in most psychology courses, even at some Christian colleges. Students need to recognize and be able to refute the anti-Christian and anti-scientific philosophies embedded in modern psychology. Failure to recognize those assumptions may lead Christian students to inadvertently compromise their Christian worldview.

If it is true that many Christian students walk away from their faith after the first year of college, and if that has anything to do with the teaching in college, it may be, at least in part, because of the subtle worldview challenges embedded in psychological theories. By simply forewarning and preparing students in advance, they are better able to resist believing false assumptions.

The time to deal with psychology is now because Darwinian evolution is the "new" psychology. Freudian psychology, behaviorists, humanists, and cognitive psychology are considered by many yesterday's news. Today, neuro-biology and evolution are psychology's main theories. Darwin anticipated evolution's impact on psychology in 1859 when he wrote:

> "In the distant future I see open fields for far more important research. Psychology will be based on a new foundation, that of the necessary acquirement of each mental power and capacity by gradation. Light will be thrown on the origin of man and his history (Darwin, 1859)."

According to Darwin, all mental activity, even what we think of as our God-likeness, is ultimately nothing more than a "capacity" that humans acquired, bit by bit, through variation and natural selection. Darwinian evolution, when applied to human psychology, reduces our consciousness, our morality, our capacity to make decisions and judgments, religious experience, love, empathy, altruism, hate, greed, dreams, and everything else that makes us human to nothing more than a bunch of neurons doing their thing.

Psychology, more so than biology, is where the theory of evolution has the most difficulty. There are no cogent evolutionary explanations for our "higher" capacities, our God-likeness. It is the author's opinion that evolution's death knell will not come from cellular biology, it will come from psychology. The fight against evolution is not likely to be won with arguments of sub-cellular irreducible complexity. It is winnable in the arena of the incomprehensible complexity of the human mind.

It is also important to deal with psychology because people are hurting. Christians have long been at the forefront of meeting the world's physical needs with food, blankets, and shelter. But are we at the forefront of meeting the world's psychological needs? Too often secular community mental health centers serve more hurting people than they can handle, while Christians debate whether nouthetic or Christian counseling or "just praying harder" is the answer. That is not right. Correcting the problem begins by re-claiming psychology for Christ.

The goal for our study of psychology, just like the study of biology, theology, history, and every other discipline, is to understand God's creation and, in the words of Johannes Kepler, to "think God's thoughts after him." Instead of surrendering psychology or falling away in the face of the world's beliefs and teaching, we have a duty to put forth reasoned explanations for our worldview in every discipline, including psychology.

That is the goal for *Psychology: A Christian Perspective*. There are many excellent works that explain a Christian worldview, and there are dozens of excellent introductory psychology texts. But there are very few introductory psychology texts that present psychology's content from a Christian perspective and none, to the author's knowledge, intended for Christian high school students.

I believe that the study of the soul, the mind, and behavior are right and proper for Christians and that Christian students should bring their worldview and become part of the future intellectual leadership in Christian psychology.

Let's get started!

Chapter 1

What is Psychology?

In This Chapter
- The Psyche
- What is Psychology?
- Psychology's Influence
- A Christian Approach to Psychology
- Psychology's Goals
- Psychology's Fields of Study
- Psychology's Approaches

Beware lest any man spoil you through philosophy and vain deceit, after the tradition of men, after the rudiments of the world, and not after Christ (Colossians 2:8).

Jesus said unto him, Thou shalt love the Lord thy God with all thy heart, and with all thy soul, and with all thy mind (Matthew 22:37).

What does it mean to have dominion over God's creation? What does it mean to love the Lord your God with all your heart? What does it mean to love the Lord with all your mind? What was Jesus talking about when He spoke of your heart? What is the nature of your heart? What is the nature of your "mind?" Does loving the Lord with your mind include a duty to humbly investigate God's creation? Does the duty to humbly investigate God's creation extend to His grandest creation: Mankind? Does that duty extend to Mankind's mind? If so, one could argue that Christians have a duty to study psychology. If Christ is Lord of all, He is Lord of theology, education, biology, and psychology.

Your college psychology text book will not be called *Psychology: The Study of the Brain, Behavior, Heart, Soul, and Mind.*

What does the word psychology mean to you? What do you think psychologists study? Many people think that psychology means mind control and manipulation. Some think psychology is synonymous with psychiatry or psychotherapy. The word psychology, in much the same way as the words religion, philosophy, and politics, has different (and sometimes contradictory) meanings to different people.

The word psychology means different things to Christians, too. Psychology is one of the most controversial and divisive academic subjects among Christians today. Many Christians see psychology as a harmless academic discipline, not at all inconsistent with a Christian worldview. To them, psychology has a place alongside biology, chemistry, and physics in high school studies. However, many Christians have serious objections to psychology and claim that psychology is a dangerous, idolatrous, and ungodly rival religion, and that the study of psychology is tantamount to declaring the Bible inadequate.

The Psyche. Psychology is the study of the "psyche." In the Greek language the word "psyche" meant "soul" and "mind." Psyche is the common root of the words "spirit" and "soul." The concepts of the soul and mind are absent from most modern definitions of psychology. As we will see in the next chapter, modern psychology's naturalistic worldview does not allow for the existence of a soul or a mind (in any meaningful sense), much less their scientific study. A Christian worldview not only recognizes the existence of the soul and mind; it welcomes the application of scientific methods to their study.

> ***What is Psychology?*** Over time psychology has been defined differently.
>
> - The scientific study of human affect, behaviors, and cognitions.
> - The scientific study of human life and human nature.
> - The science of the brain and behavior.
> - The scientific study of the human heart and mind.
> - A body of knowledge for understanding, measuring, assessing, and possibly changing people's emotions, thoughts, perceptions, and behaviors.
> - The emotional and behavioral characteristics of an individual or group.
> - Actions or arguments used to manipulate or influence others.
> - A branch of philosophy that studies the soul, the mind, and the relationship of the soul and mind to the functions of the body.
> - A system for describing human personality.
> - A system for describing emotional and behavioral disorders and strategies for their treatment.

A Christian approach to psychology recognizes that Mankind is uniquely created in the image of God. By studying God's natural revelation, guided by special revelation, we can seek understanding of how we are both like the animals and how we are unique in our God-likeness.

Most introductory psychology texts define psychology as the scientific study of the brain and behavior. *The American Heritage Dictionary* defines psychology as "the science that deals with mental processes and behavior" and "the branch of philosophy that studies the soul, the mind, and the relationship of the mind to the functions of the body." For our purposes, psychology is ***the scientific study of the ABCs – affect (emotions), behavior, and cognition (mental processes)***. As such, psychology and the Bible bring different perspectives and levels of understanding to some of the same subject matter. Of all the sciences, psychology comes closest to the issues the Bible addresses. Psychology and the Bible both deal with human nature, the human condition, and even human salvation. And of all the sciences, psychology has had the greatest influence in the culture, academia, and the church.

Psychology in the Culture. Modern society is fascinated with all things psychological. Each year Americans buy millions of books about self-help, addiction, recovery, relationships, parenting, spiritual growth, and emotional and mental health. ***Popular psychology***, promoted by seminar speakers, columnists, and celebrities, suggests techniques (that may or may not be scientifically tested) designed to improve psychological health and well-being (and maybe get rich too!). Millions of Americans seek mental health services every year. Psychology influences business, advertising, social work, nursing, engineering, and any other career path you might pursue.

Psychology in Academia. Nowhere is the extent of psychology's influence more evident than in academia. Most medical schools, liberal arts colleges, seminaries, and teachers' colleges require students to have some exposure to psychology. Psychology is one of the most popular undergraduate majors, even at Christian colleges and universities. Enrollment in psychology courses outpaces other scientific disciplines, and many high schools now offer an introductory psychology course.

Psychology's Extent. The extent of psychology's influence in the culture, academia, and the church is remarkable for its "young" age. Psychology's influence is a compelling reason for Christian students to study and understand modern psychology.

Psychology in the Church. The extent of psychology is not limited to the culture and academia. The influence of psychological theories about learning and child development, parenting practices, moral development, personality and self-esteem, problems of living and more is widespread in the Christian church. Psychological insights influence sermons across the country, and some pastors leave the pulpit for jobs in pastoral counseling or social work. Self-help books about recovery, addiction, relationships, parenting, and weight loss make up the bulk of the new Christian book titles. Sometimes these books are based on psychological theories that are fundamentally inconsistent with a Christian worldview. You need to recognize when worldview assumptions are "Christianized" by sprinkling in a few Bible verses and mentioning Jesus. You must evaluate psychology at the worldview level (even when it is wrapped in Christian language) or you risk accepting ideas that are foundationally inconsistent with your Christian worldview.

A Christian Approach to Psychology. It is essential that Christians studying psychology respect the inspiration and authority of the Bible. We must maintain a commitment to the authority and inspiration of the Bible and not underestimate the corrupting, distorting, and destructive influence of sin on human thinking. We need to remember that God is Truth and that ultimately there will be no conflict between true psychology and a Christian worldview. Christians studying and working in psychology must be faithful to Scripture, not compromise their Christian worldview assumptions, and must understand modern psychology's historical roots, philosophical assumptions, and empirical methods.

Our study of psychology must be more than a curiosity to discover something new and interesting about people. Christians studying and working in psychology must increase the body of evidence that supports a Christian worldview and effectively communicate that it is logical, internally consistent, and meaningful. We must see a spiritual purpose to our study. When a non-Christian recognizes that he has accepted as truth (by faith) psychology's philosophical assumptions, he may be closer to accepting God's Truth (by a saving faith). Christians studying psychology have, among their classmates and professors, a ripe mission field indeed.

We should humbly answer those who attack Christianity on psychological grounds with a sound apologia. We must provide a solid defense for our own assumptions. We cannot arrogantly claim that we have all the answers or that we can "prove" our positions. We must be willing to hold contradictory beliefs until better data or clearer revelation reveals that there is no genuine contradiction.

> Do not study psychology without the full armor of God: the belt of truth, breastplate of righteousness in place, feet fitted with readiness, the shield of faith, the helmet of salvation, and the sword of the Spirit, which is the word of God (Ephesians 6:10-18).

We must remember that all learning is, at least in part, the work of the Holy Spirit and that only the Holy Spirit can reveal God's ultimate Truth. As the Holy Spirit guides us, we become more Christ-like, which in turn, affects our scholarship. We must resist theological hubris by claiming that our theological beliefs are superior to, or automatically "truer," than psychological findings. To do so makes a mockery of the unifying nature of God's full revelation. Christians studying and working in psychology can also help reduce the Church's misunderstanding and fear of psychology and help remove the stigma of seeking help for emotional problems. Christians studying psychology must have excellent preparation in theology, biblical interpretation, and the principles of Christian discipleship. You must understand the rich history of Christian psychology stretching from the early Church. Though most Christians who study psychology understand that the Bible ought to influence their scholarship, too many Christians know far more about psychology than they do about their own religious traditions.

Christians in psychology must prevent modern psychology's worldview assumptions from corrupting their view of the nature of God, Mankind, knowledge, right and wrong, and the causes and cures for abnormal thoughts, feelings, and behavior, while lovingly correcting those already corrupted. We must wrestle with freedom vs. determinism vs. responsibility vs. heredity vs. environment and the concept of the self. We must produce rigorous scholarship and research to develop a body of authentically Christian psychological data. We need not bracket our faith to study psychology and we need not defend Christ from research. We can then apply psychology's methods to topics dear to Christian ministry. For example:

- What variables account for the failures and successes of Christian ministries?
- What factors contribute to the large percentage of dropouts among second generation Christians?
- Can research support the beneficial effects of prayer and meditation?
- Can research into the nature and causes of anger help fathers and mothers avoid provoking their children?
- Can psychology devise tests for assessing spiritual maturity for leadership positions in the church?
- Can psychology devise tests that help determine if missionaries are prepared for the struggles of foreign missions?
- What is the optimal size for small group Bible studies?
- What is the most effective treatment for cultic brainwashing?
- What is the relationship of the spiritual disciplines to physical health?
- What styles of parenting are most likely to produce Christian character traits in children?

- How can we improve training for Christian workers?
- Can Christians in psychology contribute to our understanding of terrorism, gang violence, holocausts and genocide, drug abuse, post-traumatic stress, divorce, abortion, prejudice, and for dealing with abnormal thoughts, feelings, and behaviors? If so, how?

The list of useful research questions is endless, but in addition to exemplary scholarship, Christians in every field must strive to live exemplary lives. Our goal is to have the "mind" of Christ, so we must reclaim psychology for Christ. Many Christians believe that there is a "cultural commission," similar to the Great Commission that requires Christians to "reclaim" the culture, education, and by extension, psychology. The Church risks marginalization if Christians ignore their responsibility to reclaim the whole culture (including psychology). The early Church showed God's way to be so much better, that even the pagans recognized it. Should we do any less with psychology? Christians who study psychology join others in physics, biology, history, the arts, sociology, and many other fields seeking a deeper understanding of all of God's creation.

Biology class can provide a good model for our approach to psychology. Modern biology teaches evolution as settled fact. When you take a biology class, you must deal with the evolutionary assumptions. Psychology professors increasingly teach evolutionary psychology as fact. As we study psychology, we must also distinguish fact from philosophy and assumptions at the worldview level.

The Bottom Line. Beginning with Charles Darwin's *Origin of Species*, all sciences, including psychology, underwent a transformation. Scientific data was interpreted in ways that excluded supernatural beliefs and assumptions. Psychology, once the study of the soul, became the study of the brain and behavior. Darwinian macro-evolution imposed itself on the Christian understanding of life (biology) and then tried to exclude anything Christian. Darwinian macro-evolution is now imposing itself on the Christian understanding of Man (psychology) and is trying to exclude anything Christian. But evolution, as a theory of the ultimate cause of all life, does not define biology. Likewise, neither evolution nor the atheism and humanism of many of its modern founders defines psychology.

No one can approach biology or psychology objectively. Our approach is subjective, subject to our worldview and to distortions of a fallen world on our understanding. But that does not mean that there is no objective psychology or biology. Though the evolutionary presuppositions of modern psychology are diametrically opposed to a Christian worldview, we need not fear or avoid the entire discipline because of them. We must, as we do with biology and every other academic discipline, recognize and refute evolutionary (and other anti-Christian) assumptions.

The humble investigation of all of God's creation is part of what it means to love God with one's mind. Christian students have a duty to explore all of God's creation, and that duty to explore extends to His grandest creation; you and your mind.

Psychology's Purpose. There are four main purposes for psychological research.

- Psychologists observe and describe psychological phenomena.
- Psychologists test theories and hypotheses explaining the phenomena.
- Psychologists attempt to identify the factors that influence our thoughts, feelings, and behaviors.
- Psychologists develop and implement techniques to predict and change thoughts, feelings, and behavior.

Psychology's Variety. In introductory "survey" classes like this one, students get an overview of psychology's topics. In advanced classes, students focus on a particular topic in more depth. Many psychologists, in their careers or research, focus on a particular topic or subfield. The American Psychological Association recognizes over 50 subfields, called divisions.

- ***Cognitive psychologists*** study the mental processes involved in sensation and perception, learning and memory, decision-making, and problem solving.
- ***Physiological psychologists*** (also called ***neuroscientists***) study the brain, how nerve cells communicate and transmit information, and the role of genetics in psychology.
- ***Personality psychologists*** study the unique characteristics of people. Some personality psychologists use tests to measure and compare people according to personality characteristics.
- ***Developmental psychologists*** study changes in behavior and mental processes across the life span.
- ***Counseling, clinical***, and ***community psychologists*** study the causes of mental and behavioral disorders and devise techniques to help people recover from those problems. Counseling psychologists differ from psychiatrists, who are medical doctors who specialize in treating people with mental disorders.
- ***Educational psychologists*** develop strategies to improve teaching and learning.
- ***School psychologists*** test and diagnose learning and academic problems and provide early intervention and crisis intervention services.
- ***Social psychologists*** study the way that people interact with other people and in groups.

As you will see in later chapters, there are five main approaches to psychology. The main approaches, also known as "schools" of psychology (also called schools of thought), make worldview assumptions about the nature of Mankind. In this book, we will look at each in detail.

- The ***biological school of thought*** views mental processes and behaviors in terms of biological structures and electro-chemical processes.
- The ***behavioral school of thought*** emphasizes the relationship between environmental influences and behavior.
- The ***cognitive school of thought*** emphasizes the influence of cognitive processes like perception, problem solving.
- The ***psycho-analytic school of thought*** emphasizes unconscious processes.
- The ***humanistic school of thought*** emphasizes innate goodness and potential and the influence of feelings and needs on thoughts and behaviors.

In Chapter 3 we will explore the history and characteristics of each of psychology's major schools of thought. In the remaining chapters, we will examine and explore each topic from the worldview perspective of the major schools and compare that perspective with a Christian worldview. In Chapter 2, we turn next to describing a Christian worldview.

Chapter Summary.

Psychology is one of the most controversial and divisive academic subjects among Christians today. Many Christians think that psychology is harmless and has a place alongside biology, chemistry, and physics in high school studies. Many Christians claim that psychology is a dangerous, idolatrous, and ungodly rival religion. If Christ is Lord of all, He is Lord of theology, education, biology, and psychology.

Psychology is the scientific study of human affect, behavior, and cognition. Its theories influence the culture, academia, and the Church. Christians studying and working in psychology must be faithful to Scripture, not compromise their Christian worldview assumptions, and must understand modern psychology's history, worldview assumptions, and methods.

Evolution, atheism, and humanism are common threads in psychology, but they do not define the discipline. Christians need not fear or avoid the entire discipline. We must, as we do with biology and other academic disciplines, recognize and respond to anti-Christian assumptions and claiming psychology for Christ.

The main purposes for psychological research include:

• Observing and describing psychological phenomena.
• Creating and testing hypotheses to explain the observations.
• Discovering the factors that influence mental processes.
• Developing techniques to predict, improve, or otherwise change behavior, thoughts, learning, and emotions.

When psychologists focus on a particular aspect of study or practice, they enter one of psychology's subfields.

• Cognitive psychologists study mental processes.
• Physiological psychologists (also called neuroscientists) study the brain and nervous system.
• Personality psychologists study the unique characteristics of people.
• Developmental psychologists study changes in behavior and mental processes across the life span.
• Counseling psychologists study the causes of and the cures for mental and behavioral disorders.
• Educational psychologists study teaching and learning.
• School psychologists test and diagnose learning and academic problems.
• Social psychologists study the ways people interact with other people and in groups.

There are five main approaches to psychology also known as "schools." Each makes worldview assumptions about the nature of Mankind.

• The biological approach emphasizes biological structures and electro-chemical processes.
• The behavioral approach emphasizes the relationship between environmental influences and behavior.
• The cognitive approach emphasizes thought processes.
• The psycho-analytic approach emphasizes unconscious processes.
• The humanistic approach emphasizes the belief in Mankind's innate goodness and potential.

For Review.

1. Define psychology in your own words.
2. Describe reasons that psychology is controversial among Christians today.
3. Explain and provide examples of psychology's influence in the culture and in the Christian Church.
4. Why does the author of this text say that "psychology is not a harmless academic discipline nor is it inherently anti-Christian?"
5. Describe the impact of Darwin's theory of evolution on the study of psychology.
6. Name and describe five of psychology subfields.
7. What advice does the text offer about a Christian approach to psychology?
8. The text named four things psychologists do. Identify and describe them.
9. The text named five main approaches to psychology. Identify and describe them.
10. Describe three helping careers Christians might pursue and the ways that psychology influences those careers.

Chapter 2

A Christian Worldview

In This Chapter

- What is a Worldview?
- What is a Christian Worldview?
- What Do You Believe About God?
- What is the Nature of Mankind?
- How Can We Know Things With Certainty?
- Are There Moral Absolutes?
- What Are the Causes of and Cures for Abnormal Thoughts, Feelings, and Behaviors?

Weltanschauung. Sigmund Freud, the father of psychiatry, defined weltanschauung as an intellectual construction which gives a unified solution of all the problems of our existence… a comprehensive hypothesis in which no question is left open and in which everything in which we are interested finds a place. Freud's own weltanschaunng was wholly inconsistent with a Christian weltanschauung.

This book is about psychology vis-à-vis a Christian worldview. It is about how psychology and your worldview relate. This chapter delves into some specifics about a Christian worldview.

When psychologists ask questions about the human mind, they are asking about an incomprehensibly complex system. Even simple mental processes involve the complex interactions of millions of neurons spread across the brain. The more complicated mental processes like "thoughts" or "feelings" involve complex interactions between the brain, the body, and the outside world. We think of thoughts and feelings as though they were distinct mental processes, but they are not. Our genetic makeup and the environment also influence our mental life. By necessity, introductory psychology texts describe complexity with broad strokes on only a few issues.

One's worldview is also a complex system. It is a system of core attitudes, beliefs, and values. This text does not claim to define "*the*" Christian worldview. It does, however, claim to describe "*a*" Christian worldview. By necessity, this text describes a narrow slice of "*the*" Christian worldview, hopefully in terms on which all Christians can agree.

Everyone has a worldview. Christians, Muslims, atheists, agnostics, and every other faith has a worldview. Each of us holds core foundational beliefs or convictions through which we perceive and understand the world. Those foundational beliefs define your worldview. A worldview is, as the word suggests, a way of looking at the world. Your worldview is the conceptual framework that you use to give meaning to the world. Your worldview is made of your core beliefs and your most fundamental assumptions about the world. You may not

Schema. Psychological theories define a "schema" as a mental structure used to organize and understand the world around us. You probably won't hear psychology professors use the word "worldview," but they will speak of schemas.

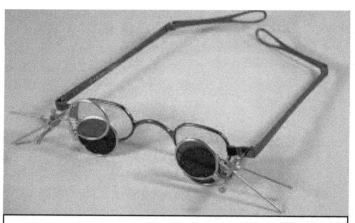

Multi-lensed glasses are a way to think about your worldview. Glasses however, are passive. Your worldview is an active and changeable part of you. You should actively think "Christianly" about psychology.

think about your worldview very often, but it includes your answers to the really big questions of life. All human intellectual activities, including scientific research and theories, happen in a worldview context and are guided by one's worldview. Ultimately, truth is only discernible from error at the worldview level. In second Corinthians, the Apostle Paul instructs us to submit every thought to the obedience of Christ. That means intentionally examining everything you learn in light of your worldview.

A Christian Worldview is a Biblical Worldview. The Christian worldview begins with the biblical account of God, creation, the fall, and redemption. The biblical account of where we came from, our nature, and how we should live is *"the"* Christian worldview. Your worldview includes your beliefs about dating, divorce, music, gifts of the Holy Spirit and other issues. Those are important issues, but our interest is in five questions where a Christian worldview and modern psychology's underlying assumptions definitely intersect.

1. What do you believe about God?
2. What is the nature of Mankind?
3. How can we know things with certainty?
4. Are there moral absolutes?
5. What are the causes of and the cures for abnormal thoughts, feelings, and behaviors?

1. What do you believe about God? God exists or He does not. Either He created you and the universe or not. The most basic piece of your worldview includes whether you believe God exists, what you believe about His nature, and the extent to which He influences your life. The Christian worldview is that there is one true triune God who is personal, loving, just, infinite, self-revealing, all-powerful, all-knowing, ever-present, self-existent, sovereign, eternal, and active in the world today.

2. What is the nature of Mankind? Your beliefs about the nature of Mankind are fundamental to your worldview and to your study of psychology.

And the Lord God formed man of the dust of the ground, and breathed into his nostrils the breath of life; and man became a living soul. (Genesis 2:7 KJV)

Are we the creation of a purposeful and relational God, or the product of evolutionary forces? Or both? Are we born "good?" Do we have a mind that is greater than the sum of our brain activity? Do we have a soul that survives the death of the body?

Your worldview of the nature of Mankind builds on your beliefs about God and the accuracy of the Bible. A Christian view of Mankind, or **biblical anthropology**, describes us as the purposeful creation of God, made in His image and likeness, and as sinners in rebellion against Him by nature and by choice. We were made from the dust of the earth and are part of the natural order. As such, we have much in common with the animals. We are born, we grow old, and our bodies eventually die. However, like God, we are spiritual beings. Unlike the animals, we have moral discernment, freedom to choose, and responsibility for our behavior. We experience guilt, grace, and love. We are relational beings. We have consciousness, a mind, and a soul.

Monism, Dualism, or Tripartite. Christians for centuries have debated whether we are one, two, or three-part beings. As we will see in Chapter 3, modern naturalistic psychology is united in its worldview. In that monistic worldview, all mental life is nothing more than complex brain activity. There is no mind or soul in any "supernatural" sense.

Christians believe that Mankind is material, made from the dust of the earth. We also believe that we are something more. The Bible is clear that there is something about us that makes us distinct from the animals. But what is the nature of our God-likeness?

God created us to be in a relationship with Him. **Dualism**, the traditional Christian belief, is that because God is spiritual (non-material), we must also have a non-material nature in order to have that relationship. Dualists believe that our brains and our minds are distinct in essence, but operate in interaction. Some Christians have a **trichotomous** worldview, which describes Mankind in terms of body, mind, and soul. A **Christian monist,** as opposed to a naturalistic monist, sees us as one in essence, as embodied souls in an irreducible unity of mind, body, and soul.

3. How can we know things with certainty? How do you know? How do you know that what you know is true? How do we know anything with certainty? *Epistemology* is the study of the nature, sources, and limits of knowledge. Is science the only valid path to knowledge? Is the scientific method the only way we can know anything with certainty? Is the Bible a valid source of psychological information? Is the Bible the only valid source of information about our nature?

> We are more than products of conditioning, unmet needs, chemical imbalances, and traumas. We are not autonomous, but we are more than the sum of our parts, and more than complex machines in closed cause-and-effect systems.

> When a prophet speaks in the name of the Lord, if the thing follow not, nor come to pass, that is the thing which the Lord hath not spoken (Deuteronomy 18:22). Christians studying psychology must be willing to put their worldview to empirical tests and be willing to view psychological science under the light of the Bible. God's Truth will survive experimental confirmation.

Is "all truth God's Truth?" Can naturalistic psychology contribute anything to a Christian understanding of the care for abnormal thoughts, feelings, and behaviors?

A Christian worldview is that Truth, objective and independent Truth, absolutely exists. According to a Christian worldview, God reveals Himself in His creation (nature), the Bible, and supremely in His Son. The Bible is accurate in all its teachings and the universe operates in accordance with orderly natural laws that we can study and understand. Because the world is orderly and predictable, the methods of science are an appropriate way to discover truths about the world. Mankind was given dominion over the earth, and dominion includes a duty to explore and understand creation.

Faith/Science Conflict? Many people believe that a Christian worldview and science are inherently in conflict. Many believe that the Bible has no place in science and that science is the Bible's enemy. In other words, they believe that there is a *faith/science dichotomy*. Some historians have made the case that the Church (especially the Catholic church) fought every new scientific idea. Though it is true that through history the Church disputed many major scientific discoveries, it is not correct that the Christian church is necessarily "anti-science." In fact, science (and by extension, psychology) was born of the Christian worldview.

A Christian worldview sees God as immutable, sees the world as orderly and rational, and believes that we can and should seek to understand creation. The historical Christian approach to science (though not without exception) was that faith and science were complementary. The fathers of modern science, many of whom were Christians, were not surprised to discover, on the basis of reason, truths about the universe. They saw science as one tool to explore creation, to discover how God operates in natural processes, and to understand what it means to be human. Descartes, Bacon, Newton, and Galileo explored God's creation and then  tested their ideas with scientific methods. Christians today should not be surprised or conflicted to discover truths through science and reason and should reject the idea that a Christian worldview and science are enemies.

Truth is not merely a personal preference. It is objective and absolute and can be diligently searched out.

Likewise, psychologists should not be surprised or conflicted that some questions are beyond the scope of their methods.

To dichotomize "science" from "faith" destroys true science and marginalizes true faith. This text presumes that true psychology and Christianity are complimentary.

Natural and Special Revelation. A Christian worldview believes that God reveals things to us in two ways: general or natural revelation and special revelation. *Natural revelation* refers to truths revealed through the world. We can learn truth by observing creation, by scientific experiments, by logic, and by the study of history (that is, any technique apart from reading the Bible or the working of the Holy Spirit). *Special revelation* refers to biblical details about God's character, His purpose, our nature, His plan for us, and our relationship with Him. Special revelation refers to God's works in history and the work of the Holy Spirit in humanity. A Christian approach to the study of psychology rests on a worldview that God reveals truths through both special and natural revelation.

God's natural and special revelation have "convergent validity;" they are parts of an overarching and non-contradictory whole. Understanding that natural and special revelation are ultimately all-encompassing and completely harmonious, Christians can be in awe of what has been revealed while seeking to discover what has not. It is science's purpose to better understand natural revelation. It is psychology's purpose to better understand natural revelation as it relates to the brain and behavior. If Truth is a unified whole and there is no inherent faith/science dichotomy, true science and true faith must agree. If Truth is a unified whole, natural revelation cannot contradict special revelation. The appearance of a contradiction is only an appearance. In terms of psychology, the appearance of a contradiction is the result of bad research, bad interpretation, or bad theology.

The role of natural revelation in the study of Mankind troubles many Christians. The role of special revelation in psychology troubles many psychologists. Some Christians believe that there is nothing modern psychology can contribute to our understanding of Mankind. In other words, because God created us, only the Bible can explain us. This text presumes that because special and natural revelation cannot ultimately conflict, valid psychological data will ultimately fit with *"the"* Christian worldview. A Christian approach to psychology must recognize the value of all of

God's revelation, special and natural. Special revelation provides a context or framework in which science can clarify and illuminate biblical truths. The error of Christians who limit God's communicative power about the nature of Mankind exclusively to the Bible is similar to the error of modern psychologists who discount the Bible's psychological insights.

A Christian worldview includes the understanding of the effect of sin on our behavior and our thinking (called the *noetic effect of sin*). So, by extension, what we know (about psychology and theology) is limited and impaired by sin (Romans 8:20-21; 1 Corinthians 13:12). Our personal bias and depravity should cause us to maintain a sense of humility and hold our conclusions tentatively.

4. Are there moral absolutes? What do you believe about the nature of right and wrong? Is there such thing as moral absolutes? Are there absolute rules governing human behavior and consequences for violating those rules, or is morality "relative?" A Christian worldview recognizes moral absolutes described in the Bible and lived by Jesus Christ.

5. What are the causes of and the cures for abnormal thoughts, feelings, and behaviors? Your worldview about the causes of and the cures for abnormal thoughts, feelings, and behavior includes whether you believe that pain, suffering, and guilt have meaning and purpose or that they are unfortunate circumstances to be avoided at all costs. A Christian worldview holds that through pain we are refined and made more Christ-like. The Christian worldview believes that redemption and restoration makes us "whole" but that "wholeness" does not necessarily equal ease and comfort. Christians disagree about whether extra-biblical techniques (e.g., medication) are ever proper approaches to caring for abnormal thoughts, feelings, and behaviors. A Christian worldview emphasizes sin as the primary, if not exclusive, cause of abnormal thoughts, feelings, and behaviors. Modern psychology attributes it to anything but sin! A Christian worldview sees guilt, pain, and suffering as tools God uses to conform us to Christ's image. Jesus himself was a "man of sorrows." It is noteworthy that many in Christendom share modern psychology's view that emotional pain must be avoided at all costs. In fact, a "feel good" gospel has much in common with modern self psychology (see Ch. 3).

Stop Reading. Do not keep reading until you are clear about your Christian worldview. Remember, the Christian worldview is Truth, but we can not prove it with science. It is important to remember that everyone's worldview is a matter of faith and no one's worldview is ultimately a matter of science. The foundational beliefs of a Christian worldview, of an atheist's worldview, and of a psychology professor's worldview are matters of faith and philosophy and not of data and science. In the next chapter we will explore psychology's history by examining its philosophies and assumptions.

Chapter Summary.

Everyone has core beliefs and assumptions – a worldview. All psychological research and theorizing happen in a worldview context. Ultimately, truth is only discernible from error at the worldview level.

The Christian worldview begins with the biblical account of God, creation, the fall, and redemption. A Christian worldview and modern psychology intersect around five questions.

- What Do You Believe About God? This is the most basic piece of one's worldview.
- What is the nature of Man? Are we the creation of a purposeful God, or the product of evolutionary forces? Are we born "good?" Do we have a mind that is greater than the sum of our brain activity? Do we have a soul that survives the death of the body?
- How can we know things with certainty? A Christian worldview is that Truth absolutely exists. God reveals Himself in His creation and through the Bible. Many people believe there is a faith/science dichotomy when in fact, science (and by extension, psychology) was born of the Christian worldview. Because special and natural revelation cannot ultimately conflict, valid psychological data will ultimately fit a Christian worldview.
- Are there moral absolutes? A Christian worldview recognizes moral absolutes that are described in the Bible and were lived by Jesus Christ.
- What are the causes of and the cures for abnormal thoughts, feelings, and behaviors? A Christian worldview emphasizes sin as at least one cause of mental and emotional pain; modern psychology attributes it to anything but sin. A Christian worldview holds that through pain we are refined and made more Christ-like.

For Review.

1. What is a worldview?
2. What is epistemology?
3. What is natural revelation? What is special revelation?
4. What do you believe about God?
5. What do you believe about the nature of Mankind?
6. What do you believe about moral absolutes?
7. What do you think causes abnormal thoughts, feelings, and behaviors?
8. Describe a monistic, dualistic, and tripartite view of human nature.
9. Describe the faith/science dichotomy. Do you believe there is a dichotomy between science and a Christian worldview? Explain your answer.
10. How have your thoughts and opinions about psychology and worldviews changed?

Chapter 3

Psychology's History and Worldviews

In This Chapter
- Naturalism
- New Ways of Knowing
- Rationalism
- Empiricism
- Phrenology
- Psychology as a Science
- Charles Darwin and Evolutionary Psychology
- Neuro-biology
- Behavioral Genetics
- Behaviorism
- Sigmund Freud
- Cognitive Perspective
- Humanism
- Moral Absoulutes

Is psychology old or is it new? It is both. Psychology is a very young science and a very old topic. Throughout history people have thought deeply about psychology's topics. Poets, theologians, and philosophers wrote about the mind centuries before psychology became a "science." Most histories of psychology date its beginning to 1879 with Wilhelm Wundt's psychological laboratory in Germany, but Wundt did not discover or invent psychology. Prior to Wundt, mental processes had not been systematically studied with scientific methods, but they had been studied extensively. Psychology is new in terms of the application of scientific methods to the study of the human mind. Psychology is also new in terms of the worldview assumptions of its modern fathers and major schools of thought. This chapter traces modern psychology's history through its worldview assumptions and schools of thought.

Naturalism is the worldview assumption that defines the difference between the old and new psychology. Worldviews are built on beliefs about first things. A Christian worldview begins with the belief that God exists and He created the universe and all life. Naturalism begins with the belief that something (anything) besides God is responsible. Why do we think, feel, and behave the way we do? In the Christian worldview, the Bible provides those answers. Biblical anthropology, also called the doctrine of Man, describes a view of Mankind in light of God's biblical revelation. Early scientific psychologists offered naturalistic alternatives to biblical descriptions of Mankind. Freudian, behavioral, cognitive, humanistic, and evolutionary theories all have roots in naturalism. As a Christian student, you must approach every discipline, including psychology, from the vantage point of faith, refusing to replace your theistic assumptions with naturalism.

A key point is that psychology was not discovered, invented, or created in the 19th century; it only became modern and scientific.

In the seventh century B. C., an Egyptian pharaoh conducted a psychological experiment on the acquisition of language. Psamtik I ordered that two infant children be removed from their parents to be raised by a mute shephard, in isolation from other people and from language. Psamtik's hypothesis was that children raised without hearing the spoken language would spontaneously begin to speak in Mankind's natural in-born language. The children were reported to have spontaneously spoken the Phrygian word for bread, "bekos," leading Psamtik to conclude that Phrygian was the Mankind's "native" language.

New Ways of Knowing.

Modern psychology traces its roots to the **Reformation** (16th century) and the rejection of **"authority"** as the sole source of knowledge about God and the world. Prior to the Reformation, theologians believed that everything we were meant to know had already been revealed. The Bible, as interpreted by Church authority, was the sole and definitive source of knowledge. In religion, **Martin Luther** rejected Church authority in favor of individual, Spirit-led understanding. By the 17th century, scholars in astronomy, physics, and medicine were doing the same thing. Without rejecting their core Christian beliefs, many of the fathers of science (the grandfathers of modern psychology) rejected human authority in favor of new ways of knowing about the world.

Rationalism. Modern science and psychology also trace their roots to the Christian philosopher **Renee Descartes** (1596 – 1650). Descartes believed that we can use "reason" to know things about the world with certainty. Descartes believed that our physical senses were less trustworthy than reason. His method is known as **deductive reasoning**. Beginning from a premise ("Cogito" or "I think..."), Descartes deduced a rational conclusion ("ergo sum" or "therefore I am"). Deductive reasoning involves beginning from a premise or truth that is certain and deducing one conclusion from another. Descartes did not reject his Christian worldview, but he did believe that "reason" was an important confirming measure of truth. As you might guess, at a time when Church authority was believed to be the God-ordained sole way of knowing such things, Descartes' approach was not well-accepted by many. Unlike Descartes, many rationalists today emphasize reasoning to the exclusion of other ways of knowing about the world.

Cartesian Dualism. Descartes applied deductive reasoning to questions of the nature of Mankind. Descartes concluded that we are made of body and soul, and that though distinct, the body and soul interact with one another. Descartes believed that the physical and spiritual connected at the **conarium**, now known as the pineal gland. Descartes' idea, known today as Cartesian dualism, was not new. He, like Christians and others for centuries, believed Mankind was both physical and spiritual. The ancient Greeks thought our spiritual and physical natures connected in the lungs (after all, when you quit breathing you die), and Hippocrates, who was ahead of his time, thought it happened in the brain. The

Descartes believed that because the soul was immaterial, it did not occupy space, but it needed a point of contact with the material body. Descartes believed that the soul interacted with the body specifically in the pineal gland. It was at the pineal gland that the mind controlled the flow of animal spirits to the body.

Renee Descartes, the father of rationalism

significance is that Descartes arrived at his conclusion through a nascent scientific method and without reference to biblical or other "beliefs."

Modern psychology generally rejects Cartesian dualism in favor of naturalistic monism, a belief that there is no spiritual/non-material part of human nature.

Descartes was also interested in the nervous system. He believed that there are two types of human behaviors that operate in interaction. ***Involuntary behaviors*** (e.g., reflexes and sensations) were thought to be completely mechanical and physical. ***Voluntary behaviors*** (e.g., reasoning, decision-making, initiating voluntary movements) were thought to be spiritual. The involuntary/physical and voluntary/spiritual connected at the conarium. Descartes thought that sensations traveled from the body via nerves to the pineal gland in the brain where "animal spirits" were released. The animal spirits traveled back to the body along tube-like nerves causing muscles to inflate. The cycle came to be known as the ***reflex arc***. According to Descartes, the reflex arc could explain human involuntary behavior and all animal behavior. Before Descartes, the suggestion that human behavior had anything in common with animal behavior would have been viewed as ludicrous and perhaps blasphemous.

Empiricism. ***Francis Bacon*** (1561 – 1626) has been called the father of modern science and a major prophet of the ***Scientific Revolution***. Bacon's philosophy is called empiricism and its method is known as ***inductive reasoning***. Where Descartes distrusted the senses, Bacon favored them. Beginning with repeated observations of nature, one can discover the natural laws of nature in a process that came to be known as the scientific method.

About 400 B. C., the Greek doctor and philosopher ***Hippocrates*** proposed an early theory of human personality types. Hippocrates thought that personality types were determined by levels (balance) of body fluids called ***humors***. The humors – ***blood, yellow bile, black bile***, and ***phlegm*** – represented the best "scientific" medical knowledge of the time. According to Hippocrates, an excess of blood (relative to the other humors) made one ***sanguine*** (extroverted, creative, and sensitive). An excess of yellow bile made one ***choleric*** (charismatic, ambitious, and a leader). A little too much black bile makes one ***melancholic*** (thoughtful, introverted, and reserved) and likewise an excess of phlegm leads to a ***phlegmatic*** (calm, not emotional, even-tempered) personality type. The terms sanguine, choleric, melancholic, and phlegmatic were used to describe personality types for about 1700 years.

Early psychologists like Wilhelm Wundt wanted to establish psychology as a "hard" science like chemistry or physics and embraced empiricism as a guiding principle. They, like many psychologists today, differentiated psychology from philosophy and religion by limiting their study to

> **Mesmerism.** In 1774 Franz Mesmer detailed his cure for some mental illness, originally called mesmerism and now known as hypnosis.

observable and quantifiable phenomena. By doing so they, like psychologists today, were still able, perhaps more clearly, to discover truths about our collective humanness. The emphasis on empiricism led to psychology's definition "evolving" from "the study of the mind, spirit, and soul," to "the science of the brain and behavior."

Many people criticize psychology's reliance on empirical methods. The difficulties applying empirical methods to psychological research (e.g., inability to control variables, bias, placebo effects) have even led many to argue that psychology does not fit the definition of a true empirical science. A psychology that leaves out intangibles like the mind, love, and faith is seen as sterile and trivial. Strict empiricism only allows psychologists to study our creatureliness, it makes no meaningful contribution to what it means to be human, and it relegates Christian beliefs to a topic of study, along with mysticism, rituals, and other primitive belief systems.

Phrenology. Around 1800, about 75 years before the founding of Wilhelm Wundt's psychology laboratory, **Dr. Franz Gall** (1758-1828), an anatomist and physiologist, popularized a "science" called phrenology. Phrenology, now discredited, suggested that the shape of the skull was an indicator of a person's character and personality. Dr. Gall believed that various mental functions and personality traits resided in specific parts of the brain. He thought that more or less of a particular characteristic or trait would correspond with more or less brain matter in a specific region of the brain. Gall thought that the shape and size of the skull mirrored the shape and size of the brain. If one portion of the brain was better developed (e.g., bigger), Gall believed that the skull would reflect that difference. Gall believed that the tendency to lie and steal was assoicated with a bump behind the ears, that one's "individuality" was apparent by the shape of the skull above the bridge of the nose, and that a close examination of the skull enabled him to identify those with special abilities in a number of areas.

Phrenology is noteworthy for several reasons. Gall's ideas were condemned by many Christians as heretical. The Catholic Church labeled phrenology "heretical" for claiming that characteristics of the "mind," created in the image of God, had a seat in brain matter. Mainstream science rejected phrenology as fakery. Phrenology was right, however, in its basic belief that the brain is involved in mental activity and that many mental functions are localized in specific parts of the brain. In that sense, phrenology was an important step toward modern day neuro-biology.

> The expression "You ought to have your head examined" goes back to phrenology and Frances Gall, who literally examined people's heads in order to analyze their personalities.

Broca's Area. Paul Broca (1824 - 1880) discovered that speech was controlled by a specific part of the brain. Broca's area, on the left temporal lobe, does play a role in speech, but today psychologists understand that speech is complicated and involves several brain structures.

Psychology as Science.

In the first half of the 19th century, most psychologists studied **psychophysics**, the measurement of sensations, perceptions, and motor responses. Psychophysicists explored how sensory and motor nerves work, the function of sense organs, and individual differences in perception. According to the great historian of psychology **E. G. Boring**, **Gustav Fechner** (1801 - 1887) is the real father of modern scientific psychology. Father or not, Fechner was one of the very first to apply scientific procedures to mental processes. Fechner was a psychophysicist who made precise measurements of sensory functioning to answer questions like, *"What is the minimum amount of light, sound, touch, taste, or smell a person can perceive?"* The study came to be known as psychophysics, the "physics" of mental life.

Structuralism. In the second half of the 19th century scientific psychology rapidly matured and expanded. Psychologists like Fechner, Herman von Helmholtz, Wilhem Wundt, and Edward B. Titchener explored the "structure" of mental processes. **Structuralism** was an early approach to psychology interested in describing mental experiences in terms of complex structures made from increasingly simpler component structures.

Herman von Helmholtz (1821 - 1894) made great contributions to our understanding of hearing and vision. Helmholtz was the first to measure the speed of nerve impulses. Like Wundt, Fechner, and Titchner, Helmholtz was interested in the physical structures involved in mental experiences. As a structuralist, Helmoltz sought to discover the simple components upon which complex mental experiences were thought to be made.

Wilhelm Wundt (1832 - 1920) gets the credit as the founder of scientific psychology. Wundt established a psychology laboratory at the University of Leipzig in Germany in 1879. His interest was the **structure of consciousness**, and his goal was to identify the components, or elements of mental experiences in a type of periodic table of mental elements. His method was **introspection**, meaning the researcher looked inward to describe subjective mental experiences. Despite rigorous attempts to be precise, introspection was not reliable and it faded from use. It is noteworthy that introspection was reintroduced by Sigmund Freud and humanist psychologists years later.

Dr. Charles Bell (1774 - 1842) discovered that nerves travel from the brain to the organs and support both sensory and motor functions. Bell's palsy, named for Dr. Bell who first described the condition, is a weakness or paralysis in the muscles controlling expressions on one side of the face. **Bell's Palsy** is caused by damage to one of a pair of facial nerves running beneath each ear to the muscles in the face.

Edward B. Titchener (1867 - 1927), who trained under Wundt, wrote *Experimental*

Psychology: A Manual of Laboratory Practice, the first guide for conducting psychological research. Titchener, who actually coined the term **structuralism**, examined sensations, attention, perception, and a host of other mental phenomena. Though a structuralist, Titchener recognized that the functional aspects of mental processes were relevant and important topics for study.

Charles Darwin and Evolutionary Psychology.

Early scientific psychologists worked during a time of major worldview shifts. Atheism, naturalism, and evolution sought to exclude God, creation, and the Bible from all sciences, most notably biology and geology. The impact of Darwin's theory of evolution on psychology was both tremendous and immediate. Darwin's theory cast doubt on biblical authority and suggested that human psychology and animal psychology differed only in degrees and not in essence. Evolutionary psychologists since Darwin have tried to explain how evolutionary processes alone were sufficient to produce the human brain. Darwin's theory requires that psychology explain and interpret everything about us (including what we think of as our God-likeness) in terms of adaptive traits passed down from one generation to the next according to natural selection. Darwin set the stage for psychology's full departure from philosophy and religion.

By the late 19th century, Darwin's ideas about evolution were well known to scientists, and psychologists began to propose theories explaining mental processes in terms of evolutionary forces. Darwin's theory led to a new focus in psychology called **functionalism**. **Herbert Spencer**, **William James**, and **Charles Darwin** himself were influential early functionalists. Functionalists saw human behavior and mental processes as complex combinations of increasingly simple component behaviors and processes. Each evolved to serve a purpose or function. **Functionalists** focused on discovering the survival and reproductive advantage a particular behavior or mental function provided. A Christian worldview is that the purpose of our brain and mental life (and everything else) is to glorify God and serve Him. Functionalists describe purpose in terms of survival and reproductive advantages.

Naturalism, by definition, excludes the possibility of the demonic. A Christian worldview recognizes that Satan and demons are real and active in the world. Modern psychologists often cite the Christian belief in Satan as prima facie evidence that all Christians are "screwball wackos."

Modern psychologists will often use the account of the demoniac at Gerasenes in Mark Chapter 5 as an example of a primitive understanding of mental illness. The argument is that because the Bible writers did not understand mental illness, they used the best metaphor they knew. If your professor uses that example, you might ask if he or she believes that means Jesus miraculously healed schizophrenia.

Herbert Spencer (1820 - 1903), a famous evolutionist and contemporary of Charles Darwin, coined the phrase "survival of the fittest." Spencer applied evolution principles to the development of mental processes and suggested that behaviors that produce pleasurable results were more likely to be repeated. If a behavior increased the chances of survival, it would be passed to subsequent generations.

Proximate Cause refers to the mechanics of a behavior or cognitive process – what happens and how? *Ultimate Cause* refers to the "why" of behavior and mental processes. The ultimate cause of any behavior or mental process, in terms of evolutionary psychology, is always a survival and reproductive advantage. The ultimate cause in a Christian worldview is always, ultimately, to glorify God.

Williams James (1842 - 1910), known as the father of American psychology, applied Darwin's theory to explain emotions and consciousness. In James' theory, consciousness and emotions evolved as a complex mix of physical processes that individually and collectively equipped our ancestors for the challenges of survival.

Many modern psychologists see in evolution a grand unifying psychological theory and a reason for all behavior and mental processes. For many, evolutionary psychology is the "new" psychology. Evolutionary psychologists search for the genesis of the human mind in animal biology. All behavior and mental processes exist, as the reasoning goes, because they, and their component parts, were each sequential adaptations "chosen" by natural selection. Mental disorders, from an evolutionary perspective, are the remnants of behaviors that once were adaptive and beneficial. Though evolutionary psychologists assert evolution as fact, it is nonetheless a worldview assumption ultimately grounded in faith.

Neuro-biology, also called psychobiology and neuro-anatomy, is the study of the nervous system's structures and processes. Neuro-biology and cognitive psychology are the primary schools of thought and the most productive research fields in psychology today.

Advances in technology allow psychologists today to observe and precisely measure brain activity at the level of individual neurons. It has allowed psychologists to precisely locate the specific brain locations associated with subjective mental experiences. In other words, we can "see" the parts of the brain that are active when we think, remember, dream, meditate, or pray. In the tradition of Dr. Gall and phrenology, new technology has revived and strengthened the worldview that we are no more than complex biochemical processes operating in brain matter.

Modern neuro-biology focuses "reductively" on brain structures and functions. *Reductive* means that each mental structure and behavior consists of ever simpler component structures and behaviors. Reductionist psychology is not necessarily inconsistent with a Christian worldview. But following it to its natural conclusion, Man becomes nothing but a collection of pieces and parts. In fact, a reductive perspective is behind descriptions of Man as complex machines or computers. We are complicated

Francis Crick, codiscoverer of DNA, proposed what he called "*The Astonishing Hypothesis*." Crick hypothesized that our mental life, consciousness, morality, decision-making, and judgment is the product of a material physical brain. According to Crick, "*You, your joys, and your sorrows, your memories and your ambitions, your sense of personal identity and free-will, are in fact no more than the behavior of a vast assembly of nerve cells and their associated molecules.*"

but reducible to simpler underlying parts. All mental processes, including love, hope, prayer, and worship, are just brain activity, which is ultimately nothing more than electrical and biochemical processes occurring in a very advanced neural network. A reductive approach also underlies psychiatry and the neuro-pharmaceutical industry's efforts to target chemical "fixes" at the molecular level.

Behavioral Genetics. Sir Francis Galton (1822 - 1911) first described the heritability of physical characteristics. Behavioral geneticists apply the same principles to examine the role of genes in our thoughts, behaviors, and even our personality. Behavior geneticists study twins (raised together and separately) to determine which behaviors are inherited and which come from environmental influences.

Behaviorism. Chapter 9 covers the principles of behaviorism in more detail. Behaviorism is one of psychology's most famous approaches. As an area of research, the goal of behaviorism is to explain the natural laws of behavior, and behavioral psychology has provided rich and valuable information. As a worldview, behaviorism radically redefined what it meant to be human. As a worldview, behaviorism saw Mankind as nothing other than very complicated machines that react to stimuli or input in predictable ways. According to B. F. Skinner, Ivan Pavlov, and John Watson, each a "radical behaviorist," *all* human behavior is determined by the environment in a closed cause and effect system. Radical behaviorism is a deterministic worldview in which free-will is an illusion.

A Christian worldview is inconsistent with behaviorism's deterministic assumption. A Christian worldview balances God's sovereignty with human freedom and responsibility. A Christian worldview does not exclude an element of predictability in human behavior and the Bible provides many examples of God's use of rewards and punishments. A Christian worldview recognizes that rewards and punishment are important to learning but does not see us as robots programmed by environmental stimuli or childhood experiences. We have minds, will, foresight, judgment, and the ability and responsibility to control our impulses. It is essential that Christians studying psychology grapple with the theological issues of God's sovereignty with free-will, choice, and responsibility.

Sigmund Freud. As we will see in Chapters 8 (Human Development), 9 (Consciousness), 11 (Personality), 12 (Abnormal Psychology), and 13 (Treatment), Sigmund Freud was both a tremendously influential and controversial figure in the history of modern psychology. His theories continue to influence academia and the culture. Today, scholars in business, economics, education, sociology, philosophy, and other disciplines apply Freud's theories to their own discipline, and many of the terms used by Freud (e.g., ego, denial, unconscious, oral fixation, libido, and Freudian slip) have become part of everyday language.

The Christian and Freudian worldviews could hardly differ more and criticisms of his theories by Christians are not surprising. Freud presumed that God did not exist. Despite his Jewish heritage, Freud was an atheist who made it clear that his theories were an alternative to theistic beliefs. Freud believed that Mankind invented gods and religions as ways to cope with psychic fears. Freud's was a deterministic worldview that emphasized sex and aggression as the prime motivations for human behavior and personality development. Freud believed Mankind is tripartite in nature (id, ego, and superego) and that we are not consciously aware of most of the influences on our thoughts, feelings, and behavior. According to Freud, our consciousness is like the tip of an iceberg. The bulk of who we are is below the surface and unconscious, meaning we cannot bring it to conscious awareness except by psycho-analytic techniques.

You will be taught about Darwin's Theory of Evolution in college. You will be taught about Freud's personality theory in college, too. Please do not forget that understanding the material and accepting the worldview are different. You can do one without the other. Christians should approach Freud's theories with skepticism and caution.

> Sigmund Freud said that religion was a neurotic fantasy and that as knowledge became more accessible, religion would soon fade away.

Cognitive Psychology. Cognitions are thoughts. Cognitions are also emotions, perceptions, problem-solving techniques, memories, and any other mental process. A cognitive approach to psychology has its roots in Wundt's structuralism and is a dominant school of thought in psychology today. Cognitive psychologists emphasize the ways we acquire and process information and construct meaning from the world. Rather than being controlled by irrational passions and instincts (i.e., Freud) or objects conditioned by the environment (i.e., behaviorism), cognitive psychology is interested in how we interact with the world, make sense out of what goes on around us, and understand ourselves and others. Cognitive psychology is the foundation for theories of learning, motivation, development, and personality and for much of modern counseling, including Christian counseling.

Humanism. Humanism is a philosophy. Humanism, also known as ***secular humanism***, describes a set of principles for living a fulfilled life. Humanism places human values, reason, free-will, meeting needs, and individual self-worth above all else. Humanism is an atheistic worldview, a type of ethical system for atheism. Humanism appeared in psychology around the 1970s when Skinnerian behaviorism and Freudian psycho-analysis, which both seemed so cold and deterministic, were falling from favor.

Humanism specifically rejects God and relies on reason and science to define morality. Humanism promises to help people live happy and fulfilled lives. Secular humanism presumes not only that God does not exist, but that Mankind is the self-existent culmination of evolutionary development. Humanist psychology claims that people in their "natural state" are inherently good and that in accepting and nonjudgmental environments we can recover that original goodness through a process of "self-actualization." Humanism presents a stark contrast to the Christian beliefs in original sin, depravity, and the need for redemption, justification, and sanctification.

Self-actualization means achieving personal fulfillment and full potential. A Christian worldview sees personal fulfillment and full potential in terms of the extent to which we have the mind of Christ. Jesus is the standard for our "actualization." In a Christian worldview, we paradoxically achieve fulfillment through giving and self-sacrifice. Humanism's emphasis on personal growth and potential has gained wide acceptance among psychologists today, and its influence is also felt in the church.

Self Psychology. Naturalism and humanism led to a perspective that believes people should feel good about themselves, learn to love themselves, and rid themselves of needless shame and guilt. That perspective is known as *self psychology*, *selfism*, and most recently, *positive psychology*. Positive psychology, a new "branch" of psychology, focuses on the study of positive emotions, strengths, and virtues. As a worldview, self psychology believes that high self-esteem, personal fulfillment, self-expression, self-acceptance, and self-fulfillment are what it means to be human. Personal subjective well-being and social functioning are of primary importance. Guilt is to be avoided at all costs, and suffering is absurd.

Self psychology is very popular. Most psychologists believe that self-esteem is the foundation of sound mental health. Self-esteem, self-fulfillment, self-expression, self-love, and individualism are appealing ideas, but their relative value in a Christian's life is a subject of debate among Christians. Some Christians equate high self-esteem with idolatrous pride. Others, like Dr. James Dobson, integrate self-esteem into their theology by balancing our sinfulness with our special status in creation. God does not create junk, but Mankind is sinful and in revolt against God through the assertion of the self. It is Jesus' example, not a subjective view of happiness, that defines actualization and toward which we should strive. Jesus lived the true psychology. Contrition, self-denial, and humility are means by which we achieve spiritual growth. A Christian studying psychology must reconcile those ideas with a recognition that, though pride is a form of idolatry, beings created in God's image do not exalt God by denigrating His creation. The Christian worldview sees self-actualization as glorifying God through obedient service.

Abnormal Thoughts, Feelings, and Behaviors. Modern psychology's worldview is most distinguishable from a Christian worldview in its beliefs about the meaning of, causes of, and cures for abnormal thoughts, feelings, and behaviors. We will examine the worldview issues in depth in Chapter 12 and Chapter 13. For now, understand that no topic in psychology comes closer to the core Bible message of sin and redemption than abnormal psychology. Psychology's naturalistic foundation requires that abnormal thoughts, feelings, and behaviors be explained in terms of heredity, chemical imbalances, repressive parents, unconscious psychic conflicts, infections, or even refined sugar and house cats – anything except sin and disunity with God!

> Humanistic psychology was also known as psychology's *"Third Force."* Humanism rejected the "dehumanizing" determinism in both psycho-analysis and behaviorism (the 1st and 2nd "forces") in favor of an emphasis on human autonomy and potentiality.

Morality. *Moral relativism* is a worldview in which standards of behavior are based on some temporal framework of values and beliefs and not on any moral absolutes. Moral relativism is the application of a naturalistic worldview to ethics and personal responsibility. Modern psychology's approach to sex illustrates the difference between a theistic and a relativistic moral worldview. Modern psychology describes attraction, mate selection, and sexual behavior in terms of evolutionary purposes. Where evolution provides the moral backdrop for behavior, fulfilling any number of sexual urges and impulses is not wrong; it is adaptive and, by definition, "morally" right. A Christian worldview recognizes that the Bible prescribes moral absolutes. When we violate those absolutes, we are personally responsible for our actions.

Feminist Psychology. Feminist psychology grew out of the feminist movement of the late 1960s. *Feminism* is humanistic worldview focused on helping women achieve self-actualization, as defined by humanist values, in a male dominated world. Feminist psychology grew out of a belief that psychological research was biased toward males. At the time, there were few women in psychology. Psychological research was generally done by male researchers on male participants. Feminist psychology rejects male-generated, religious, and traditional approaches to understanding women. Psychologists who study lesbian, gay, bisexual, and transgender (LBGT) issues on sexual orientation focus on research, education, and influencing public policy.

Chapter Summary.

Psychology is old and psychology is new. Poets, theologians, and philosophers throughout history have thought deeply about the mind, the soul, and the nervous system. Most histories date the beginning of modern scientific psychology at in 1879 with Wilhelm Wundt's psychological laboratory in Germany.

The fathers of modern psychology proposed alternative non-biblical models of Mankind. Psychology's history is best understood in the worldviews expressed in its major theories and schools of thought.

Modern psychology can trace its roots through Renee Descartes and rationalism and Francis Bacon and empiricism. Early modern psychology embraced empiricism as its guiding principle, and it is its primary approach today.

The structuralists were interested in describing the characteristics of mental "structures." Functionalists like Herbert Spencer, William James, Edward Thorndike, and Charles Darwin were interested in describing mental processes in terms of survival and reproductive advantages. Darwin set the stage for describing complex mental processes as collections of simpler underlying processes, each with a development and purpose explained by adaptation and survival. Modern psychology sees evolution as a unifying explanation for all behavior and mental processes.

Neuro-biology is the study of the nervous system's structures and processes. Neuro-biology focuses "reductively" on brain structures and mental processes as collections of simpler component structures and processes. Behaviorism, as a worldview, sees Mankind as nothing more than very complicated machines that react to stimuli (input) in predictable ways.

Freud explained the mind in terms of psychic conflicts and opposing unconscious forces. The cognitivists approached psychology in terms of the ways we acquire, process, and understand information.

Humanism is a philosophy that emphasizes human values, reason, and individual self-worth above all else. Humanist psychology suggests that high-self-esteem, personal fulfillment, self-expression, self-acceptance, and self-fulfillment define good mental health.

Psychology's naturalistic worldview sees the causes of abnormal thoughts, feelings, and behaviors as anything except sin and disunity with God. A Christian worldview recognizes sin as a primary (if not exclusive) cause of mental and emotional pain.

Moral relativism is a worldview in which standards of behavior are based on some temporal framework of values and beliefs and not on any moral absolutes. A Christian worldview recognizes that the Bible prescribes moral absolutes. When we violate those absolutes, we are personally responsible for our actions.

For Review.

1. What is Cartesian dualsim?
2. How did a naturalistic worldview affect modern psychology?
3. How did rationalism contribute to the development of modern psychology?
4. How did empiricism contribute to the development of modern psychology?
5. What are some criticisms of modern psychology's reliance on empirical methods?
6. What is phrenology and how are phrenology and modern neuro-biology similar?
7. How did Sigmund Freud's view of Mankind differ from a Christian view?
8. What were radical behaviorism's assumptions about the nature of Mankind?
9. What was the influence of Herbert Spencer, Charles Darwin, and William James on modern psychology?
10. In what way is secular humanism inconsistent with a Christian worldview?

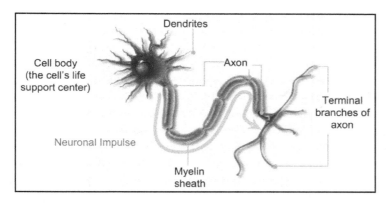

is divided into two main divisions called the **somatic** and **autonomic** divisions in a network of nerves traveling throughout the entire body.

The Neuron. The neuron is the most basic building block of the nervous system. Every movement, thought, sight, sound, emotion, or memory involves neurons. Neurons are some of the largest cells in the body and can be several feet long (i.e., from the tip of your big toe to the base of your spine). Neurons vary by their size, shape, location, and purpose. All neurons receive, transmit, and/or process information.

Neurons differ from other cells in that they communicate with each other via specialized extensions called **dendrites** and **axons**. The axon of one neuron initiates a chemical signal that is received by dendrites on another neuron. The dendrite extends from the cell body much like the branches of a tree (**dendritic tree**). The axon is a long, very thin tube leading away from the cell body. The axon has appendages called **axon terminals** or **terminal buttons**. The cell body or **soma** contains the **nucleus**, which in turn contains **mitochondria,** which provide the neuron's energy, and other complex cellular "machines." Each neuron generally has one axon that serves to carry signals away from the cell. Each neuron has several dendrites that can receive signals from different neighboring cells.

Types of Neurons. There are three types of neurons:

- Sensory
- Motor
- Interneurons

Sensory (afferent) neurons, as the name implies, carry signals from the sense receptors in the body to the brain. **Motor (efferent) neurons** carry signals from the brain and spinal cord to the muscles and glands. Sensory and motor neurons are present throughout our bodies. **Interneurons**, the third type of neuron, exist exclusively in the brain and spinal cord and make up about 90% of all human neurons. Interneurons make the connection between sensory and motor neurons and are involved in all mental activity.

The axon is generally long and thin and ends in a tree-shaped structures called axon terminals. The axon is covered in a fatty myelin sheath that insulates the axon and enables signals to move more quickly.

Glial cells, though technically not neurons, support neural functioning by digesting dead neurons, producing the myelin sheathing, and providing nutrition to neurons.

Neurotransmission. The process by which neurons communicate is known as neurotransmission. Neurotransmission is an electro-chemical process that occurs within and between neurons. Within the neuron, neurotransmission describes the movement of an electrical impulse. Between neurons, neurotransmission describes the process of one neuron sending chemical signals to other neurons across the synaptic cleft, or the gap between neurons. When a neuron is sufficiently excited, it "fires," sending an electrical impulse (***action potential***) down the axon. Neurons do not partially fire; it is an all or nothing event. The threshold level is the minimum level of excitement required for the neuron to fire. The recovery time after firing is called the ***refractory period***. Neurons recover quickly. A neuron can fire 1,000 times per second. The action potential travels the length of the axon at speeds up to 260 miles per hour.

> ***Psychiatric or psychotropic medications*** operate at the level of neurotransmitters. The phrase ***chemical imbalance of the brain*** refers to a belief that mental health problems are due to imbalances in neurotransmitter levels. Psychotropic medications affect the supply of neurotransmitters or the way in which neurotransmitters are absorbed. ***Agonists*** make more of a neurotransmitter available in the synapse. ***Antagonists*** decrease the amount of a neurotransmitter or block it from delivering its signal.

Neurotransmitters. When the electrical impulse reaches the axon, appendages called terminal buttons release chemical signals called neurotransmitters to other nearby neurons. Neurons do not communicate directly. The chemical signal must cross the synaptic cleft, the gap between the axon of one neuron and the dendrite of another. Dendrites on neighboring neurons receive those chemical signals. If the receiving neuron is sufficiently excited, it in turn will fire. A single neuron can send and receive signals to and from thousands of other neurons. Neurotransmitters crossing the ***synaptic cleft*** chemically bind or "fit" into receptor sites on the dendrites of the receiving neuron. Neurotransmitters are either excitatory or inhibitory. ***Excitatory*** means that the chemical signal increases the likelihood that neighboring neurons will fire. ***Inhibitory*** means the signal lowers the likelihood that other neurons will fire.

> ***Neurotransmitters.*** Neurotransmitters are the chemical messengers that neurons send and receive. Psychologists have identified about 100 neurotransmitters. Important examples:
>
> - ***Acetylcholine*** is active in memory formation and plays a role in controlling motor movement, slowing the heart rate, and activating digestion. A low level of acetylcholine is associated with the symptoms of Alzheimer's disease.
> - ***Norepinephrine*** affects arousal, wakefulness, learning, and mood.
> - ***Dopamine*** is involved in movement and the experience of pleasure. Dopamine plays a role in the addictiveness of drugs like cocaine. Dopamine levels are associated with the shakiness of patients with Parkinson's disease. Dopamine levels may be associated with the symptoms of schizophrenia and other mental illnesses.
> - ***GABA*** (Gamma-amino butyric acid) is different from most neurotransmitters in that it is inhibitory. GABA makes it less likely that neurons will fire. GABA is active when we sleep and is involved in the action of many drugs that sedate brain activity.
> - ***Serotonin*** affects sleep and mood. Medications like ***Prozac***, ***Zoloft***, and ***Paxil*** increase the availability of serotonin.

The Peripheral Nervous System. The peripheral nervous system (PNS) consists of the neurons running throughout the body outside of the brain and the spinal cord. The PNS controls voluntary and involuntary muscle movement, sensory information, and automatic functions of the body. The peripheral system is made up of three subsystems: the somatic, autonomic, and enteric systems.

> ***Enteric Nervous System.*** The enteric nervous system is a network of nerve fibers in the stomach, intestines, pancreas, and gall bladder controlling the digestive process.

The Somatic Nervous System. Somatic means "of the body." The somatic nervous system controls voluntary muscle movement. The somatic system makes the connection between the motor cortex of the brain and the skeletal muscles used in movement.

Autonomic Nervous System. The autonomic or involuntary nervous system controls automatic body functions. The autonomic system makes the connection between the brain and smooth muscles found in places like the stomach, intestines, blood vessels, glands, and bladder. The autonomic nervous system controls respiration, perspiration, digestion, and heartbeat.

> ***Reflexes.*** If you touch fire, you will experience a monosynaptic reflex. Sensory neurons carry the signal "hot" to the spinal cord. The spinal cord transmits that signal to the brain, but it does not wait on a reply before taking action. The spinal cord activates the motor neurons in what is known as a ***reflex arc***.

The autonomic nervous system is further subdivided into the sympathetic and parasympathetic nervous systems.

The Sympathetic Nervous System. The sympathetic and parasympathetic systems operate as opposites. The sympathetic system creates an excited state (as in "fight or flight" situations). The sympathetic nervous system mobilizes the body for action by accelerating some functions and decelerating others.

Parasympathetic Nervous System. While the sympathetic system acts like an accelerator, the parasympathetic systems acts like a brake. The parasympathetic system restores the body to a state of rest and relaxation. It slows your heart and respiration rate, diverts blood flow from the muscles, and restores the digestive process.

> ***Fight or Flight.*** Imagine you've just had a big evening meal, it is late, and you are taking a walk in your neighborhood minding your own business. Your parasympathetic nervous system is directing your body to a calm and relaxed state. Blood flows from your extremities to digest the food and you feel a little drowsy. And then, out jumps a grizzly bear! Your sympathetic nervous system kicks-in, directing your body to a very excited state.
>
> - Pupils dilate increasing visual acuity (better to see the bear).
> - Blood flows to the muscles and the brain (digesting dinner can wait!).
> - Heart rate, blood pressure, and respiration increase (all needed for fast running).
> - Blood clots more readily (in case you don't get away).

The Brain. The Bible does not mention the brain directly. The Bible mentions the heart, mind, blood, bowels, liver,

The crude method of trephining wit

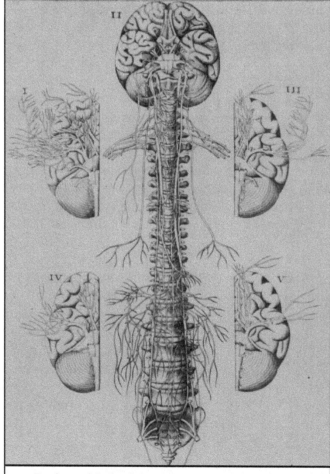

Brain and Spinal Cord (Eustachi, circa 1750)

and kidneys, but not the brain. The history of our efforts to understand the human brain is perhaps as old as Mankind. Throughout most of history, access to the brain was limited. Autopsies were often forbidden. Often advances in knowledge came by studying the effects of **brain injuries**, **lesions**, and **psychosurgery**.

The ancient Egyptians believed that the brain was unimportant and discarded it during the embalming process. An ancient South American people and others performed **trepanation**; surgically opening the skull to expose the brain. **Hippocrates** believed that the brain was the seat of our mind; and in the first century A.D., **Galen**, a physician to the gladiators, demonstrated that that nerve fibers control movement. He cut nerves at different locations along the spinal cord producing paralysis in different parts of the body.

During the **Renaissance**, knowledge of the structure of the brain increased dramatically and scientists began to understand the importance of the brain. **Andreas Vesalius** (1514 – 1564) produced one of the first known neuro-anatomy textbooks, containing descriptions and illustrations of the workings of the nerves and the brain.

As mentioned earlier, in the early 1800s Dr. Franz Gall, the founder of **phrenology**, proposed that various mental functions and personality traits were linked to specific locations in the brain. Around the

Stroke. The result of a cut-off of blood supply to a part of the brain is called a stroke, or *cerebrovascular accident (CVA).* Strokes are caused by deposits to the brain's arteries (*atherosclerosis*), hardening of the arteries (*arteriosclerosis*), clotting in the arteries (*thrombosis*), a clot from somewhere else carried to the brain (*embolism*), arteries bulging out (*aneurysm*), or arteries bursting (*cerebral hemorrhage*).

same time Dr. Charles Bell published *Idea of a New Anatomy of the Brain* in which he described the connection between the mind (seated in the cerebrum), the senses, and motor activity. Phineas Gage's accident in 1848 demonstrated that there is a connection between the brain and personality.

Paul Broca (1824 - 1880) studied the effect of brain lesions and other brain damage on one's capacity to speak. Broca's most famous patient, named "Tan," could understand language but had no capacity for speech. He could only speak the word "Tan." In his autopsy in 1681, Broca found a lesion on Tan's brain. Broca concluded that the lesion was the cause of Tan's inability to speak and that he had identified the speech production area of the brain. The part of the brain responsible for speech production is known as Broca's Area. Disorders in speech due to damage to the language center of the brain are known as **aphasias**. Aphasia of speech production is known as Brocha's Aphasia.

Shortly after Broca's discovery, **Carl Wernicke** (1848 - 1905) discovered an area in the temporal lobe involved in understanding language. An aphasia in **Wernicke's Area** results in impairments in understanding written and spoken language.

Brain Stimulation. Twentieth century psychologists discovered that weak electric currents, applied directly to the brain, stimulated neurons to fire. Applying electrical current to an area of the brain caused groups of neurons to fire. Because there are no pain receptors in the brain, subjects were awake and could report what it felt like to have an area of the brain stimulated. Methodically stimulating different areas of the brain seems to confirm what the phrenologists believed, that there was localization of function. **Localization of functioning** means that different parts of the brain carry out different functions. **Cortical mapping** refers to the graphic illustration of the localization of brain functioning. In the 1940s, **Wilder Penfield** (1891 - 1976), by methodically stimulating different area of the brain, created a famous map of the brain called the **homonculous**, Latin for "little man." The homonculous shows the areas of the brain that control movement of specific body parts. Another map showed the brain areas that receive sensory information from the body. Psychologists have used brain electrical stimulation to trigger emotions, thoughts, auditory and visual hallucinations, tastes, smells, and detailed memories (some of which were real and others were not).

The brain makes up only 2% of the body's weight, but uses 20% of the body's oxygen.

The Pleasure Center. In 1954 **James Olds** and **Peter Milne** discovered that the hypothalamus is involved in the experience of pleasure as a type of "pleasure center." Direct electrical stimulation to the hypothalamus produces feelings of mild to intense physical pleasure. Similarly, the **amygdala** is involved in the experience of fear. Electrical stimulation to the amygdala produce feelings of fear, anxiety, and sometimes, violence. Animals whose amygdala is removed show no fear.

The case of Phineas Gage suggested a connection between personality and the brain. Experiments on dogs and monkeys had shown that surgically removing parts of the cerebral cortex calmed the animals. With the knowledge that mental activity was localized in the brain, psychologists sought ways to surgically alter the brain as a type of treatment for severe mental disorders. In the 1930s **Egas Moniz** (1874 - 1955) developed of a type of psycho-surgery known as a **lobotomy** or **frontal lobotomy**. Lobotomies are a type of intentional brain injury. Moniz opened the skull and severed the nerve fibers connecting a portion of the frontal lobe to the rest of the brain. He reported that after surgery, patients were less agitated and less paranoid.

Walter Freeman (1895 - 1972) perfected a quick and seemingly barbaric procedure to perform lobotomies. Freeman performed "ice pick" lobotomies. Freeman drove an ice pick-like tool into the brain through the eye socket with a hammer and then swept it from side to side cutting the connections to and from the prefrontal cortex. His procedure was so fast that eventually Freeman performed outpatient lobotomies using local anesthesia in assembly line fashion. Freeman personally performed over 3,400 lobotomies and taught the procedure in over 50 psychiatric hospitals. Between 1939 and 1951, over 18,000 lobotomies were performed in the United States. Lobotomies were misused and caused serious problems for the people who received them. In some cases, families would submit troublesome relatives for a lobotomy. Moniz won a Nobel Prize for his work even though the procedure had serious and lasting consequences for patients.

Brain Imaging. Until recently, there was no way for psychologists to "see" the living brain in action. Today, brain-imaging technologies provide a way for psychologists to see and measure brain activity.

Electroencephalograph (EEG). Until about 1970 the main brain-imaging technology was the EEG. The EEG records electrical voltage produced when neurons fire. EEGs show brain activity but not brain structure.

Computer axial tomography (CT scan) involves rotating an x-ray machine around the brain to produce a series of images. The combined images produce a three-dimensional x-ray of the brain. CT scans show brain structure but not brain activity.

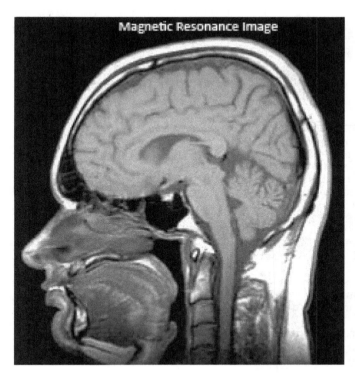

Magnetic Resonance Image

Positron Emission Tomography (PET scan) and ***Single Photon Emission Computed Tomography (SPECT scan)*** produce real-time three-dimensional images of the brain at work. PET scans show blood flow, oxygen use, drug activity, and glucose metabolism in specific regions of the brain. PET scans show both brain structure and activity and have provided important information about the brain activity associated with auditory hallucinations, multiple personality disorders, and other mental conditions.

Magnetic Resonance Imaging (MRI) uses powerful magnetic fields and radio waves to create detailed images of the brain. Like PET and SPECT scans, MRIs allow psychologists to see brain structure and brain activity.

Functional Magnetic Resonance Imaging (fMRI) uses the magnetic properties of blood to produce pinpoint images of blood flow as it is occurring. An fMRI scan can produce a precise image of brain activity as fast as every second.

Brain Anatomy. The living brain appears pink and soft weighs about 3 lbs. It is shielded by the ***skull***, cushioned and nourished in ***cerebrospinal fluid***, and protected from toxins by the blood-brain barrier. The ***blood-brain barrier*** is a separation that protects the brain by allowing glucose from the blood to enter the brain, and by keeping out other substances and some toxins. The ***spinal cord*** connects the brain with the body and transmits signals from the brain to the body and back again. It too is shielded by bone (the ***spinal column***) and nourished in ***cerebrospinal fluid***.

Divisions of the Brain. The brain consists of three major divisions. In the embryo, the brain develops as a tube of cells that rapidly divide into three distinct parts: the ***forebrain***, ***midbrain***, and ***hindbrain***. As it develops, the brain folds into deep wrinkles called convolutions. ***Convolutions*** allow more brain surface area to fit in the limited space in the skull. Convolutions continue to form and deepen for years after birth. Looking at a brain from above, you see only forebrain. It is the largest division of the brain. Beneath the forebrain, near the center of the brain, is the midbrain. Below and behind the midbrain, near the base of the skull at the top of the spinal cord, is the hindbrain.

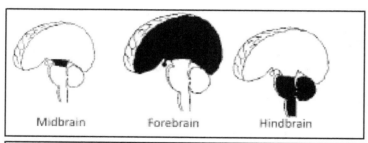

Midbrain   Forebrain   Hindbrain

Functional Areas of the Cerebral cortex

- The *Motor Cortex* controls voluntary body movement.
- The *Sensory Cortex* spans the parietal, occipital, and temporal lobes. Different locations in the sensory cortex receive information from the different senses.
- The *Association Cortex* combines sensory and motor information. Damage to association areas can create serious problems in a wide range of mental abilities.
- The *Prefrontal Cortex* is involved in problem solving, emotion, and complex thought.
- The *Somatosensory Cortex* processes sensations of touch.
- The *Visual Cortex* receives visual stimuli.
- The *Auditory Cortex* is involved in the processing of sound.
- *Wernicke's Area* is involved in language comprehension.
- *Broca's Area* is involved in speech production and articulation.

The Forebrain. The forebrain is the largest part of the brain making up about two-thirds of the brain's size. The forebrain includes the c*erebral cortex*, **thalamus**, **hypothalamus**, **amygdala**, and **hippocampus**.

The Cerebral Cortex. The outer layer of the forebrain, just under the skull and forehead is the cerebral cortex. The cerebral cortex contains the majority of the brain's neurons. The image most people have of the brain is the folding tissue of the cerebral cortex. The cerebral cortex is responsible for "higher-order" functions like language and reasoning.

Brain Hemispheres. The cerebral cortex is divided into hemispheres, lobes, cortexes, and areas. A deep fissure called the **longitudinal sulcus** splits the cerebral cortex down the middle into the left and right hemispheres. The cerebral cortex has **bilateral symmetry**, meaning that each hemisphere is a mirror image of the other. The left and right hemispheres are connected by a dense bundle of nerve fibers called the **corpus callosum**. The corpus callosum allows the two halves of the brain to communicate.

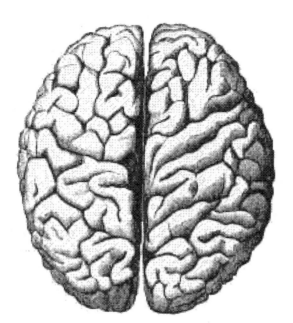

Hemispheric specialization refers to the different roles each hemisphere plays in mental life. For example, each side of the cerebral cortex controls movement in the opposite or contralateral side of the body. Touch receptors on the left side of the body transmit signals to the right cerebral hemisphere. Handedness (left or right-handed) is a function of the dominance of the opposite cerebral hemisphere. Generally, language is localized in the left hemisphere and spatial processing in the right, but most complex mental activity involves areas on both sides.

Visual processing is localized in the occipital lobe at the back of the brain. The *occipital lobe* collaborates with other brain structures in the formation of memory. The *parietal lobe* is the middle area of the brain. The parietal lobe is involved in spatial processing and in interpreting touch sensations. The *temporal lobes*, on the sides of the brain near the ears, are involved in hearing and collaborate with other parts of the brain in memory and emotion. The *frontal lobe*, in the front of the brain, is related to executive functions like attention, organization, planning, judgment, problem solving, and creativity.

Brain Lateralization. Though the cerebral hemispheres work together, brain lateralization refers to the localization of some brain activity in the right or left hemisphere. Generally the right cerebral cortex (right "brain") is dominant for spatial abilities, face recognition, and creativity. The left hemisphere is dominant for language, math, and logic. Much of what is known about brain lateralization comes from studies of people who have had the corpus callosum surgically severed as in cases of severe epileptic seizures.

Lobes. Each hemisphere is further divided into four lobes named for the parts of the skull under which they are located. As with hemispheric specialization, some mental activity is localized in specific lobes and some activity involves several lobes. The cerebral cortex can also be divided into functional areas.

The Thalamus. The thalamus is a small structure at the top of the midbrain. The thalamus plays an important role in sensory processing and movement. It serves as a type of relay station by receiving sensory information from the senses and sending it to the cerebral cortex. The thalamus also receives motor instructions from the cerebral cortex and sends them to other areas of the brain and to the body via the spinal cord.

The Hypothalamus. The hypothalamus is a very small structure, about the size of a pea, resting under the thalamus. The hypothalamus plays a major role in the autonomic nervous system, the experience of pleasure, and in control of body temperature, hunger, and thirst. The hypothalamus controls the pituitary gland and other endocrine glands.

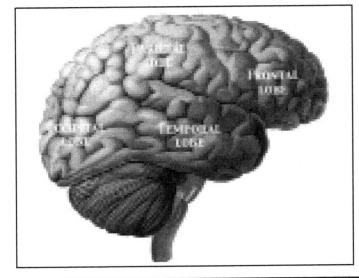

The Amygdala. The amygdala is an almond shaped structure located deep in the temporal lobe. The amygdala plays a role in fear and other emotions, learning, memory, attention, and perception.

The Hippocampus. The hippocampus is a seahorse-shaped structure in the temporal lobe. The hippocampus is involved

Brain Stem. The brain stem is a general term for the area of the brain between the thalamus and spinal cord. The brain stem includes the medulla, pons, tectum, reticular formation, and tegmentum. The brain stem supports basic functions of life such as breathing, heart rate, and blood pressure.

in processing memories, emotion, and spatial navigation. The hippocampus becomes smaller with age, which is thought to be related to declines in memory that many experience as they age and with Alzheimer's disease.

The Hindbrain. The hindbrain sits under the cerebral cortex at the base of the skull and the top of the spinal cord and is comprised of the cerebellum, pons, and medulla. The structures in the hindbrain co-ordinate movement, equilibrium, and sleep patterns and regulate involuntary body functions such as respiration and circulation.

The Cerebellum. The cerebellum is the second largest structure in the brain. The cerebellum (Latin for "little brain") is a walnut-shaped structure situated at the base of the brain responsible for movement, co-ordination, balance, and motor-related memory.

The Reticular Formation. The reticular formation is a mesh-like network of neurons involved in sleep and consciousness, arousal and attention, coordinating signals from the senses, and pain modulation.

The Pons. The pons (Latin for "bridge") serves in coordinating communication between the two cerebral hemispheres and between parts of the brain and the spinal cord.

The Medulla. The medulla, or medulla oblongata, is part of the brain stem located at the top of the spinal cord. The medulla is responsible for many vital functions including breathing, temperature regulation, and some aspects of speech.

The Midbrain. The midbrain is a small area of the brain (approximately 2 cm long) that sits between the forebrain and the hindbrain. It forms a major part of the brainstem and is comprised of the *tectum*, *tegmentum*, and *cerebral peduncles*. These structures connect the cerebral cortex with the brainstem and spinal cord. The tectum is involved in processing visual and auditory signals. The tegmentum is a network of neurons involved in reflexes, involuntary body functions, and attention. The cerebral peduncles are large fiber bundles of neurons that connect the midbrain and the cerebellum.

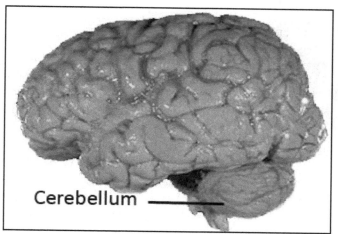

Cerebellum

Brain Plasticity. Our nervous system grows and changes throughout life. Brain plasticity refers to the lifelong process of creating, pruning, and reorganizing neural connections. Making new memories, learning a new skill, or recovering from a neural injury requires that there be persistent changes in the brain that represent the new information. Following some brain injuries, brain cells surrounding the damaged area change their function and shape to take the place of the damaged cells. God heals brains, too.

Circadian Rhythm. Your circadian rhythm or internal clock operates many physiological functions (e.g., sleep, body temperature, and alertness) on a 24-hour cycle. The suprachiasmatic nuclei is thought to be the brain's timekeeper.

Endocrine System. The endocrine system is a collection of glands that secrete hormones into the blood stream. **Hormones** are a type of chemical messenger (neurotransmitters are another). The endocrine system works with the nervous system to control growth and development, mood, metabolism, and reproduction.

Two parts of the endocrine system are found in the brain. The pineal gland, thought by Descartes to be the seat of the soul, produces **melatonin** which helps regulate the sleep cycle. The hypothalamus plays a major role in the endocrine system, controlling the pituitary gland and other endocrine glands.

The Limbic System. The thalamus, hypothalamus, amygdala, and hippocampus make up the limbic system. The limbic system plays an important role in our sense of smell and in memory and emotions.

Conclusion. The preceding pages present a very basic and simple overview of the brain and nervous system. The brain and nervous system are marvels of God's creation. You could spend your life studying it and not comprehend its complexity. Our brains are the most complex structures in the known universe, perhaps more complex than the universe itself. Each neuron contains irreducibly complex chemical and electrical machines in perfect synchronization.

The "God Spot." Many psychologists believe that belief in God is programmed into our brains. Because beliefs in gods are common across peoples and throughout history, as the theory goes, it must be programmed or "hard-wired" in our brains. If so, there must be a highly-evolved structure somewhere in the brain. The god spot, in the left temporal lobe, is said to be that structure. The discovery that some people with temporal-lobe epilepsy were prone to religious hallucinations led to the discovery that electrical stimulation to the temporal-lobe induced a religious-like experience. fMRIs show that the same area of the brain is active when subjects engage in religious activities.

Worldview Check. It should come as no surprise that our brains are involved in our experiences with God. The God spot may be the region of the brain where we experience God; it is not a region of the brain that creates that experience.

Was the nervous system designed or did it evolve? Does its complexity prove or disprove God? In Psychology 101, even in the face of evidence of design, the hypothesis of intelligent design will be excluded from consideration. Intelligent design is inconsistent with a naturalistic worldview. Evolutionist **Julian Huxley** explained that though we "seem" to be purposefully designed, the purpose is "only an apparent one." Huxley's is a worldview assumption, not a scientific statement. Evidence of intelligent design, though abundant, can not change a naturalist's worldview.

Evidence of similarities between your mental life and a primate's mental life is no threat to a Christian worldview.

The challenge for a naturalistic worldview is showing how "numerous, successive, and slight modifications" can explain our unfathomably complex nervous system, at the macro and the cellular levels. Do not believe it if the professor tells you the challenge has been met.

Chapter Summary.

The human nervous system is the most complex and coordinated structure in the known universe and a wonder of God's creation. The study of the brain and the nervous system is called neuro-psychology, neuro-anatomy, and neuro-biology.

The human nervous system consists of two sub-systems; the central nervous system (CNS) and the peripheral nervous system (PNS). The central nervous system consists of the brain and the spinal cord. The peripheral nervous system consists of those nerves outside of the brain and the spinal cord.

The neuron is the basic building block of the nervous system. Neurons communicate with each other via specialized extensions called dendrites and axons. At rest, a neuron has a slightly negative electrical charge. When it becomes sufficiently positively charged, a "spark" of electricity moves down the axon. Between neurons, neurotransmission occurs when a neuron releases neurotransmitters into the synaptic cleft where they are received by neighboring neurons. Psychotropic medications operate by affecting neurotransmission.

The peripheral nervous system (PNS) controls voluntary and involuntary muscle movement, sensory information, and automatic functions of the body. The PNS is made up of two main subsystems: the somatic and autonomic systems. The somatic system controls voluntary muscle movement. The autonomic system controls automatic body functions. The autonomic nervous system is further subdivided into the sympathetic and parasympathetic nervous systems which act as opposites. The sympathetic system creates an excited state and the parasympathetic system restores the body to a state of rest and relaxation.

Understanding of the structure and function of the brain came by studying the effects of brain injuries, lesions, psychosurgery, brain stimulation, and brain-imaging. Phrenology, a 19th century pseudo-science, proposed that mental functions were linked to specific areas of the brain. Phineas Gage's accident demonstrated the connection between the brain and personality. Cortical maps are graphic illustrations of the localization of brain functioning.

Brain imaging technologies provide a way for psychologists to see and measure brain activity. The electroencephalograph (EEG) records electrical voltage produced when neurons fire. The computer axial tomography (CAT scan) produces a three-dimensional x-ray of the brain. Positron emission tomography (PET scan) produces real-time three-dimensional images of blood flow, oxygen use, drug activity, and glucose metabolism. Magnetic Resonance Imaging (MRI) uses powerful magnetic fields and radio waves to create detailed images of the brain.

The brain is shielded by the skull, cushioned and nourished in cerebrospinal fluid, and protected from toxins by the blood-brain barrier. The brain consists of three major divisions: the forebrain, midbrain, and hindbrain. The forebrain makes up about two-thirds of the brain's size and includes the cerebral cortex, thalamus, hypothalamus, amygdala, and hippocampus. The hindbrain sits under the cerebral cortex at the base of the skull and is comprised of the cerebellum, pons, and medulla. The midbrain is a small area that sits between the forebrain and the hindbrain and forms a major part of the brainstem.

The cerebral cortex is the outer layer of the forebrain under the skull and forehead containing the majority of the brain's neurons. The cerebral cortex is divided into hemispheres, lobes, cortexes, and areas. The longitudinal sulcus divides the cerebral cortex into the left and right hemispheres, connected to each other by a dense bundle of nerve fibers called the corpus callosum. Each hemisphere is further divided into lobes, named for the parts of the skull under which they are located, and into cortexes and "areas" named for their functions.

The cerebellum, the second largest structure in the brain, is a walnut-shaped structure at the base of the brain involved in movement, co-ordination, balance, and motor-related memory. The brain stem supports basic functions of life such as breathing, heart rate and blood pressure.

Brain plasticity refers to the lifelong process of creating, pruning, and reorganizing neural connections.

The endocrine system is a collection of glands that work with the nervous system to control growth and development, mood, metabolism, and reproduction. The limbic system plays an important role in forming memories, the experience of emotion, and our sense of smell.

For Review.

1. Identify the major divisions of the nervous system.
2. What are the major structures of the neuron?
3. Name the three types of neurons and describe their function.
4. Describe neurotransmission, both within the neuron and between neurons.
5. Name and describe the three subsystems of the peripheral nervous system.
6. Respond to the following statement from a Christian worldview perspective. *"All mental experience is nothing more than brain activity."*
7. Describe important historical discoveries about the structure and function of the brain.
8. Discuss the case of Phineas Gage as an example of how brain injuries led to knowledge about brain function.
9. Describe the psycho-surgery known as the frontal lobotomy.
10. Name and describe five brain-imaging techniques.
11. Identify and describe the midbrain, forebrain, and hindbrain.
12. Identify 4 lobes of the cerebral cortex.
13. Describe hemispheric specialization.
14. Describe brain lateralization.
15. Describe "the god spot" from a naturalistic perspective and from a Christian perspective.

Chapter 5

Sensation and Perception

Wondrous. Take just a moment to look at something. It could be the scene outside of your window or simply the words on this page. As you "see" an object, light bounces off the object, enters the eye, and is focused on your retina. Receptor cells in the retina convert the light into neural signals that activate neighboring cells, which transmit millions of electrochemical messages, in an instant, to your brain. That is wondrous.

In your brain, separate specialized structures process information about color, form, motion, and depth, and then in ways psychologists only partially understand, combine that information to form a consciously perceived image that is instantly compared to images previously stored in your memory.

The whole process is like taking a house apart, molecule by molecule, and transporting it somewhere else where millions of specialized workers put it back together again. That this happens instantly, effortlessly, and continuously is better than cool; it is truly wondrous.

The processes through which we sense the world around us are very complex. The beauty and wonder of God's creation is for us to enjoy, but in order for us to enjoy it, it must first pass through our senses. Philosophers and scientists wonder at the marvel of the processes by which we experience and understand the physical world. In this chapter we review the basic processes through which sensory organs convert physical energy into nerve impulses and through which the brain interprets and understands those impulses.

Sensation and Perception. A sense is a system that transmits to the brain, information about the world outside of the brain. A sense converts characteristics of the physical world into nervous system activity. Sensations are processes by which external physical energy and chemicals stimulate our sense organs to transmit neural signals to the brain. Sensation refers to the experience of the environment through touch, taste, sight, sound, and smell and to our experience of ourselves in the world. Our sensory organs and sensory neural pathways to the brain are similar to those of other mammals.

Perception, on the other hand, is the process through which we organize, interpret, and give meaning to the raw neural impulses. Perception is tied to our consciousness. It involves an awareness and understanding unlike any animal. Sensation and perception are distinct processes that must operate seamlessly for us to experience and interact with the world around us.

Everything we know about the world we learned through our senses. This chapter explores our senses and how we perceive or "make sense" of sensory information.

Sensation. Sensation begins with sensory receptors – highly specialized cells designed to respond to particular types of energy. The brain can not directly experience light, sound, taste, or touch. Because the brain only experiences electro-chemical impulses, specialized sensory receptor cells, known as transducers, convert external physical energy into internal neural energy. Transduction is the process of converting physical stimuli into neural energy. There are three primary types of receptor cells:

- ***Photoreceptors*** are activated by electromagnetic energy (i.e., light).
- ***Chemoreceptors*** respond to chemical substances (i.e., odors).
- ***Mechanoreceptors*** respond to mechanical energy (i.e., touch, movement, vibrations).

Coding Sensations. Each sight, sound, touch, taste, and smell is qualitatively different. When receptors convert energy into neural activity, they code the physical properties of the sensation (brightness, color, volume, etc.) into patterns of neural activity. The coded patterns are transmitted to the central nervous system where the thalamus processes and relays the information to other parts of the brain where it is decoded, given meaning, understood, and perhaps remembered.

Signal Detection Theory. Early modern psychologists interested in the relationship between external stimuli and internal sensations developed signal detection theories to understand, describe, and predict responses to various stimuli. Psychologists create mathematical models of the relationships between the characteristics of the stimulus, the characteristics of the individual, and background noise.

> ***Seeing stars.*** Sensory cells are generally found within a sense organ and respond by design to specific stimuli. Sensory cells can be made to respond to other forms of strong stimulation. For example, a bump on the head (a mechanical stimulus) may stimulate the eye's photoreceptor cells. The result is seeing stars.

Absolute Thresholds
- Vision - A candle flame seen at 30 miles on a clear night.
- Hearing - The tick of a watch in quiet conditions at 20 ft.
- Taste - One teaspoon of sugar in 2 gallons of water.
- Smell - One drop of perfume diffused into the entire volume of air in a six-room apartment.
- Touch - The wing of a fly on your cheek from a distance of 1 cm.

Absolute Threshold. Absolute threshold refers to the minimum intensity of a stimulus that will stimulate an organ to operate. In other words, the absolute threshold is the lowest intensity of a light, sound, touch, taste, or smell that we can sense. Because the absolute threshold varies from person to person and from time to time for the same person, *absolute threshold* is defined as the point at which a very weak stimulus could be detected 50% of the time. The threshold varies because of internal noise and response factors. Internal noise refers to neurons firing randomly "in the background." *Response factors* are characteristics of you, your motivation, and your expectations, which affect your responsiveness to stimuli.

Sensory Adaptation. Sensory adaptation, also called *sensory habituation*, refers to the tendency of neurons to become less sensitive to constant or familiar stimuli. For example, people who live near airport runways experience sensory adaptation when they do not "notice" airplane noise. After living near an airport, the sound of crickets in the country would be a *novel stimulus* to which one would be very sensitive. *Dark adaptation* is the process in which the visual receptors become more sensitive to light, and *light adaptation* is the process by which our eyes become less sensitive to light. Sensory adaptation is the reason you are not constantly aware of the feeling of your clothes and you adjust to the water temperature of the swimming pool.

Just Noticeable Difference. We not only have the ability to detect stimuli, but we can recognize differences between similar stimuli. The *just noticeable difference* (JND) refers to receptor cells' ability to detect subtle changes in stimulus strength. How much brighter, louder, warmer, or smellier must a stimulus be before we notice the change? The just noticeable difference is the smallest change in a stimulus which a person can detect 50% of the time. It is easier to notice differences between weaker stimuli. Nineteenth-century psychologist *Ernst Webe*r (1795 – 1878) discovered the relationship between signal strength and JND. Weber found that we can not detect changes in signal strength unless the magnitude of the change is more than a fixed proportion. The relationship of sensation to change in stimulus strength is known as *Weber's Law*.

Weber's Law has important applications in marketing. With information about Weber's Law and the just noticeable difference, product manufacturers can make changes in product packaging that we will not notice (i.e., we might not notice the difference between a 16 oz. jar and a 15 ½ oz. jar or a $.10 price change). They might also use Weber's Law to make positive changes to their product very apparent.

The JND tends to be a constant expressed as a fraction of the stimulus intensity. For example, if you could just notice the difference between a 100 pound object and a 102 pound

Accessory structures modify the incoming sensory stimuli. For example, the lenses in your eyes focus light on the retina, and your external ear gathers sound and funnels to the inner ear.

The cornea is one of the parts of the body most sensitive to pain.

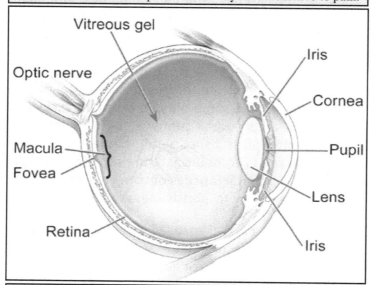

Vitreous gel

Optic nerve

Iris

Cornea

Macula

Fovea

Pupil

Lens

Retina

Iris

Eye Color. The color of the iris and thus the eye is determined by the amount of pigment contained in them.

Near-sightedness (myopia) and far-sightedness (hyperopia or hypermetropia) occur when images are not focused correctly on the retina. As we age, the lens becomes less flexible (presbyopia). Glasses and contact lenses change the refraction to correctly focus the image on the retina.

Alternately focus on your finger (near vision) and an object on distance. You can feel the lenses changing shape.

Because rods are concentrated around the outer edges of the retina, it is best to star gaze by not looking directly at a star. Gazing directly at a star casts its dim image on the fovea, where there are no rods, causing the star to disappear. Try it.

object (2% JND), it does not mean that you would notice the difference between 1000 pounds and 1002 pounds. Instead, it would take 1020 pounds (2%) before you noticed the difference. Like the absolute threshold, JND varies according to several factors. The amount of extraneous stimuli or background noise, the strength of the stimulus, the amount of repeated information in the stimulus, and bias affect JND.

Sight. For much of its modern history, the study of sensation and perception was psychology's main emphasis. The visual system was an important part of that emphasis. Sight is our most dominant sense, and more of our brain is involved in sight than in any other sense.

Light. Human sight is a highly sophisticated sensation of reflected *electromagnetic radiation* from a portion of the electromagnetic spectrum. For humans, only a small section of the electromagnetic spectrum is visible. We see the visible portion of the spectrum in the colors of the rainbow (red, orange, yellow, green, blue, indigo, and violet, commonly remembered by the acronym ROY G. BIV). We experience light as color or hue, brightness, and saturation. The light's wavelength is seen as *color*. The light's amplitude or energy is experienced as *brightness* or intensity. *Saturation* refers to the extent to which the light contains only one wavelength or color. Highly saturated colors look bright and vivid.

Cornea. The sensation of sight begins when reflected light enters the eye. The cornea refracts (i.e., bends and concentrates) the light into the iris. The *anterior chamber*, behind the cornea, is filled with a transparent liquid called the *aqueous humor*, which further refracts and focuses the image.

Blind Spot. The spot where the optic nerve leaves the eye contains no rods or cones. It is known as the blind spot. To draw the blind spot tester on a piece of paper, make a small dot on the left side separated by about 6-8 inches from a small + on the right side. Hold the image about 20 inches away and close your right eye. With your left eye, focus on the +. Slowly bring the image closer while focusing on the +. At some point the dot will disappear from sight. It happens when the image of the dot falls on the blind spot in your retina. (Try it with the other eye, too.)

Iris. The iris, the colored part of the eye behind the cornea, contains small muscles that open or close the **pupil**, the dark center of the iris, to allow in more or less light. The **pupillary reflex** accommodates varying light levels by **dilating** (enlarging) or **constricting** (shrinking). The pupillary reflex is controlled in the brain stem. Emergency medical personnel assess brain stem functioning by observing whether the pupils constrict in reaction to light.

Lens. The lens, located behind the iris, has primary responsibility for focusing the image onto the retina. The lens is flexible and controlled by a set of muscles that allow it to adjust its focus on objects near or far away.

Retina. The retina is comparable to a rounded screen at the back of the eye. The retina contains specialized photoreceptors called rods and cones. Rods and cones are named for their shapes. They are photoreceptors, meaning they contain chemicals that respond to light energy, triggering the neuron to send fire.

Rods. Rods are most sensitive to low levels of light and give us our night vision. Rods, named for their rod-like shape, do not respond to different wavelengths of light, so they do not sense color. The human eye has over 100 million rod cells concentrated around the outer edges of the retina. Rods provide peripheral vision and detect motion.

Cones. Cones are photoreceptor cells that operate best at high levels of light and are responsible for color vision and vision acuity. Cones are concentrated in the center of the retina, most densely in an area called the fovea.

Fovea. The fovea is at the center of our field of vision. It is a small area, densely packed with cones, in the center of the retina. The fovea only contains cones and is where we have our highest visual acuity.

Optic Nerve. Rods and cones transmit their signal to ganglion cells. Over 1 million ganglion cells' axons exit the eye and form the optic nerve. The optic nerve is a bundle of nerve fibers that travel from each eye and cross at the optic chiasm. At the optic chiasm, about half of the nerve fibers cross over to the opposite cerebral hemisphere. The thalamus routes the signals to the visual cortex in the occipital lobe. Visual images from the right visual field are processed in the left visual cortex; images from the left visual field are processed in the right hemisphere.

Feature Detectors. Feature detectors are specialized neurons (or groups of neurons) that respond to specific characteristics of visual stimuli (e.g., lines, angles, curve, and movement). Feature detectors fire when a visual image contains its specific characteristic.

> ***Color Blindness.*** People who have difficulty seeing color are said to be color blind. Total color blindness is rare. Red-green color blindness (the most common color blindness) and blue-yellow color blindness describe the inability to see certain colors.

Color Vision. Cones in the retina are responsible for our color vision. Two theories, the trichromatic and the opponent process, explain color vision.

Trichromatic Theory. The trichromatic, or three-color theory of color vision, one of psychology's oldest, suggests that we experience all colors as mixtures of red, green, and blue light. Later research showed that there are three types of cones, each responding to red, green, or blue light. Each type of cone contains chemicals designed to respond to light in the red, green, or blue light range of the spectrum.

Opponent-process Theory. If you stare at a bright object and then look away, you will see an after-image. The trichromatic theory of color vision could not explain after-images. There are some color combinations that we cannot see. The opponent-process theory of color vision suggests that in addition to the mixing of three colors, we sense color through the activity of two opponent systems – a blue-yellow system and a red-green mechanism. Cones respond to opposing colors with excitatory or inhibitory responses. The ratio and combination of cones responding to colors in an excitatory/inhibitory blend is thought to best explain color vision.

Hearing. The eye senses electromagnetic radiation. Hearing is the sensation and perception of pressure changes in a medium, usually the air. Sound waves, like light waves, have amplitude and frequency. Amplitude describes the wave height or the amount of pressure change. Amplitude is the loudness. A sound's pitch is a function of its frequency (i.e., the number of waves per second).

The Ear. The funnel-shaped outer-ear, also called the auricle or pinna, gathers sound pressure waves and directs them down the auditory canal to the eardrum or tympanic membrane. The auricle, auditory canal, and tympanic membrane, also called the eardrum, make up the outer ear. The eardrum is a thin, skin-like stretched membrane,

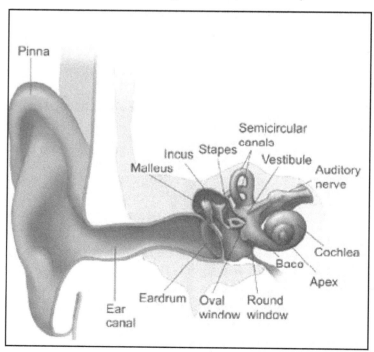

much like the skin of a drum. When the sound waves hit the eardrum, it vibrates. Those vibrations pass through a series of small bones or ossicles in the middle ear. The ossicles consist of the hammer or *malleus*, anvil or *incus*, and the stirrup or *stape*. The ossicles are the smallest bones in your body and work to magnify the eardrum's vibrations and to transmit them to the inner ear. Those magnified vibrations enter the inner ear at the *oval window*. The *cochlea* is a hard, snail-shaped fluid-filled structure lined with the basilar membrane. The *basilar membrane* is covered with microscopic hair-like cells called *stereocilia* that connect with the *auditory nerve*. As vibrations enter the cochlea, the fluid moves, bending the stereocilia and stimulating a neural impulse that travels along the auditory nerve to the auditory cortex of the temporal lobe. The stereocilia are mechanoreceptors; they convert mechanical stimulation (vibrations) into neural activity.

Coding Sounds. The auditory system must communicate or "code" the qualities of sounds like *volume* and *frequency*. Neurons fire more rapidly to code that a sound is loud. There are two main theories explaining how we experience differing sound frequencies. *Place theory* suggests that the stereocilia in specific parts of the cochlea fire in response to specific frequencies. *Volley theory* suggests that neurons along the cochlea fire in a wave that matches the frequency of the sound.

Chemical Senses. Humans sense chemicals via two connected sense systems. The *olfactory system* (smell) detects airborne chemicals. The *gustatory system* (taste) detects chemicals that come in contact with the tongue.

Smell (Olfactory System). At the roof of your nasal cavity is a lining of specialized tissue known as the *olfactory epithelium* (mucous membrane). The olfactory epithelium holds the olfactory receptors. Olfactory receptors are designed to respond to particular chemicals. The receptors join the *olfactory nerve* and feed directly into the *olfactory bulb* in the brain, not through the thalamus as with other senses. From the olfactory bulb, signals travel to other parts of the brain including the *amygdala*, which processes emotion, which may be why the link between smells and memories is so strong. We have receptors for thousands of different chemicals, but what we experience as an odor is a pattern of responses to a variety of individual chemicals.

Taste (Gustatory). What we experience as taste is actually more about smell than taste. Psychologists suggest that as much as 75% of what we experience as taste actually comes from our sense of smell. Taste begins with taste

There are no pain receptors in the cerebral cortex, which allows patients to remain conscious and alert during brain surgery.

receptor cells called *gustatory cells* clustered primarily in the *papillae*, commonly called the taste buds. Papillae are open to the surface of the tongue and contain clusters of taste receptors. Taste receptors are specialized and respond best to a single taste. We can sense sweet, salty, bitter, and sour. Some psychologists suggest that we have unique receptor cells that respond to two other tastes called umani (glutamates) and astringent (tannins).

Touch, Temperature, and Pain (The Cutaneous System).

The skin is our largest sense organ. Our sense of touch is part of a larger system known as the somatic senses. The *somatic senses* provide the brain with information about the body, its condition, and its relationship with the outside world.

Touch receptors wrap around individual hair follicles allowing you to feel slight movement in a single hair. Try it by moving a single hair on your arm.

Touch. Our sense of touch is extremely complex and involves several types of receptor cells. One square inch of skin contains nearly 20 million cells. Your fingertips are especially densely packed with *cutaneous receptors*, which makes them very sensitive to touch. Specialized cutaneous receptors respond either to pressure, shape, texture, movement, and temperature. Touch receptors fire at varying rates and combinations to signal characteristics of touch.

Phantom Pain. Phantom pain is the experience of pain in a part of the body that is not there. Psychologists report that phantom pain is a common experience of amputees.

Pain. Specialized neurons called *nociceptors* extend from the spinal cord to the skin or any other part of the body that can experience pain. Specialized nociceptors respond to sharp pricking pain or to dull gnawing pain. *Gate control theory* suggests there is a type of gateway in the spinal cord that can cut off pain signals from reaching the brain.

The Proprioception System.

Proprioception means "from one's own perspective." The proprioception system provides the brain with information about body movement, position, and balance.

The Kinesthetic System.

Our kinesthetic sense informs us about the position and movement of parts of the body. Without this sense, we could not control voluntary movements like walking. The kinesthetic sense allows you to know where your foot is, relative to the rest of your body, even when your eyes are closed. The kinesthetic sense plays a big part in allowing you to stumble but not fall. Neurons in muscle fibers and joints send information via the thalamus to the sensory cortex.

Motion Sicknesses. Motion, car, and seasickness happen when the visual system and the vestibular system disagree about whether you are moving. If you read while in the car, your vision tells the brain you are stationary, but the vestibular system tells it you are moving.

The Vestibular System. The vestibular system provides information about the position of our body relative to gravity and movement. Fluid-filled organs in the inner ear are oriented along three different planes. Head movement along one of those planes causes the fluid to move, which in turn is detected and converted to neural impulses. A similar system detects acceleration and deceleration.

Perception. Perception is the process through which our brain and nervous system selects, organizes, interprets, adds to, and gives meaning to sensations. Perception is what we do with the information that our senses send to the brain and how our motivation, expectations, and experiences affect how sensations will be perceived.

Top-down and Bottom-up Processing. A number of different psychological processes are involved in perceiving the world around us. Along each sensory pathway, sensory information is automatically sorted, organized, identified, selected, and grouped before it reaches the cerebral cortex in a process psychologists call ***bottom-up processing***. When sensory information arrives in the cerebral cortex, our "higher level" mental processes, past experience, expectations, context, and mental and emotional states affect how we perceive the information in a process called ***top-down processing***.

We sense the presence of a stimulus. We perceive what it is.

Figure-ground perception. See the vase? If so, it is the "figure." Everything else is background. See two faces? It is difficult to see the faces and the vase (figure and ground) at the same time.

Figure-ground Perception. Two basic principles, figure-ground perception and gestalt, explain our initial bottom-up organization of sensations. When we perceive a scene, we pay attention to or emphasize certain objects or features. Those features you attend to are "figures" and everything else is the "ground" or background.

Gestalt. Early psychologists recognized that we group the characteristics of sensations into a "whole" experience. The word gestalt means overall,

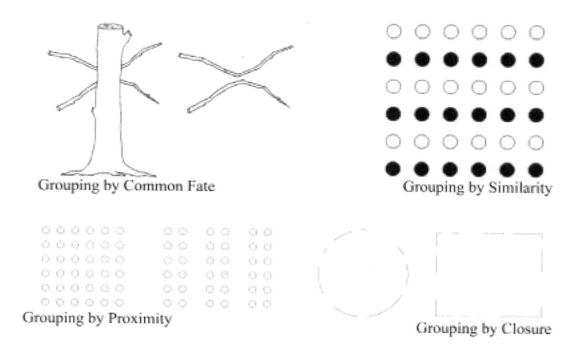

Grouping by Common Fate

Grouping by Similarity

Grouping by Proximity

Grouping by Closure

Gestalt principles (also called laws) by which we automatically group stimuli.

- *Proximity*. When objects and events appear close to one another (in space or in time), they are perceived as though they belong together.
- *Similarity*. We tend to group objects with similar properties (i.e., color, shape, texture).
- *Continuity*. We tend to group objects according to smooth lines or curves.
- *Common fate*. We tend to group objects moving in the same direction and perceive them as a single object.
- *Closure*. We tend to fill in the gaps in incomplete figures.

whole, and totality. Gestalt psychologists focus on the ways that we create a "whole" experience from the many and varied sensory inputs. When describing perception, gestalt refers to the ways we perceive stimuli by grouping sensations together in meaningful ways.

Perceptual Constancy. Our perceptual processes are designed to interpret characteristics of stimuli as constants, even as sensory input changes. For example, size is a characteristic of a visual stimulus. When we see an object moving away, its image on the retina gets smaller. We do not "see" the object shrinking, however. ***Size constancy*** means that the brain interprets the shrinking retinal image as the object moving away. ***Shape constancy*** refers to the brain's understanding that objects maintain their shape even when viewed from different perspectives. Similarly, the brain is designed to understand that an object's brightness and color remains constant under varying light conditions.

Depth Perception. Our brains are designed to experience the world in three dimensions, even though the images projected on the retina are two-dimensional. We perceive depth based on stimulus cues, or the characteristics of the scene and from the position of our eyes.

Do you see a young lady or old woman? This 1888 advertisement is a classic example of perceptual ambiguity.

Monocular Cues. Physical characteristics of a scene that provide cues to depth are called monocular cues. **Interposition** refers to our tendency to perceive objects blocking other objects as closer to us. Our brains perceive relative size as a cue of depth. In other words, the brain understands that a tiny retinal image of a person means that a regular-sized person is far away, not that there is a tiny person standing nearby. Other **depth cues** come from the **relative height** of objects, the apparent **convergence of parallel lines**, **light and shadow**, and **texture and clarity**.

Binocular Cues. Some information about depth and distance comes to us from the way our eyes are shaped and positioned. The shape of the eyes change as they focus on objects near or far. Information about the shape of the eye helps create the perception of depth. Similarly, convergence, or the degree to which the eyes rotate toward the nose, provides a cue of distance. Retinal disparity refers to differences between retinal images. The disparity is greater for objects nearby than for objects in the distance.

Movement. Cues about characteristics of objects in motion come from patterns and changes in retinal images in the visual field known as the optical flow. An example of a pattern of optical flow is called **looming**. When the retinal image of an object grows rapidly, we automatically perceive it as an approaching object.

Perceptual Selectivity. The brain receives a tremendous amount of sensory information every second. We only attend to a small part of that information. Attention to sensory information is influenced by characteristics of the input and characteristics of ourselves.

The movement of an image on the retina is not the only factor in perceiving motion. If it were, we would perceive images as moving when we move our head and eyes. Try this. Close one eye, focus on an object, and shake your head from side to side. Notice that the object is perceived as stationary. Now, focus on the same object with one eye closed, gently tap the other eye through the eyelid. The object will appear to jump around with the movement of your eye.

Stimulus Factors. Stimulus factors are those characteristics of objects that affect our perception of the object. We tend to focus on objects that are in **contrast** (physically different), **more intense**, and

Look at the black and white shapes and try to recognize the image before reading on. Do you see it? Look again. Bottom-up processing is hard at work. Once you "see" the Dalmatian sniffing the ground at the center of the image, it is part of your schema and becomes almost impossible not to see it every time you look at the picture. This illustrates the power of previous experience and learning on our perceptions.

bigger than objects around them. We tend to focus on objects in *motion* and on objects that are *new* or *unusual*.

Personal Factors. Your worldview affects your perceptions. Mental set and schema are terms psychologists use to describe the effect of our beliefs, knowledge, and assumptions on perception. Our *mental set* predisposes us to perceive new experiences in predictable ways. Past experience, values, expectations, context, and mental and emotional states affect our perception. We do not just passively receive stimuli; we are actively engaged in perceiving the world. Psychologists have shown that one's cultural background influences perception, too. A Christian worldview believes that sin affects perception (Jeremiah 17:9).

Illusions. Illusions are a type of perceptual short circuit – perceptions that are at odds with reality. We experience an illusion when we perceive *conflicting sensory information*, *paradoxes* (impossible shapes), and *ambiguity*.

Extrasensory Perception (ESP) and Paranormal Psychology.

Ask most people to name the five senses and they will answer with taste, touch, sight, smell, and hearing. They are right, in a sense (pun intended). But we also have a kinesthetic sense, vestibular sense, and a host of other sensory systems. Each body sense has a natural explanation and physiological processes. But can we sense things through non-physiological, extra-sensory processes? Do we have ESP?

Extrasensory perception is said to be the sensation of energy that cannot be measured or studied in replicable experiments. People with extrasensory perception are said to be *psychic*. The study of ESP is part of parapsychology. Parapsychology is the study of paranormal psychological phenomena. *Paranormal* refers to any phenomena that is not replicable, "physically" impossible, not explainable by natural processes, or beyond the range of normal experience.

Parapsychologists research phenomena like:

- Extra-sensory perception.
- Psychokinetics, or moving or affecting physical objects by non-physical methods (i.e.,"mind over matter").
- Survival of consciousness after death, near-death experiences, and out-of-body experiences.
- Mental telepathy or the sending and receiving of thought through brain waves.
- Clairvoyance or the ability to see or predict the future.
- Ghosts, mediums, spirit communication, and automatic writing.

A naturalistic worldview leads most psychologists to dismiss ESP and parapsychology. Most Christians also dismiss ESP and parapsychology, but for different reasons. Modern psychology dismisses parapsychology because modern psychology denies the existence of the supernatural, but a Christian worldview acknowledges that there is a natural and a supernatural world. A Christian worldview believes that the spiritual can affect the physical world (Matthew 17:20), that we survive after death (John 3:16), and that we can receive messages through "extra sensory" means (Ephesians 1:18). A Christian worldview distinguishes between good spiritual forces (of God) and Satanic forces (Ephesians 6:12). Though parapsychologists generally attribute spiritual power to some benign universal consciousness or power, the Christian must remember that there is no middle ground and should approach parapsychology with the most extreme caution.

Chapter Summary.

A sense is a system that transforms information about the outside world into nervous system activity and transmits it to the brain. Perceptions are the subjective experience of sensations, the ways that we organize, interpret, and give meaning to raw neural impulses.

- Sensation begins with highly specialized cells designed to respond to particular types of energy.
- Photoreceptors are activated by electromagnetic energy.
- Chemoreceptors respond to chemicals substances.
- Mechanoreceptors respond to mechanical energy.

Absolute threshold refers to the minimum intensity of a stimulus that will stimulate a sense organ to operate. Habituation, a simple type of learning, refers to the tendency of neurons to become less sensitive to constant or familiar stimuli. Just noticeable difference (JND) refers to receptor cells' ability to detect subtle changes in stimulus strength. The relationship of sensation to change in stimulus strength is known as Weber's Law.

Sight is our most dominant sense, and more of our brain is involved in sight than any other sense. Human sight is the sensation of reflected electromagnetic radiation. The light's wavelength is seen as color. The light's amplitude is experienced as brightness or intensity. The cornea refracts light into the iris. The pupillary reflex opens and closes the pupil and the lens focuses the image onto the retina. The retina is lined with specialized receptors called rods and cones. Rods are most sensitive to low levels of light and cones are sensitive to high light levels of light and are responsible for color vision and vision acuity. Cones are most concentrated in the fovea, the center of the field of vision. The optic nerve extends from the eye, across the optic chiasm, to the cerebral hemisphere. There are no rods or cones at the blind spot where the optic nerve leaves the eye.

Hearing is the sensation and perception of sounds. Sounds are pressure changes or waves passing through the air. Sound frequency is perceived as loudness and frequency as pitch. The outer ear directs sound down the auditory canal to the tympanic membrane, the vibrations from which pass through a series of small bones in the middle ear called the ossicles. The ossicles magnify the eardrum's vibrations and transmit them to the inner ear via the oval window. The cochlea is a snail-shaped fluid-filled structure lined with the basilar membrane. The basilar membrane is covered with stereocilia that connect with the auditory nerve.

The olfactory system detects airborne chemicals. Olfactory receptors in the mucus membrane (olfactory epithelium) at the roof of the nasal cavity connect to the olfactory nerve and feed into the brain. We have receptors that are sensitive to thousands of airborne chemicals, but what we experience as an odor is usually a pattern of responses to a variety of chemicals.

The gustatory system detects chemicals that come into contact with the tongue. What we experience as taste is actually more about smell than taste. Taste receptor cells are clustered in papillae on the tongue. The cutaneous system is part of a larger sensory system known as the somatic senses. The somatic senses provide the brain with information about the body, its condition, and the body's relationship with the outside world. Cutaneous receptors respond to pressure, shape, texture, movement, and temperature. Nociceptors extend from the spinal cord to the body and are involved in the experience of pain.

The kinesthetic system provides the brain with information about body position and movement. The vestibular system provides information about the position of our body relative to gravity and movement.

Perception is the process through which we select, organize, interpret, and give meaning to sensations.

Figure-ground perception and grouping are ways we begin to organize and understand sensations. Perceptual selectivity describes reasons we select of some sensory inputs for attention and ignore others. Stimulus factors are those characteristics of objects that affect our perception of the object. Personal factors including experience, values, expectations, context, and mental and emotional states affect our perception.

For Review.

1. Define sensation and perception.
2. Define sensory threshold, just noticeable difference, absolute threshold, and Weber's Law and sensory adaptation.
3. Describe the major structures and processes of the visual system.
4. Describe the trichromatic and opponent-process theories of color vision.
5. Describe the major structures and processes of the auditory system.
6. Describe the place and volley theories of coding sounds.
7. Describe the major structures and processes of the olfactory system.
8. Describe the major structures and processes of the gustatory system.
9. Describe the major structures and processes of the cutaneous system.
10. Describe the kinesthetic system.
11. Name the three primary types of receptor cells.
12. Describe top-down and bottom-up processing.
13. Explain Gestalt concepts and principles, such as figure-ground, continuity, similarity, proximity, closure, and so on.
14. Describe the influence of environmental variables, motivation, past experiences, culture, and expectations on perception
15. Explain extrasensory perception and paranormal psychology.

Chapter 6

Motivation and Emotion

In This Chapter
- Motivation?
- Instincts
- Drive Reduction Theory
- Arousal Theory
- Incentive Theory
- Abraham Maslow
- Social Motivation
- Freudian Psycho-dynamic Perspective
- Emotions
- Categorizing Emotions
- Theories of Emotion
- Stress

Why do we do the things that we do? Why do we feel the ways we feel? What is motivation and what are emotions?

Motivation and emotions are closely related, and sometimes it is hard to distinguish between them. Combined, motivation and emotions drive and define how we respond to every situation we encounter.

The Bible is far from silent about motivation and emotions. In a Christian worldview, our chief motivation is to glorify God. God and our relationship to Him is pivotal to everything, especially our motivation and emotions. Modern psychology's theories do not reference God.

Motivation. Motivation is defined as an inner state and a process that arouses, directs, maintains, and terminates behavior. Motivation is a force that starts and keeps you moving toward goals and leads you to do everything from getting up in the morning to studying psychology and to choosing a spouse. Motivation is said to be *intrinsic,* a force from within, or *extrinsic.* a force from outside of us.

Worldview Check. Evolutionary psychologists explain human motivation in the same ways that evolutionary biologists explain human anatomy and physiology, but it goes much further. Evolutionary *biologists* explain human anatomy in terms of adaptive physical structures that became progressively more complex over time. Evolutionary *psychologists* explain motivation and emotion in terms of adaptive mental structures that have become progressively more complex over time. Every human motivation and emotion exists because it served an adaptive function that increased the chances of survival and reproduction. Love, art, faith, sacrifice, determination, envy, anger, and more, from a naturalistic psychology perspective, are not transcendent, supernatural, or even special. They are illusions — ways of understanding and interpreting innate patterns of behaviors and mental processes that themselves are no more than biochemical processes which exist solely to help us pass along our genes to the next generation.

Modern psychology's main theories of motivation come from the biological, behavioral, and humanistic perspectives. The biological perspective produced theories explaining motivation in term of instincts, drives, and needs. The behavioral perspective explained motivation in terms of external forces, rewards, and consequences.

> *Intrinsic Motivation:* Motivation coming from within, not from external rewards; based on personal desire to complete a task.
>
> *Extrinsic Motivation:* Based on obvious external rewards or obligations, or to avoid a negative event.

The humanistic perspective explained motivation in terms of an intrinsic human need to grow and achieve.

Instincts. Early modern psychologists used instinctive animal behavior as the basis for theories of human motivation. Instincts are automatic, involuntary, and unlearned patterns of behavior that are triggered by particular stimuli. *William McDougal* (1871 - 1938) and others proposed that human behavior is not intentional; it is the playing-out of as many as 10,000 instinctive behaviors individually and in combination. Some human behavior is clearly instinctive (i.e., the infant sucking and grasping reflexes), but few psychologists at the beginning of the 20th century believed that instinctive processes alone were sufficient to explain the wide range of human motivations. It is noteworthy that modern psychologists today do not explain motivation in terms of instincts, but they focus instead on locating the connection between DNA and motivation. McDougal's instinct theory and contemporary theories of the genetics of motivation both presume that motivation is reducible to natural biologic processes.

Drive Reduction Theory. Other early theories explained motivation in terms of various "drives" and "needs." According to drive reduction theory, biological *needs* are the primary motivator of human behavior. We all need food, water, and shelter. The psychological experience of biological needs is called a *drive*. According to *Clark Hull* (1884 - 1952), organisms seek biological balance or homeostasis. *Drives* are unpleasant internal states of tension which arouse us to take action to meet a biologic need, to restore *homeostasis*, and to reduce internal tension. *Secondary drives* are not biological; they are said to be learned through association with a biological drive. For example, according to drive reduction theory, you are motivated to study hard, a secondary drive, because you've associated studying with being able to buy a nice home, eating good food, and feeling safe and secure; primary drives.

> *The Psychology of Hunger.* Why do we feel hungry? Why is it so hard to think of anything else when we are hungry? Why do some people eat when they are not hungry and others starve themselves? Hunger, like most topics in psychology, is complicated and involves a number of factors.
>
> The hypothalamus plays an important role in hunger. The hypothalamus monitors blood glucose and insulin levels. Electrical stimulation to the hypothalamus stimulates hunger. Animals whose "hunger center" in the hypothalamus is destroyed starve to death unless forced to eat. Electrical stimulation to "the satiation center" of the hypothalamus terminates hunger. Animals with damage to this portion of the hypothalamus will eat larger than usual quantities of food. External (situational) cues and internal cues can also trigger feeling hungry. The smell of fresh baked bread, the sight of hot pizza, and the sound of the dinner bell can trigger feeling hungry as can stress, your mood, and boredom.

Arousal Theory. Drive reduction theory's focus on biologic needs was insufficient to explain the full range of human motivations. There is no biologic "need" to sky dive, bungee jump, or play sports. Arousal theory

The Yerkes–Dodson Law describes the relationship between optimal arousal and performance. According to Yerkes-Dodson, performance on a task increases with physical and mental arousal, but when levels of arousal become too high, performance decreases.

states that we are driven to achieve our individually optimal state of arousal. Some of us are "programmed" to operate at higher levels of arousal than others. Arousal theory explains why some people climb mountains, ride roller coasters, watch sad movies, or curl up with a book. Arousal theory also explains why we perform better on tasks when we are at our optimal state of arousal for that task. For example, your optimal arousal level for a soccer game is different than for studying psychology.

Incentive Theory. Behaviorism, as a theory explaining behavior, is necessarily interested in the motivations prompting behavior. Incentive theories apply behavioral principles to questions of motivation. Drives are forces within us that "push" behavior. Incentives are forces in the environment that "pull" behavior. Incentives are pleasant consequences of behaviors that tend to reinforce the behavior. According to incentive theory, we are motivated by what we expect to gain by a certain behavior.

Abraham Maslow (1908 - 1970) is known as the *father of humanistic psychology*. Maslow's is probably the most influential modern theory of motivation. In his theory, Maslow proposed that Man is innately and naturally motivated to grow and progress through a series, or *hierarchy*, of physical and psychological steps or stages. Maslow's idea that people are born with a motivation to grow toward self-actualization, as defined by humanist morals and values, is central to a humanistic worldview today.

Maslow's hierarchy of needs

In Maslow's theory, our primary motivations are *physiological needs* – food, water, and shelter, and *safety needs* – security and protection from harm. When those most basic needs have been met, our motivational focus changes to *affiliation –*, a feeling of belonging, love, family ties, and group membership. Next, according to Maslow and humanism, we are propelled to meet *esteem* needs – to be recognized for our achievement, for social status, and for respect. Once our need for affiliation and esteem are

> **Achievement and Subjective Well-being.** Psychologists describe subjective well-being as each person's satisfaction with life, characterized by frequent positive moods and emotions and infrequent negative moods and emotions. Research suggests that close relationships and religious faith are more associated with well-being than achievement, wealth, or power.

met, according to Maslow, we can then pursue *"self actualization,"* a distinctly human drive to fulfill one's potential through self-awareness, knowledge, and creativity.

Maslow's theory illustrates the need to examine theories at the worldview level. Intuitively, Maslow's hierarchy makes sense. Unless we have food, clothes, shelter and security, we are motivated for little else. Unless we feel connected with other people, we feel incomplete. Unless we feel good about ourselves, we cannot achieve our full potential.

The Christian worldview sees human potential differently. Maslow did not explain why some people postpone affiliation (i.e., marriage) to pursue esteem goals (i.e., pursuing a career). Maslow does not explain why some people (e.g., Jesus, Mother Theresa, Gandhi) choose to forgo basic needs in pursuit of higher goals. The Christian worldview has the explanation. A Christian worldview recognizes that despite being hungry, unsafe, and alone, one can be fully "actualized" in one's relationship with Jesus. We should first seek the kingdom of God and trust that our physical, safety, and other "needs" will be met. Contrition, self-denial, and humility are means by which we achieve spiritual growth, not group membership, achievement, or social status. Jesus, not knowledge or self-awareness, is the measure of Mankind's "actualization." You will be taught Maslow's hierarchy in college. Please do not forget that understanding human development and accepting the humanistic worldview are different. As stated before, you can do one without the other.

> **Lie Detector Tests.** The physiological responses that accompany emotions are activated by the autonomic nervous system which is largely outside of conscious control. The polygraph, which literally means "many writings," measures and records a subject's heart rate, blood pressure, respiration, and perspiration (galvanic skin response) as the subject responds to questioning. Polygraph examiners, trained in the study of deception, compare test results to the known patterns of responses typical of deception. The American Polygraph Association (APA) estimates that polygraphs are 87.5% accurate.

Social Motivation. Since Maslow, psychologists have put forward a number of theories that explain human motivation in terms of a variety of social needs. The **need for achievement** describes a drive to meet high personal standards of excellence. The **need for affiliation** is said to motivate forming friendships and associations, and the **need for intimacy** motivates forming intimate relationships. The **need for power** is said to motivate those who want to be in charge and to control others.

Freudian Psychodynamic Perspective. Freud believed that human motivation was a product of instinctive in-born forces. According to Freud, everything we do is ultimately motivated by our pursuit of aggression and sensual pleasure.

Sexual Motivation. Sexual motivation and sexual behavior are hot-button issues. Like many other psychological topics, a Christian worldview understands human sexuality as a reproductive necessity and as an expression of our God-likeness. A Christian worldview sees the sexual union between a man and wife as an expression of God-like intimacy and unity. A Christian worldview interprets sexual behavior in relation to moral absolutes.

Modern psychology sees sexuality as evolution's driving force. It interprets sexual behavior in terms of non-religious beliefs, humanistic values, and social and cultural factors.

Psychologists describe sexual behavior in terms of the **sexual response cycle**. The sexual response cycle refers to the physiological processes involved in sex. Sex hormones (e.g., estrogen, progesterone, and testosterone) play a role in the biology and the psychology of sexual behavior.

Emotions. What are emotions? We experience emotions every day; our emotions are with us constantly. What are emotions and where do they come from? Emotions like love and joy are some of life's greatest blessings. Grief and loss can seem unbearable. We experience emotions with great intensity, and most of us will at some point struggle to control our emotions.

The Bible does not use the word "emotion," but it is filled with instructions about emotions (e.g., anger, three types of love, peace, and joy). A Christian worldview sees emotions as part of our God-likeness. Emotions are an expression of our inner person, our heart. We are commanded to experience certain emotions, avoid others, and not to let emotions control us. A Christian worldview holds that sin corrupts every emotion, but by living in a relationship with God through Christ, our emotions are changed and renewed.

Emotions are complex. Emotions involve both physiological and psychological processes. The experience of emotions is characterized by at least two components: **subjective feelings** and **physiological responses**. Emotions are **subjective** experiences. We feel what we feel. Various regions in the cerebral cortex work together to process and understand the sensations, thoughts, and memories that make up the experience of emotions. In concert with the personal subjective experience of emotions, we experience objective and universal physiological changes. In the limbic system the amygdala, hippocampus, and thalamus trigger changes in our heart rate, blood pressure, respiration, perspiration, and even pupil dilation.

We understand that some emotions are positive (e.g., joy), some negative (e.g., grief), and some a mixture of both (i.e., the bittersweet feeling your parents will have when you leave for college). Emotions are generally short-lived whereas moods which last longer. Emotions influence thoughts and behaviors, and thoughts and behaviors influence emotions in a reciprocal relationship. We experience emotions in varying intensities, and sometimes they seem to overwhelm us.

Categorizing Emotions. A number of psychologists have proposed models of emotions that number, name, describe, and categorize human emotions. Psychologist *Robert Plutchik* described eight basic emotions, each with a polar opposite basic emotion.

Basic emotion	Opposite emotion
Joy	Sadness
Trust	Disgust
Fear	Anger
Surprise	Anticipation
Sadness	Joy
Disgust	Trust
Anger	Fear
Anticipation	Surprise

According to Plutchik, all human emotions are comprised of varying degrees and combinations of the eight basic emotions and their polar opposites. For example, contempt is a combination of anger and disgust. *Psychologist Paul Ekman* (1934 -) is renowned for his study of emotions, facial expressions, and lying. Ekman described six basic emotions that he thought were biological. Ekman observed that anger, disgust, fear, happiness, sadness, and surprise were accompanied by universal facial expressions.

Communicating Emotions Not only do we experience emotions on the inside, but we communicate our emotions to others through our words, movements, posture, tone of voice, facial expressions, and behaviors. A smile means happy and a frown means sad, whether you are in Blue Ridge or Budapest. We interpret and understand other people's emotions by reading their *emotional cues.*

Theories of Emotion. What is the connection between the physical and psychological experience of emotions? Does the subjective experience of an emotion trigger the body's response, or does the body's physical response trigger the subjective feeling? Are emotions culturally-determined or biological?

The Evolution of Emotions. As noted earlier, psychologists have observed that some human emotions are universal and that specific recognizable facial expressions universally accompany those emotions. Psychologists have also

"We feel sorry because we cry; angry because we strike; afraid because we tremble." - William James

Love. Robert Sternberg (1949 -) proposed a "triangle" model explaining the experience of love. According to Sternberg, love consists of three interdependent parts: intimacy, passion, and commitment. *Intimacy* refers to feelings of closeness and connectedness. *Passion* refers to romance and physical attraction, and *commitment* is the decision to love and stay in a relationship with another person.

In Sternberg's model, the presence of one, two, or all three parts of love defines the nature of love. For example, a relationship with passion but not intimacy or commitment is infatuation. Sternberg called intimacy without romance or physical attraction, "liking." Consummate love is said to be the presence of intimacy, passion, and commitment.

observed that primates and other species display patterns of facial expressions and appear to experience emotions. According to an evolutionary theory, human emotions are highly evolved special physiological states that provided our ancient ancestors a survival or reproductive advantage.

James-Lange Theory. William James (1842 - 1910), who is known as America's first psychologist, and Carl Lange (1834 - 1900) proposed that the body triggers the experience of emotions. In the James-Lang theory, the body responds automatically to environmental circumstances, and the brain interprets the body's response as emotion. Using the scenario of meeting a bear in the woods, James theorized that seeing a bear triggers automatic physical reactions. According to James, we do not fear the bear; we react physically to the risk of death and we interpret the experience of the body's reactions to the bear (rapid pulse, increased respiration, and adrenaline rush) as fear.

The Cannon-Bard Theory. In this theory, also known as the *central theory of emotions*, the physical response and the conscious experience of an emotion both originate in the thalamus. The thalamus is involved in receiving and relaying sensory information. According to the central theory of emotion, the thalamus receives the sensory input of the bear and instantly creates the experience of fear and sends that information to the limbic system, which triggers the physiologic response, and to the cerebral cortex, where the emotion becomes conscious.

Cognitive Theories of Emotion. Sometimes it is difficult to be certain which emotion we are experiencing. Physically, we experience fear, excitement, and happiness the same way. Cognitive theories suggest that the experience of an emotion is a function of both the physiologic response and our interpretation of what is causing the response. A racing heartbeat, sweaty palms, and rapid breathing could be interpreted as excitement (during the last seconds of a close game) or as anxiety (just before a psychology exam) or as joy (just before your wedding day). *Cognitive theories of emotions* suggest that physiological responses and cognitive processes work together to produce the experience of emotions.

Understanding love is central to a Christian view of God, Man, and morality. The Bible speaks extensively about love. In a Christian worldview, the capacity to love is part of our uniquely human God-likeness. Love is tripartite (agape, eros, and phileo) and love is transcendent. We are told to love because we are loved.

Louis Armstrong sang that when you are smiling, the whole world smiles with you. *Emotional contagion* is a term psychologists use to describe our tendency to feel the same emotions being felt by those around us. When someone else is smiling, it is hard not to smile too (try it). When we are with someone who is sad, we may also feel sad.

When motivations conflict. Stress can result from motivations that conflict with other motivations. Psychologists describe four situations in which motivations conflict:

- *Approach-approach* conflicts occur when we must choose between two desirable goals.
- *Avoidance-avoidance* conflicts occur when we must choose between two undesirable alternatives.
- *Approach-avoidance* conflicts occur when desirable activities have both attractive and unattractive features.
- *Multiple approach-avoidance* conflicts occur when multiple alternatives have attractive and unattractive features.

Type A Personality. Psychologists have associated certain personality characteristics with stress and its negative effect on health. The Type A personality is characterized by time-urgency, aggression, and a need to achieve. The Type A personality is associated with an elevated risk of hypertension and heart attack.

Psychologists describe a hardy personality as a personality type with good stress resistance. *Hardy personalities* are said to view events as challenges, not threats, and tend to feel that they are in control of their lives.

Recent discoveries show that there are two distinct emotional pathways in the brain. One is fast acting, largely unconscious, and involves the limbic system. The other emotional pathway involves the cerebral cortex, is closely related to memories, and produces emotions more slowly.

Stress. Stress-related illnesses are a leading cause of death in America. College students report record high levels of stress and worry. Stress affects every area of our lives. The Bible contains very simple-to-understand but difficult-to-apply instructions about worry (don't do it!) and stress (have peace). Though psychologists have shown the benefits of religious beliefs in reducing stress, they generally attribute the benefit to the belief rather than to God.

Even though God would have Christians live stress and worry-free lives, sometimes we experience stress. When it happens, there are common characteristics of the experience. *Stress* is defined as a generalized (non-specific) response to a perceived threat. Stress reactions are said to be caused by failing to adapt to stressors. *Stressors* may be physical (e.g., fatigue), psychological (i.e., our thoughts and feelings about events), or environmental (i.e., a catastrophe, major life change, or even daily hassles).

Signs of Stress. Stress impacts our thoughts and emotions, it affects us physically, and it can change our behavior. The effects of stress include:

- *Psychological.* Slowed thinking, poor judgment, difficulty making decisions, worrying, inability to relax.
- *Emotional.* Depressed mood, anxiety, agitation, irritability.
- *Physiological.* Aches and pains, diarrhea or constipation, nausea, dizziness, chest pain, rapid heartbeat.
- *Behavioral.* Disruption to diet, sleep, social activity, and meeting responsibilities as well as possible drug and alcohol use.

Social Readjustment Rating Scale (Holmes and Rahe)	
Life Event	*Life Change Units*
Unwed pregnancy	100
Death of parent	100
Getting married	95
Divorce of parents	90
Acquiring a visible deformity	80
Fathering an unwed pregnancy	70
Jail sentence of parent for over one year	70
Marital separation of parents	69
Death of a brother or sister	68
Change in acceptance by peers	67
Pregnancy of unwed sister	64
Discovery of being an adopted child	63
Marriage of parent to stepparent	63
Death of a close friend	63
Having a visible congenital deformity	62
Serious illness requiring hospitalization	58
Failure of a grade in school	56
Not making an extracurricular activity	55
Hospitalization of a parent	55
Jail sentence of parent for over 30 days	53
Breaking up with boyfriend or girlfriend	53
Beginning to date	51
Suspension from school	50
Becoming involved with drugs or alcohol	50
Birth of a brother or sister	50
Increase in arguments between parents	47
Loss of job by parent	46
Outstanding personal achievement	46
Change in parent's financial status	45
Accepted at college of choice	43
Being a senior in high school	42
Hospitalization of a sibling	41
Increased absence of parent from home	38
Brother or sister leaving home	37
Mother or father beginning work	26

The General Adaptation Syndrome. The general adaptation syndrome describes human reaction to prolonged stress in terms of three stages. The **alarm reaction** is similar physiologically to the fight-or-flight response. If the stressor persists, as the initial alarm reaction fades, we enter the **resistance stage** in which an elevated state of arousal "settles in" for the long-haul. In the **exhaustion stage** signs of physical weakening appear, which can contribute to sickness and disease.

Sources of Stress. When you think about stress, you may think of negatives such as conflicts, frustration, or catastrophes, but not all stressful situations are negative. Getting married, a promotion at work, and having children are examples of "good" stress. In a effort to quantify the impact of both good and bad stressful life events, psychologists **Holmes and Rahe** created the **Social Readjustment Rating Scale** (SRRS) to quantify and rank stressful life events. Life events with greater "**life change units**" are said to be more stressful. Experiencing several less stressful life events has a cumulative effect and may be more stressful than a single major event. Highly stressful life events and combinations of less stressful events are associated with stress-related illnesses.

Coping with Stress. Psychologists and many others develop, teach, promote, and sometimes sell strategies to help reduce stress and improve coping. Generally the strategies include combinations of problem solving skills, prayer, meditation and relaxation, proper nutrition, sleep and exercise, using support systems, and changing thoughts, beliefs, and behaviors. As we will see in Chapter 13 on treatment, one's approach to coping with stress reflects one's worldview perspective.

Chapter Summary.

Motivation is an inner state that arouses, directs, maintains, and terminates behavior. Emotions are also inner states. Emotions are subjective psychological experiences and accompany physiologic changes.

The biological approach explained motivation in terms of instincts, drives, and needs. The behavioral perspective explained it in terms of external forces, rewards, and consequences. The humanistic perspective explained motivation in terms of an intrinsic human need to grow and achieve. William McDougal proposed that human behavior was motivated by as many as 10,000 instincts. Clark Hull's drive reduction theory explained motivation in terms of biologic drives and needs. Arousal theory explained motivation in terms of achieving an individual's optimal state of arousal. The incentive theory applied behavioral principles like association and reinforcement to explain motivation. Abraham Maslow, believed that Mankind is innately and naturally motivated to grow and progress through a hierarchy of physical and psychological stages. Social theories explained human motivation in terms of the need for achievement and affiliation and the need for power.

Emotions are complex subjective experiences involving both physiological and psychological processes. The experience of emotions is characterized by at least two components; subjective feelings and physiological responses. The cerebral cortex processes the sensations, thoughts, and memories that make up the experience of emotions. In concert with the subjective experience of emotions, the limbic system triggers changes in heart rate, blood pressure, respiration, perspiration, and even pupil dilation. Emotions influence thoughts and behaviors, and thoughts and behaviors influence emotions in a reciprocal relationship.

A number of psychologists have proposed models that number, name, describe, and categorize human emotions. William James believed that physiological responses triggered the experience of emotions. The Cannon-Bard Theory suggests that the physiological response and the conscious experience of emotions originate simultaneously. Cognitive theories suggest that physiological responses and cognitive processes work together to produce emotions.

Stress-related illnesses are a leading cause of death in America. Stress is a generalized response to a perceived threat. Stressors may be physical, psychological, or environmental. (i.e., a catastrophe, major life change, or even daily hassles). Stress effects us cognitively, emotionally, behaviorally, and physically.

For Review.

1. Describe human motivation and emotion from the biological, humanistic, social and evolutionary perspectives.
2. Describe William McDougal's theory of motivation.
3. Describe the drive reduction theory of motivation.
4. Describe Maslow's five stages of motivation.
5. Define emotions and the three components of the experience of emotions.
6. Describe the James-Lange and Cannon-Bard theories of emotions.
7. Describe cognitive theories of emotions.
8. Describe psychological, emotional, physiological, and behavioral signs of stress.
9. Describe the type A personality.
10. Describe and give examples of negative stress and of "good" stress.

Chapter 7

Learning and Memory

What is learning? How do animals learn? How do humans learn, and how are animal and human learning similar and how do they differ? What does the Bible have to say about human learning? Is there a spiritual dimension to learning? How do the various learning theories fit with a Christian worldview? Can psychological theories inform a Christian view of human learning? These are some of the questions facing Christian students as they study the psychology of learning. How we learn has been a topic of great interest throughout history and to psychologists since the beginning of modern scientific psychology.

The capacity to learn is basic to our lives. Learning involves much more than acquiring a new skill or new knowledge. We must learn to walk and talk, to read and write, to trust and believe, and to behave according to God's and society's rules.

Learning is generally defined as a mental process leading to relatively permanent changes in behavior, knowledge, or mental processes due to practice or experience. Instinctive behaviors do not require learning. Because it is impossible to directly observe mental processes, psychology's emphasis has been on the result or outcome of learning: changes in behavior. Today, much of the research on learning is focused on the changes that occur in neural circuitry as a result of learning.

There are dozens of theories of learning. Every theory of learning rests on assumptions about the nature of the learner. Based on its assumptions, each of psychology's major schools of thought crafted theories to explain learning. There are biological, behavioral, cognitive, psycho-analytic, humanistic, and social learning theories (plus countless others that combine theories). No single approach or theory of learning seems sufficient to fully explain how we learn. As with each of psychology's topics (personality, motivation, cognition, emotions, abnormal psychology, etc.), modern psychology's study of learning has shifted from a philosophical approach to a naturalistic

The key components of classical conditioning are:

- A **Reflex.** Classical conditioning always starts with a reflex. Reflexes are not learned. Dogs reflexively salivate when given meat powder.
- The **Unconditioned Stimulus** (UCS). The UCS is a stimulus that naturally elicits a biological reflex. Meat powder is an unconditioned stimulus for a dog.
- The **Unconditioned Response** (UCR). The UCR is a natural response to a natural stimulus. Salivation is a dog's unconditioned response to meat.
- A **Neutral Stimulus** (NS). The neutral stimulus does not elicit a reflexive response. The sound of a metronome (or a bell or light) is a neutral stimulus to a dog.
- A **Conditioned Stimulus** (CS). The CS is a previously neutral stimulus that, after being associated with the unconditioned stimulus, eventually elicits a conditioned response. The light begins to elicit a response after being paired with food powder.
- A **Conditioned Response** (CR). The conditioned response is the learned response to the previously neutral stimulus.

and empirical endeavor. It is important that the Christian studying the psychology of learning remembers to think about underlying worldview assumptions. As you might expect, introductory psychology texts will not address the working of the Holy Spirit (**pneumatology**) in learning. Our ability to learn is complex and reflects our nature as both physical and spiritual beings. Introductory psychology courses generally emphasize human learning as an inborn processes or a complex variation of animal learning.

Habituation. In Chapter 5 we learned that sensory habituation refers to the tendency of neurons to become less sensitive to constant or familiar stimuli. To psychologists studying learning, habituation refers to changes in behavior (i.e., learning) resulting from repeated exposure to a stimulus. People who live near airport runways "learn," through habituation, new behaviors (i.e., not jumping out of their skin) to the sounds of jet airplanes overhead.

Behavioral Learning. Modern Psychology's earliest theory of learning is known as **behaviorism**. Classical conditioning and operant conditioning are complementary behavioral theories; each describes learning in terms of organisms' responses to environmental stimuli. The simplest form of behavioral learning is known as classical conditioning.

Classical Conditioning. **Ivan Pavlov** (1849 - 1936), a Russian scientist, is famous in the history of psychology for his contribution to our understanding of learning. His interest in digestion led to a discovery that came to be known as classical conditioning. Classical conditioning refers to a type of associative learning seen in very simple animals and in humans.

The unconditioned response and conditioned response are similar, but not identical. The conditioned and unconditioned responses have different causes, and they occur and at different strengths. The conditioned response is generally weaker than the unconditioned response. A dog does not salivate as much in response to the light as it does for real meat powder. By repeatedly pairing the light or sound (neutral stimulus) with the meat powder (UCS), the light or sound alone began to elicit a response. The dogs learned to associate the conditioned stimulus (CS) with the unconditioned stimulus (UCS). The sound (neutral stimulus) became a conditioned stimulus (CS). The learned response is known as a conditioned response (CR).

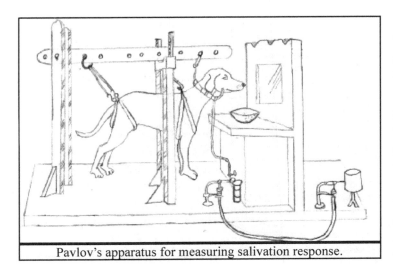

Pavlov's apparatus for measuring salivation response.

Because Pavlov needed saliva for his research, he exposed dogs' salivary glands and inserted tubes to collect and measure the secretion of saliva. He used meat powder to stimulate salivation. After some time, Pavlov noticed that the dogs started salivating before the meat powder was put in their mouths. He observed that dogs began salivating when they saw the food, when the researcher who fed the dogs entered the room, or when they heard the bell signaling the research assistant to bring the food. Pavlov eventually abandoned his research on digestion (for which he would win a Nobel Prize in 1904) and began a long series of experiments to explain associative learning, the process by which animals make associations between environmental stimuli.

In his subsequent experiments on learning, Pavlov secured a dog in a harness behind a one-way glass. Pavlov delivered the meat powder by remote control, allowing him to pair the delivery of meat powder with other stimuli. For example, after the dog became accustomed to the harness, Pavlov turned on a light and then delivered the meat powder. Initially, the dog did not salivate until the food powder was delivered. The light did not elicit a salivation response. After a number of trails in which the light was always followed by meat powder, the dog began to salivate as soon as the light was turned on. The light began to elicit a response. Pavlov's discovery, which he called **signalization**, came to be known as classical conditioning. **Conditioning** is

John B. Watson, an American who studied Pavlov's work, also conducted classical conditioning research. Watson connected subjects' fingertips to wiring, allowing him to administer mild electric shocks. Watson rang a bell and then administered a shock to the subjects' fingertips. The electricity caused the subjects to involuntarily move their fingers. After only a few pairings, the subject would move their fingers whenever the bell rang, even if it was not followed by a shock.

Conditioned Food (Taste) Aversion — One-trial Learning. Classical conditioning generally requires several parings of the conditioned and unconditioned stimuli. In some instances, however, conditioning occurs with a single paring. In the 1970s psychologist *John Garcia* conducted a series of experiments on rats in which he paired a taste with sickness. Garcia presented groups of rats with saccharin-flavored water and over the next 24 hours induced sickness by exposing the rats to radiation. Some rats became sick immediately after drinking the water, others did not become ill for as much as 24 hours, and the control group did not become sick. Garcia noted that a strong and persistent aversion to the flavored water appeared after only one pairing of the flavor and sickness, even with a six hour delay between taste and the onset of sickness.

Taste aversion may occur even when the illness is not caused by food. Psychologists have noted that children receiving cancer treatment often develop taste aversions for foods eaten before chemotherapy.

John Watson and Little Albert. John Watson's "Little Albert" experiment is famous in psychology's history as an example of conditioning in humans and for its brazenly unethical approach. In 1920 Watson and his graduate student Rosalie Raynor attempted to demonstrate that Pavlov's principles of conditioning worked with people. Watson's subject, 9 month old "Little Albert," was first exposed to a white rat, rabbit, monkey, and to burning newspaper to observe that Little Albert did not fear those things.

Watson then paired the white rat with a loud clanging noise that startled Little Albert and caused him to cry. Watson repeatedly paired the presentation of the rat with the loud clang. Each time Little Albert cried. Eventually, Little Albert cried and tried to crawl away at the presentation of the rat, even without the loud clang. After conditioning, Albert also feared other furry or white objects, demonstrating the principle of stimulus generalization.

Phobias, Desensitization, and Counter-conditioning. The results of Watson's Little Albert experiment suggested that a phobia – an irrational, intense, and persistent fear of certain situations, activities, or things – could be explained by the principles of classical conditioning. Desensitization and counter-conditioning are behavioral therapy techniques in which individuals make new associations. In Little Albert's case, desensitization and counter-conditioning would have involved pairing white rats and other furry animals with pleasant stimuli, relaxing thoughts, and pleasant visual images.

a learning process that occurs when an organism associates a natural stimulus with an environmental stimulus. It came to be known as "classical" conditioning because it was modern psychology's first major theory of learning. Pavlov noted that when a signal is paired with a natural reflex-producing stimulus, the signal alone begins to activate a learned response similar to the natural reflex. The process of learning the response is known as ***acquisition***.

Extinction. The reverse of acquisition is extinction. A conditioned response (salivation) stops when the conditioned stimulus (a sound) is repeatedly not paired with the unconditioned stimulus (meat). In the case of Pavlov's dog, when the sound no longer signaled (predicted) the arrival of food, the dog eventually stopped salivating to the sound. But extinction does not completely erase learning. Pavlov and others noted that after a behavior is extinguished (the dog no longer responds to the sound), it sometimes spontaneously reappears. ***Spontaneous recovery*** refers to the reappearance of conditioned response after a period of absence. ***Reconditioning*** refers to the conditioned response reappearing when conditioned and unconditioned stimuli are once again paired after a period of extinction.

Stimulus Generalization, as you might guess, refers to the same conditioned response occurring to similar, but not identical, stimuli. After using a particular tone to condition his dogs, Pavlov varied the tone and measured the extent to which the different tones

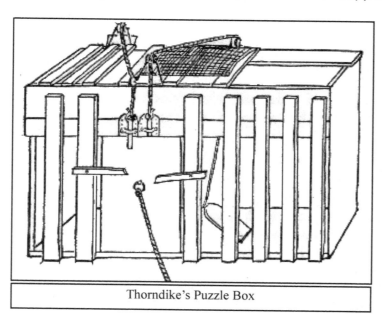

Thorndike's Puzzle Box

stimulated responses. He found that the degree to which the tones were similar was related to the amount of salivation. The reverse of stimulus generalization, **stimulus discrimination,** occurs when one stimulus triggers a conditional response but another does not. For example, a dog might associate one sound (e.g., a metronome) with meat powder but not associate another sound (e.g., a violin). The dog discriminates between two stimuli.

Second-order conditioning refers to pairing one conditioned stimulus with another neutral stimulus. Consider the dog conditioned to salivate to a sound. If a light were paired with the sound, eventually the dog would begin to salivate at the sight of the light alone even though the light had not been paired directly with the food. The light is a second-order conditioned stimulus.

Since Pavlov, a number of psychologists have explored the relationship of stimulus factors to behavioral responses. Generally, responses are stronger and learned more rapidly if the conditioned stimulus predicts the unconditioned stimulus, if they occur contiguously (close together in time), and if the unconditioned stimulus is more intense.

Operant Conditioning. The principles of classical conditioning explain much about animal learning. It seems intuitively important that animals be able to associate a stimulus with a biologically significant event. But for much behavior there is no reflex-producing triggering stimulus. Classical conditioning was insufficient to explain complex behaviors, and linking all behaviors back to reflex-producing stimuli was very cumbersome. Edward Thorndike suggested that learning depended less on reflexes and more on the organism's operations on the environment.

Edward L.Thorndike (1874 - 1949) used cats and "puzzle boxes" to study learning. He placed cats in boxes that had only one way out. To escape, the cat had to open

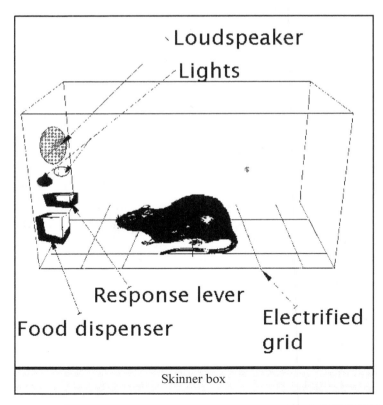

Loudspeaker

Lights

Response lever

Food dispenser

Electrified grid

Skinner box

the box door by pressing a specific area of the box. In the course of the cat's seemingly random efforts to escape, it accidentally pressed the right spot and opened the door. On subsequent attempts the cat tried to repeat what it had done before. After repeated trials, the cat could escape quickly and efficiently. Thorndike suggested a *"law of effect"* to describe the cats' behavior. The law of effect states that any behavior followed by a pleasant consequence tends to be repeated, and any behavior followed by unpleasant consequences tends not to be repeated. The key distinction between classical conditioning and the law of effect is the *stimulus-response connection*. Classical conditioning is about forming associations between stimuli. *Stimulus-response* refers to the conditioned connection between a stimulus and a response or behavior.

The key components of Operant Conditioning are:

- *Reinforcement*. A consequence of a behavior that increases the likelihood that the behavior will occur again.
- *Positive Reinforcement*. A consequence following a behavior that is usually pleasant (e.g., food, money, praise) and that increases the likelihood of the behavior occurring again.
- *Primary Reinforcer*. A consequence of behavior that is inherently reinforcing (e.g., food and water).
- *Secondary Reinforcer*. A consequence of behavior that is reinforcing through association with a primary reinforcer (e.g., money, which is associated with food and water).
- *Negative Reinforcement*. A consequence following a behavior in which a negative stimulus is removed. Remember that all reinforcement increases the likelihood that the behavior will occur again. By rewarding a behavior by removing an unpleasant stimulus, negative reinforcement increases the likelihood that the behavior will occur again. Positive reinforcement introduces a pleasant stimulus. Negative reinforcement removes a negative stimulus.
- *Punishment*. A consequence of a behavior that decreases the likelihood that the behavior will occur again.
- *Positive Punishment*. A consequence of behavior that is usually unpleasant (e.g., pain) and decreases the likelihood that the behavior will occur again.
- *Negative Punishment* (sometimes known as "time-out" or omission training). A consequence of behavior in which a positive stimulus is removed. Remember that all punishment decreases the likelihood of a response. Negative punishment decreases the likelihood of a response by removing a pleasant stimulus. Generally, positive punishment introduces an unpleasant consequence and negative punishment removes a pleasant stimulus.
- *Primary Punisher*. A consequence of behavior that is inherently unpleasant (e.g., spanking).
- *Secondary Punisher*. A consequence of behavior that is unpleasant through association with a primary punisher (e.g., a stern warning).
- *Extinction*. The gradual disappearance of a behavior when reinforcement or punishment ceases.
- *Shaping*. Shaping guides behavior toward the desired response by reinforcing successive approximations of desired behavior. In the case of the Skinner box, the rat receives reinforcement for looking at the bar, then for sniffing the bar, touching the bar, and eventually for pressing the bar.

B. F. Skinner (1904 - 1990) was an American psychologist who, like Pavlov, is famous in the history of psychology for his experiments in behavioral learning. In Pavlov's classical conditioning, the environment acts on organisms and learning happens in a sort of one-way interaction. Skinner expanded on classical conditioning to include the ways animals and humans "operate" on the environment in order to gain rewards and avoid negative consequences. Skinner did not disagree with Pavlov, and classical and operant are not opposing theories. Operant conditioning explains learning in terms of the rewards, punishments, and negative consequences of particular behaviors in a two-way interaction with the environment.

Pavlov is remembered for his salivating dogs. Skinner is known for his work with rats, pigeons, and animal boxes, called Skinner boxes. In a *Skinner box*, an animal

---

receives a food reward for performing various behaviors. A typical Skinner box contains a food pellet dispenser (*magazine*), a *response lever*, a *light* or *buzzer*, and equipment to record data about the animals' *response rates*. For some experiments, the boxes are equipped to provide electric shocks through the floor grid as punishment.

For a rat in a Skinner box, learning begins when the researcher releases a food pellet into the magazine, the hungry rat smells it, finds it, and eats it. The process is repeated until the rat "learns" the location of food and *associates* the clinking sound of a pellet dropping into the magazine with food. The rat is conditioned to respond to the sound of a pellet dropping into the magazine. A response (e.g., running to the food magazine) to a stimulus (e.g., the sound of the pellet) is reinforced with food.

Next the rat's behavior is "shaped." *Shaping* describes reinforcing *successive approximations* of the desired behavior. The researcher wants the rat to learn to press a lever, the *target behavior*. The researcher shapes the rat's behavior by first delivering a food pellet when the rat faces the lever and then when the rat is near the lever. The rat learns and soon stays near the lever. If, by chance, the rat should touch or press the lever, the researcher delivers a pellet. Eventually the rat must touch and then press the lever before it receives a pellet. Before long the rat learns to press the lever for food.

Schedules of Reinforcement. Schedules of reinforcement refers to the frequency or pattern of reinforcement. A behavior does not have to be reinforced every time it occurs. Reinforcement schedules can be continuous or intermittent.

- *Continuous reinforcement schedule*. Desired behavior is reinforced every time it occurs.
- *Intermittent reinforcement schedule*. Desired behavior is reinforced some of the time. Intermittent reinforcement schedules are more resistant to extinction than continuous reinforcement. There are two categories of intermittent reinforcement schedules: ratio and interval. There are four types of intermittent reinforcement schedules: fixed ratio, variable ratio, fixed interval, and variable interval.
- *Fixed ratio reinforcement schedule*. Reinforcement happens after a fixed number of responses. For example, the rat receives a food pellet after every fifth response. The passage of time does not make reinforcement more likely.
- *Fixed interval reinforcement schedule*. Reinforcement happens after a fixed amount of time. For example, the rat receives a food pellet for a response every two minutes.
- *Variable ratio reinforcement schedule*. Reinforcement happens after a variable number of responses. The passage of time does not make reinforcement more likely. In the case of the Skinner box, the rat receives a food pellet after an average of five responses.
- *Variable interval reinforcement schedule*. Reinforcement happens after

Token Economy. A Token Economy is a behavior management technique often used to reward desired behaviors. In a Token Economy children receive points or tokens for exhibiting a desired behavior. Tokens can be traded-in for activities, or privileges, or other reinforcers.

Vicarious conditioning describes conditioning in which one is influenced by seeing or hearing about the consequences of another's behavior.

Learned Helplessness. Psychologists have demonstrated that animals learn to associate positive and negative reinforcement with certain behaviors, but what happens if rewards and consequences are not connected to behavior? Beginning in the 1960s, psychologist ***Martin Seligman*** conducted experiments administering electric shocks to groups of dogs. Some of the dogs could end the shock by pressing a lever. Some of the dogs could not end the shock. The dogs that could not end the shock became very passive and would not attempt to escape shocks in new situations from which they could escape. Seligman termed the phenomenon ***learned helplessness*** and suggested that it may have application in understanding the causes of human depression.

Superstitions. A reward is intended to increase a behavior. Sometimes rewards reinforce behaviors that are not actually connected to the rewards at all. In his article entitled *Superstition in the Pigeon*, Skinner demonstrated that pigeons learn through coincidental association with a reward. Skinner delivered food to pigeons at regular intervals with no reference to the bird's behavior. Skinner discovered that the food reinforced the behaviors of the birds immediately before the food was delivered. Some pigeons turned counter-clockwise between rewards, some thrust their heads into a corner of the cage, and some moved their heads and bodies in a pendulum motion – whatever the birds happened to be doing at the time of the reward was delivered.

Behavioral Chaining. Psychologists have demonstrated that a series of discrete behaviors can be linked or chained together in a series. In behavior chains, each behavior reinforces the previous behavior and triggers the next behavior.

What Do You Think? Some Christians believe that behavioral learning principles are demonstrated in the Bible (e.g., the series of rewards and consequences the Jews experienced in their captivity and time in the wilderness). They apply behavioral principles at home, in the classroom, and at church. Other Christians believe that because behaviorism is grounded in naturalism, determinism, evolution, and a denial of human consciousness, that it should be shunned.

Questions about determinism, reductionism, and responsibility contribute to vigorous denunciations by many in Christendom of the application of behavioral approaches to human leaning. As a model of Mankind, behaviorism is shallow. As an explanation of all human behavior, behaviorism is woefully insufficient. As a partial model explaining some of the ways in which humans learn, behaviorism has merit.

a variable period of time. In the case of the Skinner box, the rat receives a food pellet for a response after an average of two minutes.

Avoidance and Escape Conditioning. Psychologists have demonstrated that not only do animals learn behaviors through association with positive stimuli; they learn new behaviors to avoid or escape unpleasant stimuli as well.

Escape conditioning occurs when animals learn that particular behaviors will end an ongoing negative stimulus. The behavior that ends the ongoing negative stimulus is negatively reinforced – reinforced by the elimination of the negative stimulus.

Avoidance conditioning occurs when a signal precedes a negative stimulus. After a few occurrences of a signal preceding a negative stimulus, the signal will trigger an avoidance behavior. Avoidance behaviors are persistent, meaning that the behavior continues even when there is no longer anything to avoid.

Spanking. The effectiveness and appropriateness of corporal punishment is a hot-button topic among Christians and psychologists alike. Because the Bible provides instructions to parents about the use of punishment in raising children, a Christian worldview sees spanking as a moral issue. Humanistic philosophies generally reject corporal punishment on moral grounds as well.

Some psychologists suggest that corporal punishment is ineffective. The American Psychological Association and others say the evidence is "clear and compelling" that "spanking is not a very effective strategy," suggesting that it does not teach new behaviors and that it is not useful in eliminating the behavior beyond the moment. Some psychologists suggest physical punishment is needed to establish and maintain limits on behavior and that corporal punishment is associated with good behavioral and emotional outcomes in children.

Cognitive Learning.

Cognitive psychologists emphasize the mental processes that are a part of learning. Where behaviorists believe that learning occurs without thought, cognitive theories suggest that all learning (including conditioning) involves cognitive processes. Cognitive psychologists explore mental processes such as information processing, mental representations, and expectations as central to a cognitive perspective of learning. Cognitive learning theories refer to the mental processes by which we acquire knowledge and skills and the ways we create and manipulate mental representations of physical objects and events.

Latent Learning.

In 1930 **Tolman and Honzik** conducted research on what came to be known as latent learning. Latent learning is a form of learning that is not demonstrated in an immediate behavioral response and occurs without direct behavioral reinforcement. Latent learning is said to demonstrate the importance of cognition in learning, in addition to the principles of behavioral learning. Latent learning is comparable to acquiring new knowledge (e.g., how to change a tire) that is not yet needed.

The Bobo Doll Study. In 1961, Albert Bandura published his "Bobo doll" study, famous in the history of psychology for its insight into aggressive behavior in children.

Bandura studied 36 boys and 36 girls ranging from 3 to 6 years old. Half of his subjects were exposed to aggressive adult models and half were exposed to models that were subdued and nonaggressive in their behavior. The aggressive models punched, kicked, hit with a mallet, and made angry comments toward a Bobo doll. A Bobo doll is an inflatable doll with a weight in the bottom, so each time it is knocked down, it pops right back up. The nonaggressive models quietly assembled blocks, totally ignoring the Bobo doll.

Later, Bandura secretly observed the children in a room with a Bobo doll and other toys. The children who had witnessed the adult striking the Bobo doll were far more likely to strike their own Bobo doll than the children who had not seen the adults' aggressive behavior.

In their experiments, Tolman and Honzik used mazes and three groups of rats. One group of rats always had a food reward at the end of the maze. One group never received a food reward at the end of the maze, and the third group had no food reward for 10 days, but then received a food reward for the next 10 days.

Initially, the always-rewarded group made fewer errors (wrong turns) and completed

From Bandura's Bobo Doll study. (Top) An adult models agression. (Bottom) A little girl demonstrates social learning.

Kohler's Chimpanzees demonstrating insight learning

the maze more quickly than the other groups. Beginning on the 11th day, however, after receiving the reward, the third group surpassed both the always and the never-rewarded groups on speed and accuracy. Tolman and Honzik concluded that the third group of rats had learned about the maze while wandering around it for 10 days, and that the learning had occurred without reinforcement. The rats are said to have constructed a *mental map*, a kind of mental representation of the external environment.

Social Learning. Albert Bandura (1925 -) is famous in the history of psychology for his work in social learning. Social learning theory proposes that we learn from one another through *observation*, *imitation*, and *modeling*. Social learning theory explains learning in terms of the *reciprocal* interaction between cognitive, behavioral, and environmental influences.

Insight Learning. Wolfgang Kohler (1887 - 1967) observed chimpanzees solving problems. He observed that chimpanzee problem-solving appeared to happen through sudden insights into solutions to problems.

Kohler constructed a variety of problems for chimpanzees to solve. In taped recordings of one problem, chimpanzees are unable to reach bananas that hung just out of reach. Kohler reported that after unsuccessfully reaching and jumping, the chimpanzees appear to pause and reflect on the problem, considering alternatives. In the recording chimps are seen stacking crates and using a pole in order to reach the bananas. Kohler, explicitly presuming that primate problem-solving abilities were less-evolved versions of human abilities, theorized that "insight" also plays a role in human learning.

Memory. Memory is the process by which information is *acquired*, *encoded*, *stored*, *retrieved*, and possibly *forgotten*. *Hermann Ebbinghaus* (1850 - 1909), one of the fathers of modern experimental psychology, extended empirical methods to questions of human memory. Before Ebbinghaus, memory was thought to be "too subjective" for scientific investigation. Ebbinghaus served as the sole subject of his own experiments by memorizing long lists of nonsense syllables. By treating each nonsense syllable as one unit of memory, Ebbinghaus was able to calculate the rate at which he acquired new memories (the ***learning curve***) and the rate at which he lost those memories (the ***forgetting curve***).

Encoding Memories. A memory is a mental representation of the external world. ***Encoding memories*** is the process of converting our perceptions of the external world into mental representations. Encoding memories involves the creation and strengthening of redundant neural connections and pathways known as ***engrams*** or ***memory traces***. ***Memory retrieval*** is the process of locating and bringing memories to a conscious level.

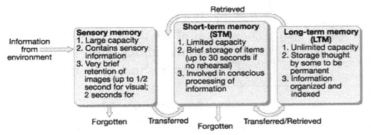

Today, psychologists compare human memory to a computer ***information-processing system***. Like human memory, a computer acquires input, codes it, saves it, and then retrieves the information when needed. If the computer crashes, the information is lost, or "forgotten." The terms ***acquisition*** and ***encoding*** refer to the process of converting information received from the senses into a form that can be placed into memory. When we create a mental representation of external information, we have encoded a memory. Psychologists divide memory into three types: sensory memory, short-term memory, and long-term memory, sometimes called the ***"three-box" model*** of memory.

Sensory Memory. Memories begin with the senses, but not all information received by the senses becomes a memory. The senses are constantly sending information to the brain where it is held in sensory memory, a sort of temporary buffer, for less than one second, during which time it is evaluated for further processing. Our sensory memory holds a large amount of information for a very short period of time. Much of the sensory information is not selected for further processing. We could not deal with all of the sensory information we receive at any given time. The thalamus, in the limbic system is thought to serve as a type of sensory filter with a separate "storage bin" for each of the five senses.

Iconic Sensory Memory — Try It. Fix your gaze across the room and very slowly allow your gaze to move as you turn your head slowly from the right to the left. You will perceive a smoothly flowing visual scene as if your eyes are moving at the same speed as your head. Instead, you will notice that your eyes focus briefly on a point then jump quickly to the next point. The scene is held in sensory memory just long enough for your eyes to focus on the next point.

- ***Iconic memories*** are associated with visual sensory memory.
- ***Echoic memories*** are associated with auditory sensory memory.
- ***Haptic memories*** are associated with the touch.

A disturbance in the thalamus' role as sensory filter is thought to be responsible for the "sensory overload" experienced by some people with schizophrenia.

Selective attention refers to the process by which we select the sensory information we attend to and which information we "ignore."

Short-term Memory. Williams James called short-term memory the primary memory. Our **short-term memory** (STM) holds a small amount of memory for a limited time. Short-term memory capacity, or immediate **memory span**, is limited to 5-9 items or "chunks" of information. Short-term memories usually last only a few seconds, but their duration can be increased by rehearsing the information. **Working memory** is a type of short-term memory that we use to manipulate and think about the information held in short-term memory.

Chunking. Short-term memory holds about seven items, or chunks. Our short-term memory recognizes one chunk as one meaningful unit of information, so one chunk might be quite large. For example, an area code consists of three digits, but your short-term memory treats it as one chunk. Chunking is a short-term memory strategy to organize and group memory items into larger units allowing for more information to be stored.

Long-term Memory. Long-term memory (LTM) is, as its name suggests, intended for long-term storage of information. Long-term memory is essentially all your knowledge of yourself and the world around you. Unless an injury or illness occurs, long-term memories last a lifetime, and we continue forming new long-term memories throughout life. The capacity of our long-term memory may be limitless.

Although the three-box model describes long-term memory as a single type of memory, psychologists today understand that we encode and store various types of long-term memories differently.

Declarative, also called **explicit memory**, is for facts, figures, and events. The President's name, your birth date, and the names of the books of the Bible are stored in declarative memory. It involves conscious effort to encode, store, and retrieve declarative memories, which is why studying takes so much effort and concentration.

Procedural, also called **implicit memory**, is for skills, abilities, routines, and processes. How to ride a bicycle, the words to a favorite song, and the steps in making a peanut butter sandwich are stored in procedural memory. It requires practice and repetition to encode and store procedural memories, but it does not require conscious effort to retrieve them.

Serial Position, Recency, and Primacy Effect. Ebbinghaus was the first to describe the effect of position, recency, and primacy in memory formation and recall. The serial position effect describes the relationship between the position of an item in a list and the ability to recall it. The primacy effect explains that items near the beginning of a list are easier to recall than those in the middle. The recency effect explains that items near the end of a list are easier to recall than those in the middle.

Episodic memories are memories of single events. The events of your life are stored in episodic memory in a mental autobiography.

A *flashbulb memory* is not a "photographic" memory. A flashbulb memory is a vivid and life-long memory of a personally important or shocking event or circumstance. Many people formed flash bulb memories on September 11, 2001; remembering exactly what they were doing, where they were, and who they were with when they heard the news of the attack. Psychologists suggest that flashbulb memories are so strong because they tend to rehearsed and retold over and over again.

Semantic memories include memories of concepts, context, and meaning. Language, your worldview, and your understanding of qualities of personal relationships are stored in semantic memory.

Amnesia. Much of our understanding of human memory comes through observations of brain-damaged patients. Psychologists have observed that damage or injury to various brain regions and structures affect memory differently. *Amnesia* refers to the inability to form or recall certain memories as the result of brain injury or trauma.

Anterograde amnesia is the inability to form memories of events after the brain injury or trauma. People with Alzheimer's disease often suffer anterograde amnesia and tend, early in the disease process, to forget recent events while recalling older memories.

Retrograde amnesia is the inability to retrieve memories of events prior to an injury or trauma. Often accident victims cannot recall the events immediately prior to the injury and in rare cases memory loss is extensive. Amnesia may affect declarative, procedural, episodic, or semantic memory encoding, storage, and retrieval. Drug and alcohol abuse and some mental illnesses can also affect memory.

Retrieving Memories. Since Ebbinghaus described the effect of primacy and recency in recalling memories, psychologists have identified a number of factors affecting memory retrieval. Some memories are *context dependent*, meaning that the environmental context in which we store a memory influences its retrieval. Some students report better results studying for a test in the classroom in which the test will be administered. Our personal emotional state influences encoding and retrieving memories. *State-dependent memories* refers to the influence of mental states and emotions. When our mood is good, we are more likely to recall memories we formed when we were feeling good. When our mood is bad, we are more likely to recall memories formed when we were feeling bad.

Recall vs. Recognition. *Recall* refers to retrieving previously stored memories. Answering the question "*Who was the second President of the United States?*" requires recall. *Recognition* requires comparing new information with information stored

Eidetic memory is a phenomenon which occurs in a small percentage of children. An eidetic memory is a vividly real afterimage that lingers for up to a few minutes. Photographic memories are a type of eidetic memory described as the ability to recall a visual image with near-perfect (photographic) detail. Photographic memory is rare and there are few (if any) documented cases.

previously. Identifying a suspect in a police line-up requires recognition – comparing the faces in the line-up with the stored image in memory. Recognition memory is generally stronger than recall, which is why students prefer multiple choice test (recognition) questions over fill-in-the-blank or the dreaded essay questions (recall).

A *retrieval cue* is anything that triggers or helps in retrieving memories. The *tip-of-the-tongue phenomenon* provides an example of the power of cues. Sometimes information that we know is not completely or readily accessible. Who is the father of modern psycho-therapy? Cues like *"starts with an F"* and *"rhymes with Boyd,"* might provide the extra association needed to retrieve the knowledge that Sigmund Freud is known as the father of modern psycho-therapy.

Psychologists suggest that we organize memories in *hierarchical categories* in a complex *semantic network.* We group memory items together based on similarities and associations. Accessing memories is not unlike using an internet search engine. The mental category "red" contains many items. The cue *"red"* activates, or "primes" us to recall networked items associated with red. Two cues, *"red and bird,"* focuses the results by forming some associations (i.e., robins, cardinals, and hummingbirds) but not others (i.e., blue jays and ravens).

Forgetting is the process by which we are unable to retrieve memories. Just as many factors influence the forming of memories, many factors influence forgetting. *Memory decay* refers to the fading of memories over time. Most forgetting occurs because the information never gets encoded into long-term memory. Sensory memories decay after less than one second unless selected for processing in short-term memory. Short-term memories fade after a few seconds unless rehearsed and encoded into long-term memory. Psychologists disagree about whether long-term memories ever decay completely or if forgetting long-term memories is a function of interference.

Cues facilitate memory retrieval. *Interference* refers to thoughts or memories that interfere with what we are trying to recall. Interference can occur either retroactively or proactively. *Retroactive interference* occurs when forming new memories prevents recalling previous ones. For example, memorizing the Preamble to the Constitution today may interfere with your ability to recall the poem you memorized last week. *Proactive interference* occurs when a previous memory interferes with a more recent one. For example, it may be more difficult to recall that there are eight planets in the solar system after learning that Pluto was one of nine planets in the solar system.

Sigmund Freud believed that we all "repress" or subconsciously prevent uncomfortable long-term memories from coming to consciousness.

In 1974 psychologists ***Loftus and Palmer*** conducted an experiment exploring the subtle influence of suggestibility and the interaction between language and memory. Subjects viewed and answered questions about a filmed automobile accident. Each subject was shown the same accident. Some subjects were asked to estimate how fast the cars were going when they "smashed" into each other. Other subjects were asked to estimate how fast the cars were traveling when they "collided, bumped, contacted, or hit." Subjects asked the speed when the cars "smashed" estimated that the vehicles were traveling faster than subjects who were asked to estimate the speed at which the cars "bumped." Although the film did not show breaking glass, subjects in the "smashed" group were more likely to report that they "remembered" seeing broken glass.

The Accuracy of Long-term Memories. Memories are mental representations, not reproductions of external events. Just as environmental and personal factors influence our perception of external events, many factors influence the construction and retrieval of long-term memories. Previous memories, biases, expectations, retelling, and past experiences all influence memory formation and recall. ***Mis-attribution***, or ***memory source confusion***, refers to the phenomenon in which information learned after an event becomes part of the memory of the event. Children will report the memory of an event based more on photographs and stories about the event than the event itself.

Improving Memory. Psychologists have suggested a number of strategies and techniques to improve memory retention and recall. A number of studies suggest that ***distributed practice***, studying material in several short sessions with rest in between sessions, is more effective than ***massed practice***, also known as ***cramming***. Psychologists also suggest that ***overlearning***, or continuing to rehearse new material after it has been mastered, contributes to stronger longer-term retention.

Rote memorization, or maintenance rehearsal, refers to holding memories longer in short-term memory by simply repeating or rehearsing the information. For example repeating the phone number for pizza delivery long enough to dial the number is maintenance rehearsal.

Elaborative rehearsal facilitates encoding long-term memories by attaching meaning and significance to the information. For example, putting the pizza delivery phone number to song and repeating the song is an example of elaborative rehearsal.

Mnemonics are techniques for retrieving memories that are otherwise difficult to recall. The rhyme *"30 days hath September"* is a mnemonic tool for remembering the number of days in each month.

Acronyms are made by taking the first letter from each item in a list to be remembered. For example, you might remember the names of the Great Lakes – Huron, Ontario, Michigan, Erie, and Superior – by the acronym HOMES. The first letter from items in a list can be used to form acrostic sentences. For example, the first letter of each word in the sentence *"My* *very elegant mother just served us nine pies"* represents, in order, the nine planets once thought to make up the solar system – Mercury, Venus, Earth, Mars, Jupiter, Saturn, Uranus, Neptune, and Pluto.

Keywords are useful when learning new vocabulary or remembering names and faces. Using keywords involves making a connection between the new word and an image involving a related word that serves as a "key" to the new word. For example, you might associate the word "anchorite" with a mental image of a religious hermit, alone in a cave, using an anchor, like a pencil, to write. Anchorites are hermits who for religious reasons withdraw from society.

Method of loci, or method of location, refers to mentally placing objects in a well-known location. For example, if you need to remember to purchase milk, eggs, and sugar at the store, you might visualize a gallon of milk at your bedroom door, a carton of eggs on your dresser, and five pounds of sugar next to your pillow. While at the store you could mentally "walk through" your room "seeing" the items you want to remember.

Chapter Summary.

Learning is generally defined as a mental process leading to relatively permanent changes in behavior, knowledge, or mental processes due to practice or experience. Every theory of learning rests on assumptions about the nature of the learner. There are biological, behavioral, cognitive, psycho-analytic, humanistic, and social learning theories plus countless others that combine theories. No single approach or theory of learning seems sufficient to fully explain how we learn.

Habituation refers to a very simple type of learning in which behavior changes as a result of repeated exposure to a stimulus. Behaviorism was modern psychology's earliest theory of learning. Classical conditioning and operant conditioning are complementary behavioral theories that describe how environmental factors influence learning.

Ivan Pavlov's discoveries, which came to be known as classical conditioning, describe a learning process that occurs when two stimuli are repeatedly paired. Pavlov noted that when a signal is paired with a natural reflex-producing stimulus, the signal alone begins to elicit a learned response similar to the natural reflex. The unconditioned response (UCR) is an organism's reflexive unlearned response to a stimulus. The unconditioned stimulus (UCS) naturally elicits the organism's reflexive response. A neutral stimulus (NS) does not elicit a reflexive response. After being associated with an unconditioned stimulus, the neutral stimulus eventually elicits a learned response, at which time it is called the conditioned stimulus. The response to the conditioned stimulus is known as the conditioned response (CR).

B. F. Skinner's discoveries, which came to be known as operant conditioning, expanded on classical conditioning to include the ways organisms "operate" on the environment in order to gain rewards and avoid negative consequences.

The key components of operant conditioning are:
- Reinforcement. A consequence that increases the likelihood that a response will occur.
- Positive Reinforcement. A consequence that is usually pleasant and increases the likelihood of a response.
- Primary Reinforcer. A consequence that is inherently reinforcing.
- Secondary Reinforcer. A consequence of behavior that is reinforcing through association with a primary reinforcer.
- Negative reinforcement. A consequence of behavior in that increases the likelihood of a response by removing a negative stimulus.
- Punishment. A consequence of a behavior that decreases the likelihood that a response will occur.
- Positive punishment. A consequence of behavior that is usually unpleasant (e.g., pain) and decreases the likelihood of a response.
- Negative punishment (sometimes known as "time-out" or omission training). A consequence of behavior in which a positive stimulus is removed.
- Extinction. The gradual disappearance of a response when reinforcement ceases.

Shaping guides behavior toward the desired response by reinforcing successive approximations of desired behaviors. Schedules of reinforcement refer to the frequency or pattern of reinforcement. Continuous reinforcement schedules reinforce a behavior every time it occurs. Intermittent reinforcement schedules reinforce behavior some of the time. In fixed ratio reinforcement schedules reinforcement happens after a fixed number of responses. Fixed interval reinforcement schedules reinforce behavior after a fixed amount of time. Variable ratio reinforcement schedules reinforce behavior after a varying number of responses. Variable interval reinforcement schedules reinforce behavior after a variable period of time.

Cognitive theories of learning describe the cognitive processes by which we acquire knowledge and skills and the ways we create and manipulate mental representations of physical objects and events. Latent learning is a type of learning that is not demonstrated in an immediate behavioral response and occurs without direct behavioral reinforcement. Social learning theory explains learning as the result of observation, imitation, and modeling in a reciprocal interaction between cognitive, behavioral, and environmental influences.

Memory is the process by which information is acquired, encoded, stored, and retrieved. Memories can be thought of as existing in one of three "boxes," sensory memory, short-term memory, and long-term memory. Sensory memory is like a temporary buffer where information is held very briefly and evaluated for further processing. Short-term memory is limited to 5-9 items or "chunks" of information and is held for only a few seconds. Long-term memory has limitless capacity and it hold information for a very long time.

For Review.

1. Define learning.
2. Describe classical conditioning and Ivan Pavlov's experiments.
3. Name and define the key components of classical conditioning.
4. Describe operant conditioning, Thorndike's law of effect, and B.F. Skinner's experiments.
5. Describe conditioned taste aversion.
6. Describe John Watson's Little Albert experiment.
7. Describe reinforcement schedules.
8. Describe cognitive theories of learning.
9. Describe latent learning.
10. Describe Albert Bandura's Bobo doll study.
11. Describe social learning theories.
12. Describe the three box model of human memory.
13. Describe factors that influence forming, storing, and retrieving memories.
14. Describe the primacy and recency effects.
15. Describe and explain mnemonic techniques.

Chapter 8

Human Development

In This Chapter

Developmental psychology is the study of the lifelong process of change. From the miracles of conception and birth until death, we are constantly changing. Early in our lives the change is dramatic, but throughout our lives, the way that we think, feel, behave, and relate with others continually changes. Developmental psychologists study the stages of our physical, sexual, cognitive, emotional, moral, and social development, and the genetic and environmental factors that influence them.

Theories of human development provide psychologists with an organizing framework for describing, explaining, and predicting developmental changes. Developmental theories describe our physical, sexual, cognitive, emotional, moral, and social growth and change. Developmental theories also provide guidance for appropriately interacting with people at different developmental levels.

Some developmental theories describe human development in terms of continuity. **Continuous development** refers to the gradual and ongoing unfolding, or maturation, of inborn characteristics. Some theories suggest we develop discontinuously, through a progressive series of distinct steps or **stages**. Some development theories suggest that human development is influenced most by genetic factors. Freud thought unconscious sexual forces drove development. Others suggested that environmental influence plays a greater role How much of who we are is determined by our genes? Is human development affected more by our genetic makeup or environmental influences? Most psychologists today believe that it is both – that we continuously develop, but we also move through stages, and that genetics and the environment are inextricably connected.

A Christian view of human development begins with the belief that God knit us together in our mother's wombs and He has a plan for our " development." A Christian worldview also recognizes that we are born corrupted by sin and are inclined to sin. Early modern psychologists rejected the notion of original sin and crafted developmental theories grounded in the worldview assumptions of the Renaissance philosophers John Locke, Jean Jacques Rousseau, and Immanuel Kant.

John Locke (1632 - 1704), like Aristotle before him, believed that children are born a "blank slate," or ***tabula rasa***. From this perspective, nurturing, learning, and the environment are the primary developmental influences. Locke's philosophy contributed to behaviorism, the theory that development is driven primarily by interaction with the environment.

Jean Jacques Rousseau (1712 - 1778), like Plato before him, believed that children are born in a state of natural goodness. From this perspective, the natural unfolding, in stages, of inborn characteristics drives development. Rousseau believed that environmental influences, especially societal and parental influences, interfered with the development of children's natural goodness. Early psychologists, observing that children develop certain motor skills at about the same age (e.g., rolling over, sitting up, standing, and walking), theorized that we develop in natural stages. *Behavioral genetics* today is the study of the degree to which genes interact with the environment in development.

Immanuel Kant (1724 - 1804) believed that the interaction between *inborn characteristics* (genetic influences) and the *external world* (environmental influences) drives development. From this perspective, children are *active agents* in their own development. We are not simply passive recipients of external forces or controlled by pre-determined genetic programming. Our inborn nature and the environment are equally important. Kant's philosophy contributed to cognitive theories of development.

More recently, *G. Stanley Hall* (1844 - 1924), an early American psychologist and the first president of the American Psychological Association, contributed one of modern psychology's early theories of child development. Hall was influenced by Charles Darwin and Ernst Haekel's idea that "*ontogeny recapitulates phylogeny*," also known as *recapitulation theory*. *Ontogeny* refers to the development of an embryo, and *phylogeny* refers to the species' entire history of evolutionary change traced all the way back to its original single-celled ancestor. *Recapitulation theory* states that the prenatal development of an embryo follows the same stages as the evolutionary development of the embryo's species. Hall applied recapitulation theory to human development, theorizing that prenatal cognitive development mirrors our species' cognitive evolution. Hall believed that maturation was the primary force in human development. The path of our development is set at birth, and as we mature, the evolved and in-born characteristics naturally unfold.

Fetal Alcohol Syndrome (FAS). A serious result of drinking alcohol during pregnancy is fetal alcohol syndrome. Fetal alcohol syndrome is characterized by a combination of mental retardation, birth defects, abnormal facial features, behavior problems, cognitive and memory problems, growth problems, and central nervous system damage. Fetal alcohol syndrome has no cure, but it is 100% preventable by not drinking alcohol, especially during any stage of pregnancy. Alcohol often does its most serious damage before the mother knows she is pregnant.

Recapitulation theory has been thoroughly rejected by most psychologists. Human prenatal physical development does not progress through evolution-like stages. The theory is, however, often cited in textbooks today as evidence supporting evolution.

By studying fraternal and identical twins, psychologists following Hall sought to discover and measure the extent to which psychological traits were inherited. The **heritability index** is an estimate of the extent to which a trait is inherited. The heritability index is calculated by measuring a characteristic in **identical twins** and comparing it to how often the characteristic occurs in **fraternal twins**. A trait that is highly heritable is more likely to occur in identical twins, who share 100% of their genetic makeup than in fraternal twins who share 50% of their genetic makeup.

Prenatal Development. Maturation is the life-long process of development that unfolds according to age independently of the environment. Maturation begins with prenatal development. **Prenatal** refers to the time between conception and birth. Life begins at conception as a **zygote**. Each parent contributed one-half of your genetic makeup, or **genotype**. To the extent that genetics influence development, each of your parents contributed equally to that influence.

After about two or three weeks of rapid cell division, the zygote forms an **embryo** and implants in the mother's uterus. At this point some cells begin to differentiate and form the **neural groove** – the beginning of the brain and nervous system. By the 7th week the brain stem develops, and by the 9th week the child begins displaying spontaneous movement. During the embryonic stage all of the major organs develop, so the embryonic stage is known as a "**critical period**" of human development. Exposure to **teratogens** are especially damaging during the embryonic stage.

Around eight weeks **gestation**, all major organs are formed. Throughout the **fetal period**, from eight weeks until birth, the brain and nervous system develop at a tremendous rate; adding as many as 250,000 new neurons every minute and making countless new synaptic connections. The unborn

Teratogens. Birth defects may be caused by genetic factors, environmental toxins, or some combination of the two. Teratogens are *environmental toxins* that can pass through the placenta and harm the developing child. Tobacco, alcohol, prescription and illicit drugs, disease, pollution, and radiation are teratogens that can damage cognitive development, behavior, intelligence and health.

child feels touch and pain and can taste, hear, smell, and see. Psychologists have demonstrated that while still in the womb, children respond to their mother's mood, have REM sleep and may dream, and form memories and preferences.

Because infants cannot speak, they cannot report their preferences. Psychologists in the 1950s and 1960s started using an infant's heart rate, sucking rate, and the amount of time spent looking at an object as external indicators of internal cognitive events.

The Newborn. At birth the newborn child, or **neonate**, has amazing God-given psychological characteristics and abilities. The **swallowing reflex** enables neonates to swallow liquids without choking. The **rooting reflex** causes a newborn to turn its head toward something touching its cheek and search around with its mouth for the nipple. The **grasping reflex** causes infants to close their fists around anything that is put in their hands. The **stepping reflex** causes newborn babies to make little stepping motions if they are held upright with their feet just touching a surface.

Cognitively, newborn children are not blank slates. Psychologists today understand that newborn children have more ability than ever thought possible. At birth, infants see, hear, taste, smell, and feel. Newborns can focus their vision within a range of 8 - 12 inches. They demonstrate a preference for bright colors and for faces over inanimate objects. Newborns prefer sweet tastes, prefer sounds in the frequency of the human voice, recognize mother's voice and smell, and communicate by crying, smiling, and cooing. Shortly after birth most parents can distinguish between their baby's cry of hunger, anger, and pain.

At birth newborn children can be classified by temperament. **Temperament** refers to individual personality traits that appear in infancy. They are thought to be inborn and are relatively stable through life. Some newborn children are more active, alert, and cuddly than others. Some babies startle easily, cry longer, and are not easily comforted. Others are calm, cry little, and are comforted more easily.

Piaget's Theory of Cognitive Development. *Jean Piaget* (1896 - 1980) is famous in the history of psychology for his theories of intellectual development in children. Piaget, like Hall and Rousseau, believed that children are born in a state of natural goodness and that development means the natural stage-wise (discontinuous) unfolding of inborn characteristics. While at the Rousseau Institute, Piaget observed and interacted with children – his own and the children of his friends and associates. He hoped to identify and describe the emergence of intelligence in children. He noticed that children at similar ages made similar types of cognitive advances and made similar kinds of cognitive errors. Piaget's theory, that intellectual development is internally driven and progresses in an orderly, sequential, and predictable way, revolutionized modern thinking about child development. Piaget's **four stage model** of cognitive development remains very influential today.

Throughout fetal development, the brain develops at a tremendous rate, adding as many as 250,000 new neurons every minute and making countless new synaptic connections.

Piaget believed that children are active participants in "constructing" or building **schemas**, or ways of organizing, representing, and understanding the world. He named the mental processes used to construct schemas **assimilation** and **accommodation**. Children develop and modify their schemas by assimilating and accommodating new information. Children **assimilate** or "fit" new information into existing schemas. For example, a child seeing a zebra for the first time might call it a horse. Children also change their schema to fit new information. **Accommodation** is the process by which children change or "expand" their schemas to account for new information. When a child learns that not all equines are horses, their schema is said to have changed to accommodate that new information.

Sensorimotor Stage. Piaget's is a stage theory of development. He believed that all children progress through the same four distinct intellectual stages at about the same rate. Piaget called the first stage the sensorimotor stage. From birth to 18 months, the developing child experiences the world solely through the senses and motor activity. Through reflexive and repetitive motions, newborn children explore, discover, and gradually learn about the world around them. During the sensorimotor stage, infants discover relationships between their bodies and the environment and begin to develop **mental representations** of objects and relationships. Infants discover **causality** – an understanding of cause-and-effect and the fact that they can control their bodies and move objects. Early in this stage, children act as though an object hidden from sight ceases to exist. Later in this stage, children understand **object permanence** – that objects do not cease to exist when out of view. Peek-a-boo is not as exciting for children who thoroughly understand object permanence.

Pre-operational Stage. The pre-operational stage, from around 18 months to 6 years, is characterized by the use of **symbols** to represent things (as in imaginary play), the ability to **classify** and **categorize** objects, and **language skills** development. During this stage thinking tends to be **egocentric**, meaning that young children cannot conceive of someone else's perspective. Children in the pre-operational stage tend to have difficulty distinguishing reality from imagination and will ascribe thoughts and feelings to inanimate objects like a favorite stuffed animal.

Concrete Operational Stage. Piaget observed that around age six, children develop **conservation**, the understanding that matter does not increase or decrease because of a change in form. Conservation is one of many concrete mental operations that characterize Piaget's 3rd stage of development,

Psychologists **E. J. Gibson** and **R. D. Walk** developed the **visual cliff** to investigate infant depth perception. A visual cliff uses transparent glass to create the appearance of a large drop from one surface to another. Gibson and Walk noted that 6-month-old infants would cross the visual cliff but 10-month-old infants would not. They theorized that the ability to perceive depths appeared around the age infants learned to crawl.

> **Conservation.** Piaget is famous in the history of psychology for his demonstration of conservation. In one experiment Piaget showed children clear containers, of various shapes and sizes, filled with equal volumes of colored water. Children under the age of six generally incorrectly believed that the tall, thin containers held more water than short, fat containers. After about age six children understand conservation – that just because the shape of the container changes, the volume of water does not.

the concrete-operational stage. From around age six until early adolescence, children begin to use logic, mental manipulations, and mathematics. Piaget thought children in this stage were limited to thinking about concrete objects and that they could not understand abstract concepts like freedom and love. Children in this stage develop the ability to perceive from another's perspective, and they realize that the stuffed animal is not really alive.

Formal Operational Stage. Piaget's final stage, from adolescence into adulthood, is characterized by the development of the ability to perform ***complex mental operations***. Not everyone reaches the formal operational stage. Those who do develop the ability to use ***abstract thinking***, think about ***hypothetical situations***, ***plan*** complex behavior, ***imagine the consequences*** of an action, use ***formal logic***, and ***draw conclusions*** from available information. The ability to think abstractly allows adolescents to begin to think using symbols and to evaluate ideas, emotions, and concepts.

Criticisms of Piaget. Piaget's theory is influential and somewhat controversial. Piaget's stage-wise model influenced theories of moral, social, and personality development and almost every other aspect of human development. Piaget's theory inspired countless follow-up studies, and today psychologists understand that Piaget underestimated childhood cognitive ability and over-stated the consistency of the four stages. Piaget was a genetic epistemologist, meaning he was interested in how knowledge developed in humans in a type of cognitive recapitulation theory. By understanding how cognitive development progresses in children, he hoped to discover how cognitive abilities evolved in Mankind.

Freudian Psycho-sexual Development Theory. While Piaget emphasized genetic influences on psychological development, ***Sigmund Freud*** emphasized unconscious sexual forces. Freud is famous in the history of modern psychology for his psycho-sexual or dynamic development theory. Freud believed that we are born with libido, a psychic drive or energy. The ***libido*** seeks physical, especially sexual, gratification. The libido propels development through psycho-sexual stages, each named for the particular gratification-seeking focus.

> **Research Methods.** Because developmental psychologists are interested in developmental change, they must study people at different times to learn how changes occur. ***Cross-sectional research*** involves studying a variety of ages at a single point in time. A cross-sectional research design might study a group of 8, 9, and 10-year-old children to learn how they differ in some characteristic. In ***longitudinal research***, psychologists study the same group of subjects for many years.

In the early 1990s at the fall of the Soviet Union, there were tens of thousands of orphans living in Romanian orphanages that were not equipped to provide for so many children. Very young children sometimes spent 24 hours a day in cribs where, although they were fed and changed, they received very little auditory or visual stimulation and were rarely touched or comforted. The majority of the children were severely delayed in physical growth, motor development, emotional expression, and cognitive ability.

Freud thought that during the *oral stage*, the first year of life, gratification was mouth-oriented. According to Freud, sucking and chewing gratified the libido's pleasure-seeking impulse and was the developmental task at this stage of life. Freud noted that during toilet training (around two years old), parents and children were very interested in elimination. Potty-training is an important step in a child's development. Freud called the developmental stage around age two the anal stage. During the *anal stage* gratification centers on feces, parental expectations, and training and discipline techniques. Freud thought that during the *phallic stage*, ages two to six, children's libidinal energy is focused on sexuality and the genitals. Freud thought that during this stage children learn sex-roles, sexual identities, modesty, and attitudes about sexuality. Freud believed that during the *latency stage*, age six to twelve, sexual urges were dormant. During this stage, Freud thought we repress sexual impulses by channeling the libido's energy into school, athletics, and same-sex friendships. We spend the rest of our lives in the *genital stage*, beginning at puberty, repressing or redirecting sexual libidinal energy.

Psycho-social Development Theories. Instead of seeing development in terms of genetic determinants (Piaget) or unconscious sexual determinants (Freud), Russian psychologist *Lev Vygotsky* (1896 - 1934) proposed one of the first *psycho-social development* theories. Vygotsky described the role that social interaction, language, and culture play in cognitive development. Like Piaget, Vygotsky believed that children are active in their development, but Vygotsky thought that social interaction, social learning, and language are fundamental to cognitive development, more so than genetic determinants.

Erik Erikson (1902 - 1994). Erikson's theory of psycho-social development incorporated ideas from Piaget, Vygotsky, and Freud. Erickson believed that social interactions were crucial to development. Like Piaget, Erikson thought that development was driven by inborn forces and progressed through stages. Like Freud, Erikson thought that development was characterized by crises and that failing to successfully move through a stage caused psychological problems. Like Freud, each of Erikson's eight stages builds on the preceding stage. and is characterized by a psycho-social crisis.

- In the *trust versus mistrust stage* – from birth to around 18 months - infants resolve a crisis of trust. Does the infant form trusting relationships or develop a sense of mistrust? Erikson thought that infants who are fed and comforted will develop trust. If trust does not develop the child will be withdrawn, suspicious, and lacking in self-confidence.

- In the ***autonomy versus shame and doubt stage*** – from around 18 months to 3 years – toddlers resolve a crisis of autonomy. In this stage children learn to walk, control elimination, and explore the world with some independence. Does the child develop a sense of positive independence and capability or a sense of incompetence, shame, and self-doubt?

- In the ***initiative versus guilt stage*** – from around 3 to 5 years – preschoolers resolve a crisis of initiative. In this stage, through play and family relationships, children learn to make plans, interact with peers, and assert their initiative. Does the child develop a sense of confidence and control or a sense guilt and timidity?

- In the ***industry versus inferiority stage*** – from around 6 to 11 years – older children resolve a crisis of inferiority. In this stage children enter the larger world of school, knowledge, societies, and cultures. Does the child develop a sense of industry, competence, and mastery, or a sense of inadequacy and inferiority?

- In the ***identity versus role confusion stage*** – from around 12 to 18 years – adolescents face an existential crisis of identity. In this stage adolescents are concerned with questions like "who am I," "why am I here," and "what do other people think about me?" In the face of rapid physical and psychological change, will adolescents develop their unique but appropriate aspirations, beliefs, interests, and identity or will they develop self-doubt, confusion, isolation, or rebellion?

- In the ***intimacy versus isolation stage*** – in young adulthood – Erikson believed we face a crisis of intimacy. In this stage young adults decide whether to give up some of their independence in order to make friends and to commit to an intimate relationship. Will we form deep, intimate, and long-lasting relationships, or will we turn to isolation and loneliness?

- In the ***generativity versus stagnation stage*** – from young through middle adulthood – the crisis is one of generativity, or the ability to generate or make something useful and valuable. In this stage Erikson believed we invest ourselves in the future in terms of raising a family, building a career, and serving the community. Will we continue to contribute, or will we become self-centered, self-indulgent, and stagnant?

- In the ***ego integrity versus despair stage*** – from middle adulthood until death – the crisis is again existential. In this stage mature adults look back and evaluate their lives and ask, "what kind of life have I lived?" If, according to Erikson, we have successfully navigated the previous crises, we will experience ***ego integrity***, a sense of life-satisfaction and no fear of death. Will we look back on life with a sense of completeness, satisfied, and peace or with bitterness, defeat, and hopelessness?

Moral Development. *Lawrence Kohlberg* (1927 - 1987) extended Piaget's theory of genetically-driven cognitive development to moral development. Kohlberg was interested in how we think about right and wrong and this theory of moral development suggests that the development of *moral reasoning*, like personality, intelligence, and social development, was inborn and progressed through levels and stages. Kohlberg described three levels of moral development (each level is made up of two stages).

> *Critique of Erikson.* Erikson's theory has been subject to criticism on a number of matters. From an empirical perspective, psychologists note that there is no agreed-upon measure for the various stages or for the "successful" resolution of each crisis. Erikson casts each crisis and its resolution in terms of humanistic values. For example, Erikson's second stage, autonomy vs. shame and doubt, presumes that autonomy and independence are preferable to submission and obedience and that rules and discipline produce shame and doubt.

- In the *pre-conventional level*, moral reasoning is based on avoiding punishment and advancing one's own interests.
- In the *conventional level*, moral reasoning is based on conforming to the expectations of others and respect for authority.
- In the *post-conventional level*, moral reasoning is based on internalized humanistic principles of justice, reciprocity, and human dignity.

Kohlberg's has been modern psychology's dominant theory of moral development for over fifty years. Many Christians criticize the theory because it describes moral reasoning without reference to God, the Bible, and sin. Many Christians believe that Kohlberg described a model of moral development that, though not explicitly Christian, is consistent with a Christian worldview.

Attachment Theories of Human Development. Do you think that early childhood attachment has an influence on relationships in later life? Many psychologists do. Attachment theories describe attachment, the factors that influence attachment, and the role that forming attachments plays in development. *Attachment* is known as a lasting psychological connection between two people. Attachment theory is based on the joint work of *John Bowlby* and *Mary Ainsworth*. Bolby and Ainsworth believed that the quality of early attachment had life-long impact on development.

> *Heinz Steals the Drug.* Lawrence Kohlberg presented people with stories of moral dilemmas to assess moral reasoning. One such dilemma is presented in Kohlberg's story called *Heinz Steals the Drug*.
>
> In Europe, a woman was near death from a special kind of cancer. There was one drug that the doctors thought might save her. It was a form of radium that a druggist in the same town had recently discovered. The drug was expensive to make, but the druggist was charging ten times what the drug cost him to make. He paid $200 for the radium and charged $2,000 for a small dose of the drug. The sick woman's husband, Heinz, went to everyone he knew to borrow the money, but he could only get together about $1,000 which is half of what it cost. He told the druggist that his wife was dying and asked him to sell it cheaper or let him pay later. But the druggist said: "No, I discovered the drug and I'm going to make money from it." So Heinz got desperate and broke into the man's store to steal the drug for his wife. Should Heinz have done that?

According to attachment theory, children who caregivers are available and responsive to infant's needs establish a sense of attachment and security.

Ainsworth observed children ages 12 to 18 months as they responded to a situation in which they were left alone and then reunited with their mothers. Based on the children's responses, Ainsworth described three major styles of attachment: secure attachment, ambivalent-insecure attachment, and avoidant-insecure attachment.

- Children who have **secure attachment** exhibit mild distress when separated from caregivers, are happy when the caregivers return, prefer parents to strangers, and seek comfort from parents when frightened. As adults, children with secure attachment have trusting relationships and good self-esteem.
- Children who have **ambivalent attachment** exhibit more severe distress when a parent leaves, may be wary of strangers, and are not comforted by the parent's return. Ainsworth thought that ambivalent attachment was a result of caregivers failure to respond when the child is in need. It is thought that ambivalent attachment produces adults who are reluctant to or have difficulties forming adult attachments.
- Children with **avoidant attachment**, when offered a choice, show no preference between a caregiver and a complete stranger, and may avoid or not seek comfort or contact from parents. Avoidant attachment may be a result of responding to a child's needs with punishment, abuse, or neglect. Avoidant attachment is said to produce adults who have problems with intimacy and who are unwilling to share personal thoughts and feelings.

Harry Harlow (1905 - 1981) is famous in the history of psychology for his studies of social behavior, attachment, maternal separation, and social isolation in primates. Harlow believed that primate research could contribute to the understanding of human psychology. Harlow's theory was that primates, and by extension humans, had a universal need for physical contact and comfort.

In one experiment, Harlow separated baby monkeys from their mothers and raised them in cages with two surrogate "mothers." Both surrogates were constructed of wire. A bare-wire mother contained a bottle with food. The other mother was padded and covered with soft cloth, but it did not provide food. Harlow noted that the monkeys clung to the cloth-covered surrogate and ignored the wire surrogate except when feeding. Monkeys "raised" by the surrogate mothers behaved strangely — autistic-like rocking, isolating, refusing to eat, and aggression. As parents themselves, the motherless mothers were either negligent or abusive to their own young— by not nursing, comforting, or protecting them, or by biting or otherwise injuring them.

> **Gender Roles.** Why do boys act like boys and girls act like girls? To what extent are gender roles a result of learning and of socialization? Are aggression, competition, risk-taking, and emotional restraint inborn in boys? Are girls naturally more emotional, nurturing, passive, and cooperative than boys? Psychologists note that young girls have better vocabulary, reading comprehension, and verbal creativity, and boys have better mathematical and visual-spatial ability. Psychologists today suggest that gender roles, sexual identity, and sexual behavior are the playing-out of evolved biological factors (e.g., hormones and brain structure) that are influenced by socialization (i.e., a process by which we learn to fit into society). A Christian worldview understands that Mankind was created male and female – equal, complementary, but different.

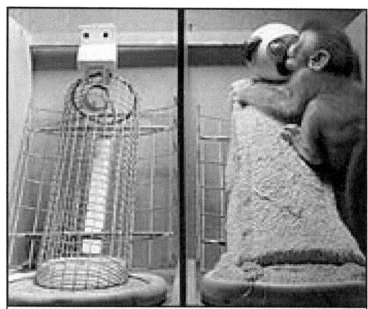
Harlow's monkeys showing preference for a comforting surrogate over a bare-wire surrogate equipped with a bottle.

Harlow's research showed the importance of mother/child bonding in primates. His techniques, however, would be cruel, immoral, and unethical if done with humans. A Christian worldview is consistent with Harlow's observation that in addition to food, safety, and warmth, humans need to feel love, acceptance, and affection to develop successfully. A Christian worldview is not consistent, however, with Harlow's assumption that human love, acceptance, and affection are reducible to, analogous to, or an extension of primate behavior.

Parenting Styles. In the 1960s psychologist *Diana Baumrind* did research to identify and describe parenting styles and to describe the influence of parenting styles on child development. Baumrind described three parenting styles:

- *Authoritarian parents* demand unquestioning obedience, give children little input in decision-making, do not display affection, and seldom praise their children. Authoritarian parenting is said to produce anxious, insecure, withdrawn, easily frustrated, and unhappy children and adults.
- *Permissive parents* allow children to do almost anything. Permissive parents make few demands of their children, rarely or inconsistently use discipline, and give children adult-like decision-making power. Permissive parenting is said to produce children and adults who are have poor emotional control, poor social skills, and little persistence in difficult tasks.
- *Authoritative parents* give children a clear sense of being loved and a sense of what is expected. Authoritative parents are reasonable, rational, and consistent. Authoritative parents are said to recognize and value a child's individual interests while also setting standards of behavior. Authoritative parenting is said to produce children who are friendly, cooperative, and self-reliant.

Adolescent Development. *Adolescence* is usually defined as ages 12 - 20, the time between puberty and adulthood. Adolescence is sometimes divided into three stages: *early adolescence* (12 - 13 years), *middle adolescence* (14 - 16 years), and *late adolescence*, (17 - 20 years). Adolescence is a time of rapid physical, intellectual, emotional, and social development.

Psychologist **Arthur Chickering** suggests that during adolescence we face seven developmental challenges including:

- Developing competence.
- Managing emotions.
- Moving toward independence.
- Developing mature relationships.
- Establishing identity.
- Developing purpose.
- Developing integrity.

Adolescence is often a time of:

- Feeling awkward or uncomfortable about one's physical changes.
- Self-doubt and worry about being normal.
- Moodiness.
- Modeling peers (dress, interests, and attitudes).
- Increased interest in the opposite sex.
- Capacity for abstract, logicial, and introspective thought.
- Seeking independence from parents.
- Testing rules and limits.

Adult Development. Daniel Levinson (1920 - 1994) is famous in the history of psychology for his comprehensive theory of adult development. Prior to Levinson's theory, most developmental theories focused on child and adolescent development and viewed adulthood as a time of developmental stability.

In 1965, eight month old **Bruce Reimer** suffered an accident during circumcision permanently damaging his penis. On the advice of psychologist **John Money**, Bruce received a sex-change operation and hormone therapy. Bruce's parents did not know that Dr. Money's real intent was to show that nurture and not biology determined gender identity. After the surgery, Bruce, now called Brenda, was raised as a little girl. Despite his parents' best effort to nurture a female identity, Bruce/Brenda behaved as a stereotypical little boy. Though Dr. Money claimed that he had demonstrated that gender identify was learned and not inborn, Bruce/Brenda did not identify as a girl and had made three suicide attempts before age 15. At 15 when Bruce/Brenda learned the truth, he decided to become male again and took the name David. At the age of 38, David committed suicide.

Like Erickson, Levinson divided adulthood into three stages of development: early, middle, and late adulthood.

- ***Early adulthood***, from around 17 to 45 years, according to Levinson's theory, is characterized by productive work and making choices. During early adulthood we make decisions about marriage, family, and career.
- ***Middle adulthood***, from around 45 to 60 years, is said to be characterized by a search for meaning and purpose in life, re-examining career goals, and leaving a legacy.
- ***Late adulthood***, from around 65 years to death, is characterized by reflecting on one's life, past achievements, and regrets, and by making peace with oneself and with others.

Aging. This chapter opened by defining developmental psychology as the study of the lifelong process of change. From the miracles of conception and birth until death, we are constantly changing. As we near the end of life, like in every other stage of development, we experience physical, cognitive, emotional, and social changes.

Psychologist Elliott Jaques coined the term *midlife crisis* to describe the existential crisis many people feel around age 40 when they fully face the reality of old age and death.

Physically, the elderly experience a decline in muscle tone, strength, endurance, and sensory ability. Socially, the elderly may experience isolation caused by the death of family and friends and by their own declining health and mobility. Emotionally, the elderly have an increased risk of depression. Illness, isolation, life changes, the death of loved ones, and cognitive decline. Depression tends to last longer in the elderly and is associated with an increased risk of heart disease and with an increased risk of death from illness.

Cognitive changes also occur near the end of life. The speed with which the elderly complete certain cognitive tasks declines, and they adapt more slowly to new situations. The stereotypical cognitive deficits in the elderly (e.g., confusion, memory lapse, and inability to care for one's self) are usually the result of dementia and not part of normal aging. *Dementia* is a loss of brain function that occurs with certain diseases and brain injuries and

Ageism is a type of prejudice or discrimination that is based on age. Ageism is usually focused on the elderly, but can be used against people of all ages.

affects memory, thinking, language, judgment, and behavior. *Parkinson's disease*, *strokes*, and *Alzheimer's disease* often cause dementia.

Flexible and Crystallized intelligence. Psychologist *Raymond Cattell* (1905 - 1998) categorized human intelligence into two types: flexible and crystallized intelligence. According to Cattell, *flexible intelligence* is made up of basic mental abilities like reasoning, abstract thinking, solving novel problems, and encoding short-term memories. Young people generally have superior flexible intelligence compared to older people and are better able to learn new things or adapt to new circumstances.

Crystallized intelligence refers to the general knowledge, vocabulary, and ability accumulated over a lifetime. Whereas flexible intelligence is the ability to learn, crystallized intelligence reflects what has already been learned. Older people are generally better at tasks requiring crystallized intelligence.

Dying. *Elisabeth Kubler-Ross* (1926 - 2004) is famous in the history of psychology for her study of death and dying. Kubler-Ross believed that when we are faced with impending death, we move back and forth through five stages or attitudes: denial and isolation, anger, bargaining, depression, and acceptance.
- Kubler-Ross' first stage, *denial and isolation*, is characterized by shock, numbness, and refusal to accept the news.
- The *anger stage* is characterized by feelings of injustice and "why me?"

- In the *bargaining phase*, many people facing death try to find a way around it. The dying may make promises of good behavior or other life change in an effort to postpone death.
- During the fourth stage, *depression*, as the terminally ill begins to accept the reality of impending death, they may feel overwhelming grief, depression, and hopelessness.
- Kubler-Ross' final stage of dying is *acceptance*. Acceptance means a quiet expectation – being neither depressed nor bitter while contemplating the end of one's life.

Kubler-Ross, who was also interested in near-death experiences and communication with spirits, did not reference Christian beliefs in her description of the experience of impending death. Though the Christian experiences many of the same feelings Kubler-Ross described, the Christian worldview includes an assurance that Kubler-Ross did not understand.

Chapter Summary.

The psychology of development is interested in describing and explaining human development in terms of physical, sexual, cognitive, emotional, moral, and social change throughout life. Continuous developmental theories describe development as the gradual and ongoing unfolding, or maturation, of inborn characteristics. Discontinuous developmental theories suggest we develop through a progressive series of distinct steps or stages. Some theories suggest that human development is influenced most by genetics and others suggest it is influenced more by environmental factors. Most psychologists today believe that it is both -- that we continuously develop, but we also move through stages, and that genetics and the environment are inextricably connected.

Early modern psychologists crafted developmental theories grounded in the worldview assumptions of the Renaissance philosophers John Locke, and Jean Jacques Rousseau, and Immanuel Kant. John Locke believed that children are born a "blank slate," or tabula rasa, and that environmental influence is primary. Jacques Rousseau believed that development was determined at birth. Immanuel Kant believed that development was influenced by the interaction of inborn characteristics and the external world.

Jean Piaget is famous for his theory of intellectual development in children. Piaget described intellectual development as an orderly, sequential, and predictable progression through four stages. Piaget believed that children were active participants in creating a schema, or way of understanding the world. Assimilation and accommodation are the processes by which children develop and modify their schema. Piaget called the first stage the sensorimotor stage. From birth to 18 months the developing child experiences the world solely through the senses and motor activity. The pre-operational stage, from around 18 months to 6 years, is characterized by the development of logical mental operations and the use of symbols to represent things. In the concrete-operational stage, from around age 6 until early adolescence, children begin to use logic, mental manipulations, and mathematics. The formal-operations stage, from adolescence into adulthood, is characterized by the development of the ability for logical, abstract, and hypothetical thinking, to plan and imagine the consequences of an action, and to draw conclusions from available information.

Lev Vygotsky described the fundamental role that social interaction, language, and culture plays in cognitive development. Erik Erikson described stages of psycho-social development. Erickson defined each of his eight stages in terms of natural crises. Sigmund Freud is famous in the history of modern psychology for his psycho-sexual or psycho-dynamic personality theory. Freud believed that personality develops through psycho-sexual stages, propelled by the life force libido. Lawrence Kohlberg described a model of moral development in which he theorized that moral reasoning also grew through three levels he called the pre-conventional, conventional, and post-conventional levels of moral reasoning.

Adolescence, the time between puberty and adulthood is characterized by rapid physical, intellectual, emotional, and social development. Early adulthood, from around 17 to 45 years, according to Daniel Levinson, is characterized by productive work and making choices. During early adulthood, we make decisions about marriage, family, and career. Middle adulthood, from around 45 to 60 years, is said to be characterized by a search for meaning and purpose in life, reexamining career goals, and leaving a legacy. Late adulthood, from around 65 years to death, is characterized by reflecting on one's life, past achievements, and regrets, and by making peace with one's self and with others. As we near the end of life, like in every other stage of development, we experience physical, cognitive, emotional, and social changes. Dementia is a loss of brain function that occurs with certain diseases and brain injuries and affects memory, thinking, language, judgment, and behavior.

For Review.

1. Describe the uses of developmental theories.
2. In what ways is development continuous, and in what ways is it discontinuous?
3. Describe nervous system development in the embryonic stage and fetal stages of development.
4. Describe fetal alcohol syndrome and how to prevent it.
5. Name and describe four reflexive abilities children have at birth.
6. Describe cross-section and longitudinal developmental research.
7. Describe development theories in terms of the philosophies of Locke, Rousseau, Kant, and Hall.
8. Piaget described four stages of cognitive development. Name and describe each stage.
9. Describe assimilation and accommodation in terms of Piaget's developmental theory.
10. Describe criticisms of Piaget's theory of cognitive development.
11. Describe recapitulation theory.
12. Describe Erik Erikson's eight psychosocial crises.
13. Describe Freudian psycho-sexual development.
14. Provide examples of moral reasoning at each of Kohlberg's levels of moral development. Evaluate your examples using biblical absolutes.
15. The text stated that "the Christian worldview includes an assurance that Kubler-Ross did not understand." In your own words, explain what Kubler-Ross' theory is missing.

Chapter 9

Consciousness

In This Chapter

- What is Consciousness?
- States of Consciousness
- Sleep
- Dreams
- Why Do We Dream?
- The Meaning of Dreams
- A Christian View of Dreams
- Hypnosis
- Meditation
- Psychoactive Drugs

What is consciousness and what does it mean to be conscious? Are animals conscious? If so, how does human consciousness differ from animal consciousness? Is consciousness subject to scientific investigation? If so, what are the brain mechanisms of consciousness? New technologies, particularly brain scanning technology, have provided much insight into conscious and unconscious mental processes. But many questions remain.

Consciousness is difficult to define, and there is no widely accepted definition. It has been defined as:

- The awareness one has of oneself and of the environment.
- The capacity to be explicitly aware of oneself and to make explicit free-will decisions.
- The ability to establish meaningful relationships.
- The subjective experiencing of a stimulus or mental state.
- The ability to attribute goals (either to oneself or to others).
- The locus for human decision-making.
- The essence of Mankind's God-likeness.

Naturalistic psychologists explain consciousness as a characteristic of the most highly evolved animals. A Christian worldview sees consciousness as part of our God-likeness and the vehicle of our relationships with God and others. Consciousness is a pre-requisite to free-will, and free-will is a pre-requisite to moral accountability. The principles of free-will and moral accountability are central to the Christian worldview. Without moral accountability, sin and salvation are meaningless. Without consciousness, humans are nothing more than very complex machine-like animals. Theories of consciousness that deny the "specialness" of human consciousness are incompatible with a Christian view of Mankind.

Human consciousness is inextricably connected to brain activity. For the Christian studying consciousness, that means understanding our God-given self-awareness in the context of the complexities of the nervous system. You must balance the discoveries made in neuroscience with the supernatural

> ***The Astonishing Hypothesis.*** The astonishing hypothesis is a concept developed by Francis Crick, co-discoverer of DNA, that every mental experience of sentient beings is nothing more than the result of electrical-chemical reactions in the brain.

component of human consciousness; they are not incompatible. Because our experience of consciousness is inherently subjective, consciousness, whatever it is, is not subject to the usual objective methods of natural science.

Modern evolutionary psychology, as you might guess, describes and explains consciousness solely in terms of brain activity. The consensus among modern psychologists is that all of mental life, including consciousness and emotions and choice and morality, are the products of brain activities. The naturalistic worldview presumes that consciousness *must* be nothing but the product of brain activity.

Psychologists struggle to define consciousness and to identify the mental structures and processes involved in it. To explain consciousness in terms of evolution, one must acknowledge that it exists, describe its structure and process in the nervous system, and describe how it enhances survival and reproduction.

States of Consciousness. The study of consciousness is made more difficult by the fact that it is not a single constant mental state. Dreams, daydreams, hypnosis, meditation, and hallucinations are states of consciousness. Psychoactive drugs alter consciousness, as do extremes of heat, fatigue, exhaustion, dehydration, and malnutrition. Different patterns of brain waves are associated with different states of consciousness.

Early modern psychologists focused extensively on the nature of consciousness using introspection in an effort to discover its nature. As psychology established itself as a natural science, its focus shifted away from introspection and consciousness toward empiricism and behavior. In the 1950s and 60s, the rise of cognitive and humanistic psychology produced a renewed interest in the study of consciousness.

Sleep. Shortly after God created Adam, He caused him to fall into a deep sleep (Genesis 2:21). Modern psychologists do not know why we spend about one-third of our lives asleep. A Christian worldveiw recognizes sleep as part of God's design. Understanding sleep is made more difficult because it is more than a simple state of unconsciousness. While we sleep, our brains continue to work. Just as there are several states of waking consciousness, sleep comprises several states or stages. We dream, we talk, and some walk in their sleep. Parents (especially mothers) waken easily at the sound of their babies and some people "program" themselves to wake at the same time every day.

There was little research into sleep until the 1950s and the discovery that our eyes move while we sleep. The 1950s and the discovery of *rapid eye movement* (REM) began a time of intensive research into the nature of sleep. REM sleep is sometimes called *"paradoxical" sleep* because the brain wave pattern during REM sleep is similar to patterns while awake. During REM sleep we dream, breathing fluctuates, heart rate varies, traces of muscle activity appear across the body, and our eyes move rapidly back and forth up to eight times each second.

In one night's sleep, we pass back and forth through stages of sleep. We move through the stages three or four times each night. Each stage is distinguished by differing patterns of brain wave activity. There are four patterns or types of brain waves: alpha, beta, theta, and delta.

- *Alpha waves* are slower and characteristic of rest, decreased attention to the environment, and the beginning of sleep.
- *Beta waves* are characteristic of alertness, thought, and concentration (an engaged mind). Beta waves have low amplitude and high frequency.
- *Theta waves* have even greater amplitude and slower frequency and are characteristic of the transition from wakefulness to sleep (i.e., when we are falling asleep).
- *Delta waves* have a very slow frequency and are characteristic of deep dreamless sleep.

Sleep begins with the transition from wakefulness to sleep. As we fall asleep, brain waves change from predominately Beta waves to predominately Alpha waves. In this state we are awake but not attentive to our surroundings.

In stage 1 sleep there are mostly theta waves. In stage 1 sleep, we lose conscious awareness of the environment, heart and breathing rates drop, body temperature drops, and muscles relax. During stage 1 sleep, we may experience odd or bizarre mental images, sensations, or even hallucinations. We wake easily from stage 1 sleep feeling un-rested.

After a few minutes of stage 1 sleep, we move deeper into stage 2 sleep. Stage 2 is characterized by short bursts of distinctive brain wave patterns called sleep spindles. A spindle is a brief burst of electrical voltage that may occur in response to sound. *Sleep spindles* are short bursts of brain activity that may represent the brain's effort to keep us relaxed. Tossing and turning often accompanies stage 1 and 2 sleep.

In stages 3 and 4, brain waves slow even more and we pass into deep sleep. In stages 3 and 4, we are difficult to rouse, breathing and heart rates slow further, and muscles relax completely. In stage 4, body functions decline to the deepest state of rest, we move little, and we are oblivious to our surroundings. Someone awakened from stage 4 sleep may be groggy, disoriented, and confused.

During the transition from wakefulness to sleep, some people experience visual or auditory hallucinations or a falling sensation. Some may interpret the experience as extra-sensory perception, ghosts, or out-of-body experiences.

Stage 5, or REM sleep, is characterized by dreams, rapid eye movements, and a dramatic loss of muscle tone – effectively paralyzing us. Brain activity during REM sleep is similar to that of wakefulness.

As noted earlier, we move through the sleep stages three or four times each night. We do not, however, move from stage 1 to 4 to REM sleep and then start over again with stage 1. For the first one or two cycles of sleep, we do progress from stage 1 to stage 4 and then to REM sleep. In later cycles we move through the cycles in reverse. Some people get all the deep sleep they need during the first few cycles and spend the rest of the night in lighter sleep. Our sleep patterns, especially following days of intense physical activity, will have more stage 4 and 5 sleep.

Why Do We Sleep? Psychologists, philosophers, and theologians for centuries have pondered the purpose of sleep. Modern psychologists, guided by their worldview presumptions, proposed a number of theories to explain the purpose of sleep. The leading theories today are the repair and restoration, information consolidation, and adaptive or evolution theories.

The repair and restoration theory of sleep suggests that the purpose of sleep is to allow the body and the brain to repair themselves. In the repair and restoration theory, REM sleep and dreams are essential to restoring mental functions. During sleep, cell division, protein synthesis, and white blood cell production increase.

The *information consolidation* theory of sleep suggests that the purpose of sleep is to allow the brain to consolidate and process the events and experiences of the day. Sleep deprivation studies suggest that without proper sleep, we tend to forget more information and are less able to encode new long-term memories.

Evolutionary theories of sleep, also known as *adaptive theories*, suggest that sleep evolved to serve some adaptive survival purpose. Sleep is puzzling to evolutionary psychologists because it is counter-intuitive, meaning that it does not make sense for an animal to spend long periods of time in a vulnerable, unprotected, and non-alert state. Nevertheless, some evolutionary theories suggest that sleep evolved to protect us from predators – that our ancestors were more likely to survive and reproduce if they slept at night while man-eaters were on the prowl.

About 70% of people report occasionally, just after falling asleep, waking suddenly to a falling sensation and a strong muscle twitch.

Do you know when you fall asleep? The average teenager takes 15 minutes to fall asleep. Many fall asleep in fewer than 6 minutes. The average teenager thinks that it takes more than 30 minutes to fall asleep.

How Much Sleep Do We Need? The amount of sleep each person needs depends on many factors, including age. As a newborn, you probably slept about 18 hours each day, and about half of your sleep was REM sleep. Teenagers need about 9 hours on average, and your need for sleep decreases until adulthood, after which it remains stable. Most adults need 7 – 8 hours of sleep each night, but some need only 4 - 5 hours each night and others need 10 or more hours. During the first trimester of pregnancy mothers-to-be often need several more hours of sleep than usual. Our need for sleep also depends on whether we have been deprived of sleep in previous days.

Though the amount of sleep we need levels off and stabilizes in adulthood, our sleep patterns change and we are more likely to experience sleep difficulties as we age. Around middle age, we begin spending less time in stage 3 and 4 sleep. As a result of sleeping less deeply, we wake more easily. Age-related hormonal and physical changes affect the quality of sleep.

Our pattern of sleep is part of a set of daily physiological cycles or rhythms. A ***circadian rhythm*** is a 24-hour physiological cycle. The word circadian comes from the Latin, meaning "around one day." Sleep, body temperature, alertness, blood pressure, elimination, and hormone levels follow circadian rhythms. Circadian rhythms are influenced by environmental cues (e.g., daylight and darkness), but they are not dependent on them. Daily rhythms will synchronize with the environment, but research indicates that circadian rhythms continue even without environmental cues, suggesting that the brain has a way to keep track of time. ***Jet lag*** refers to the fatigue and disorientation air travelers feel after a long flight when environmental cues do not match the circadian rhythm.

Sleep debt is the difference between the amount time spent sleeping and the amount of sleep needed. ***Sleep debt*** is less serious than sleep deprivation but does lead to impaired judgment, thinking, emotions, and motor activity. Eventually the body demands the debt be paid back. ***Sleep recovery*** is a pattern of sleep in which the body makes up for missed sleep with extra REM sleep.

Sleep deprivation refers to the chronic and severe lack of adequate sleep. Extreme sleep deprivation, however, can have serious effects on mental and physical health. Laboratory rats prevented from sleeping lose their ability to maintain body temperature and die in about three weeks. In humans chronic sleep deprivation impairs thinking, concentration, memory, the ability to manage stress, and the ability to fight infection. It is very difficult for humans to voluntarily go without sleep for more than 48 hours. After long periods without sleep, people lose motor coordination, have difficulty speaking, and may experience auditory and visual hallucinations.

Insomnia (too little sleep) and *hypersomnia* (too much sleep) are two of a group of conditions in which there is a disturbance in sleep patterns. *Somnambulism* is a sleep disorder in which activities normally done while awake are done while asleep. "Sleepwalkers" perform tasks (i.e., cleaning, walking around, cooking) as though they were wide-awake. The sleepwalker's eyes are generally open, but appear "glassy" or "vacant." Sleepwalkers are not conscious of their actions at a level allowing memories to form, so if the sleepwalker returns to bed before waking, he/she usually does not remember the episode. Sleepwalking is more common in children and is associated with high levels of stress and anxiety. Because sleepwalkers are in deep stage 3 or 4 sleep, they are difficult to waken and may be disoriented and groggy when awakened. Waking up someplace other than bed may be frightening, so many psychologists suggest that it is best to just lead the sleepwalker back to bed.

> The world record for the longest period without sleep is 11 days. In 1965 Randy Gardner stayed awake 11 days without using stimulants. After four days without sleep, Gardner began hallucinating and believed he was actually a famous football player.

Somniloquy, or sleep talking, is another normally harmless sleep disorder. It refers to talking out loud during sleep. Sleep talking may occur during any sleep stage, and the speech may be soft or loud, difficult to understand, nonsensical, or perhaps vulgar and offensive. It is unclear if sleep talking is always associated with dreaming, but at times it is a verbal expression of dream content. Sleep talking is common and occurs in 50% of young children. Most stop sleep talking by puberty, but about 5% of adults talk in their sleep.

Narcolepsy is a very serious sleep disorder in which people fall asleep suddenly and without warning while performing ordinary activities. People with narcolepsy experience excessive daytime sleepiness and may go directly into deep REM sleep. We all experience sleepiness, but someone with narcolepsy falls asleep at inappropriate times. Narcolepsy is particularly dangerous because it is frequently accompanied by *cataplexy*, the complete loss of voluntary muscle control.

Sleep apnea is a relatively common sleep disorder. The National Institutes of Health estimates that over 12 million Americans have it. The word apnea is from the Greek and means "without breath." During normal sleep, we occasionally stop breathing, but after a few seconds, we begin to breathe again without any disturbance to our sleep. In sleep apnea, however, each time breathing stops (as often as 20 to 30 times each hour), the sufferer briefly wakens to gasp for air. Obviously, waking 20 to 30 times each hour interferes with proper sleep. Though people at any age can have sleep apnea, it occurs most commonly in overweight males over 40 years old.

Sleep Deprivation and Driving. Sleep-deprived drivers perform as badly as or worse than those who are intoxicated. Caffeine and other stimulants cannot overcome the effects of severe sleep deprivation.

There are two types of sleep apnea: obstructive and central. In *obstructive sleep apnea*, the soft tissue in the throat collapses and closes during sleep. People with obstructive sleep apnea often snore loudly. In *central sleep apnea*, the brain fails to signal the diaphragm to breathe. Daytime drowsiness (and the accompanying risk for accidents), headaches, irritability, memory problems, weight gain, and increased risk of high blood pressure, heart attack, stroke, and diabetes are possible consequences of untreated sleep apnea.

Sleep paralysis describes the experience of being awake but temporarily unable to move or speak. Sleep paralysis occurs as we are just falling asleep or as we are just becoming fully awake. People suffering from sleep paralysis may report feeling fear and "some sort of presence," but are unable to cry out. The experience usually last a few seconds after which one feels suddenly released.

REM behavior disorder (RBD) is a sleep disorder that involves acting-out vivid, intense, and sometimes violent dreams. The behaviors include yelling, screaming, hitting, grabbing, punching, kicking, and generally flailing around. There is no known cause for RBD, but it is thought to be related to a malfunction of the area in the brain responsible for the near paralysis of dream sleep.

Dreams. Dreaming is a universal human experience and a big mystery to psychologists. When we dream, we encounter experiences, sights, sounds, ideas, and emotions. Most dreams are very ordinary. Some are extraordinary. Most are outside the control of the dreamer. My dreams and yours are not alike in length, content, emotions, or vividness.

Defining dreams is difficult. A dream is a form of thought. Dreams are powerful subjective experiences that we "see," "feel," and remember. We dream 4 - 6 times each night, but not all dreams occur during REM sleep. Dreams occur during each sleep stage. During REM sleep, brain wave activity closely resembles that of wakefulness, and dreams are more vivid. Dreams during non-REM sleep generally contain fragmented thoughts and images and are difficult to remember. Narrative dreams, bizarre dreams, and nightmares are characteristic of REM sleep. The content of dreams is similar across all cultures. Psychologists suggest that dreams of falling, being chased, being injured, a loved one being injured, flying, and being nude in public may be universal dreams.

During the typical lifespan, six years are spent dreaming.

Brain imaging suggests that dreaming involves the pre-frontal cortex. The pre-frontal cortex is known to control executive functions. Executive functions are mental processes like decision making, planning, etc. and are associated with our conscious ability to distinguish, evaluate, plan, and predict.

Why do we dream? Just as there are several theories to explain why we sleep, psychologists have proposed a number of theories to explain why we dream.

- ***Evolutionary theory*** suggests that dreams evolved as a way to rehearse strategies to survive in a hostile environment. Early humans, as the theory goes, who could dream about ways of surviving a predator attack were more likely to survive and reproduce than those who did not dream. Evolutionists suggest that the common "being chased" dream is evidence for the theory.
- In the ***activation-synthesis theory*** of dreams, the brain generates dreams to "explain" the random neural impulses (brain sparks) that occur during sleep.
- Some theories state that dreams are part of the process by which the brain eliminates, strengthens, and ***re-organizes neural connections***.
- Some psychologists believe that dreaming is the way our brains try to ***interpret*** what is going on around us while we sleep. For example, a phone ringing or your alarm clock may be incorporated into the content of a dream.
- Some use ***information-processing*** metaphors to explain dreams. The brain is like a computer and dreams are the way the brain defragments and re-organizes its data.
- Another model proposes that dreams are a safe means for experiencing powerful emotions, ***resolving psychic conflict***, and solving difficult problems.

Meaning of Dreams. What do dreams mean? Is there a Christian view of dreams? How does the experience of dreams fit in a Christian worldview? Are dreams simply subconscious mental processes, or are they a means by which God communicates with us? If God chooses to reveal Himself through the imagery of dreams, how do we understand and interpret the imagery?

Throughout history, mystics of every tradition believed that dreams held special meaning. Many people see dreams as evidence of a mystical spiritual realm—an alternate reality which we can only glimpse in dreams. Some people use dreams to diagnose illness, find game animals, predict the weather, or foretell the future. Popular literature contains countless interpretive guides promising to reveal the hidden meaning of dreams.

Sigmund Freud's ***psycho-analytic theory*** of dreams suggested that dreams were a representation of unconscious thoughts and desires. According to Freud, we are driven by aggressive and pleasure-seeking thoughts and feelings that are kept from conscious awareness. Freud suggested that these thoughts and feelings are expressed in dreams. Freud theorized that dreams provide an unconscious outlet for the violent and sexual urges we repress while conscious. Freud believed that dreams contain *latent* or hidden meanings. For example, if a dream included a cigar, Freud believed that the cigar represented the latent sexual meaning of the dream.

Carl Jung, a disciple of Freud, saw dreams as *symbolic representations* of memories and instincts shared by all people. Eric Fromm saw dreams as *unconscious problem solving*. Many today see dreams as unconscious expressions of our conscious concerns that provide unconscious insight into solving those problems. Some see dreams as cosmic messages from the spirit world, thought to provide warning, direction, advice, or inspiration. Others see dreams as evidence of their pantheistic worldview – that Mankind and the universe are "one."

A Christian View of Dreams. The Bible is rich with examples of God speaking through dreams. In the Old Testament, God chose to communicate to select people of Israel through dreams. God continued to communicate through dreams in the New Testament. He may have indicated His intent to communicate though dreams today. The early Church fathers believed dreams were a continuing source of revelation. If God continues to communicate through dreams, how are we to interpret the content?

Achieving a Christian view of dreams is made more difficult by the biblical cautions of false dreams and warnings about lies in the form of dreams. The Bible is clear that the Gospel message is complete. If dreams have no role in further "revelation," do they have a role as a means of "illumination" for the individual dreamer?

If our dream life is part of our God-likeness, if God still speaks through dreams, the Christian student of psychology must, as is the case in most of psychology's content, guard against exclusively naturalistic explanations of dreams. We should not simply dismiss dreams as meaningless unconscious imagery. If we seek meaning in our dreams, we should not accept completely secular interpretations and, as a prelude to this text's discussion of psychotherapies, the Christian student must also be cautious, skeptical, and wise when Christian dreamers claim special revelation through dreams or special ability to interpret dreams.

Hypnosis. *Hypnosis* is an altered, trance-like state of consciousness in which a person is hyper-suggestible or easily influenced. Is hypnosis real? Is it a tool of the occult? Is hypnosis just a highly focused state of attentive concentration? In a hypnotic state, is one more in tune with God's consciousness? Hypnosis is controversial and interesting. Some suggest that in Genesis 2:21-22, when Adam fell into a

> James Ryle, a prominent Christian, wrote a book published in 1993. In *Hippo in the Garden*, Ryle described a dream in which he saw a man leading a hippopotamus into a garden. Ryle interpreted the dream as a message from God announcing a coming charismatic prophetic movement.

Hypnotherapists today suggest that hypnosis can help people lose weight, quit smoking, and discover the subconscious roots of abnormal thoughts, feelings, and behaviors.

deep sleep, God performed the first hypnosis. There are references to hypnotic-like states in ancient Egyptian and Greek literature, but *Franz Anton Mesmer*, not God, is usually credited with the discovery of hypnosis.

Mesmer's technique, known at the time as *mesmerism*, was focused on healing illnesses by manipulating the *animal magnetism*, a mysterious energy field thought to surround living creatures. Using magnets and crude batteries to induce trance-like convulsions, Mesmer believed body fluids were restored to their proper flow. The *Marquis de Puysegur*, a student of Mesmer, learned that convulsions were not necessary. Puysegur induced trance-like states with words and claimed that his suggestions could heal people.

In the early 19th century, *James Braid* developed a form of *hypnotic induction* using eye fatigue to induce a *hypnotic trance*. In Braid's technique, the hypnotist held a shiny object slightly above the subject's eye level while suggesting the subject was "getting very, very sleepy" and that their eyelids were "getting very, very, heavy." With a steady gaze on an object above eye level and continuous suggestions called "sleep talk," the subject's eyelids did get heavy and they did get sleepy. Using increasingly demanding suggestions, the subject was asked to concentrate on small changes in the body or the environment and told to go to an ever deeper and more relaxed sleep. Once in the altered state, the subject acted, perceived, thought, and felt according to the hypnotist's suggestions. The hypnotized person accepted the instructions of a hypnotist much the way a dreaming person accepts strange events in a dream. This allowed the hypnotist to suggest behaviors or perceptions that otherwise would not occur.

Classic examples are taking a bite of an onion but perceiving it as an apple, accepting the suggestion that the subject's arm is paralyzed, or not experiencing severe pain. While hypnotized, people will respond to suggestions that they see things that are not there and do not see things that are there. Under hypnotic suggestion, people may remember long forgotten events, recall events that did not happen, and forget events that really happened (*posthypnotic amnesia*). Under deep hypnosis, suggestions can be issued for later execution (*post-hypnotic suggestion*). Under hypnosis, subjects have gone temporarily deaf, undergone surgery without anesthesia, and have been said to "regress" to a younger age.

Not everyone can be hypnotized, and some people are more hypnotizable than others. About 5 - 10% of people do not respond to hypnosis. Psychologists do not agree on the definition or value of hypnosis. They do not agree that hypnosis is an altered state of consciousness. The hypnotic state is not sleep; brain waves do not change as in sleep. Some theorists suggest that hypnosis causes the subject to divide their consciousness into two parts – one part that responds to the outside world and one part that does not. Some suggest that the hypnotized person is faking or playing a role.

A Christian View of Hypnosis? What is the relationship of a Christian worldview, modern psychology, and hypnosis? In terms of hypnosis, a better question may be "how do Christian worldviews differ?" Christians disagree with other Christians over whether hypnotism is acceptable for Christians. Some say that hypnosis is a type of idolatry or the practice of a false religion. They equate hypnosis with Buddhism and other Eastern religions. Christian critics of hypnosis compare the hypnotic trance with the yogic trance. Some believe that hypnosis is an occult practice (see Leviticus 19:31) and that hypnosis leaves one open to satanic attack. They see hypnosis as a religious activity in which one surrenders control of the mind to the hypnotist or perhaps to Satan. Hypnotists who claim to be able to contact the dead, lead us to past or future lives, or divine the future are, according to a Christian worldview, practicing the occult. If hypnotism is condemned in the Bible and if it provides Satan an opportunity to influence us, the Christian is well-advised to avoid it.

Some compare hypnosis, especially self-hypnosis, with deep Christian meditation and intense prayer. They compare the hypnotic trance with the examples of trances and visionary states in the Bible (see Acts 10:10). Some claim that to equate hypnosis with false religions and demon possession is to confuse the practice of hypnosis with the purpose of hypnosis. If hypnosis is a biblical tool that can draw us closer to God, refresh our minds, and open ourselves to His instruction, the Christian would be well-advised to practice it.

Some see hypnosis as a powerful tool to help get rid of bad habits, establish good habits, build confidence, lose weight, or have pain-free dental work. Others note that instead of looking inward for our help that we should look to God. The spiritual dimension of hypnosis will likely cause introductory psychology courses to dismiss hypnosis as an interesting phenomenon or a cool parlor trick. For the Christian student of psychology, it is much more.

Meditation. What is meditation? Psychologists describe meditation as a form of deep concentration in which the mind is focused on a single thing or emptied of thought. ***Meditation*** is described as the practice of calming the mind and focusing attention. In college psychology classes you may be introduced to various techniques of meditation. In Sunday school, from the pulpit, or in your personal study, you may have learned that meditation is a practice commanded by the Bible. You learned that meditation means concentrating on God, focusing on His Word, listening for God's voice, and reflecting on His works and His will.

Popular literature proclaims the benefits of Transcendental Meditation (TM), Hindu meditation, Bahá'í meditation, Buddhist meditation, Vipassana Meditation, Tafakkur, body scan meditation, and more. Meditation is said to help enhance self-awareness and self-control, to help one "get in touch" with one's "inner self", to allow one to experience "higher states of consciousness," and to "connect" to your "spirit guide." You may be told that religious beliefs or worldviews are irrelevant, that meditation is about consciousness. Do not believe it. It is all about religious beliefs and worldviews.

Meditation is associated with long-term heath benefits such as improved physical and mental health and reduced stress. There is research indicating tangible benefits for most varieties of meditation, including Christian meditation. The Christian student studying psychology must carefully evaluate those benefits and the means by which they are attained.

Psychoactive Drugs. Drug and alcohol use is the cause of unimaginable heartbreak, sorrow, sickness, and death. We were created to glorify God, to love other people, to obey human authority, to honor our bodies, and to seek the mind of Christ. Drug and alcohol use is not consistent with those objectives. Psychoactive or psychotropic drugs alter consciousness, behavior, cognition, and emotions. Since ancient times people have used psychoactive drugs to avoid reality and responsibility, cause hallucinations, relieve pain, and alter consciousness. Some drugs like caffeine, tobacco, and alcohol are so widely accepted that many do not think of them as drugs. Because caffeine, nicotine, and alcohol are psychoactive drugs, it is probably safe to say that very few people today have not at some time used psychoactive drugs. Every day millions of people abuse psychoactive drugs. ***Psychopharmacology*** is the study of the relationship between drugs and mental processes. Psychopharmacology addresses illicit (illegal) and licit (legal) drugs.

Psychoactive drugs work by crossing the blood-brain barrier and altering the way neurotransmitters work. Psychoactive drugs may cause more or less of a neurotransmitter to be released, block the reception of a neurotransmitter, or block re-absorption of a neurotransmitter. Several factors impact the effect of a drug. ***Drug effects*** vary according to the amount of the drug ingested; the drug's potency; the route of administration; the user's previous experience and expectation; the user's age, body weight, and mood; and the environment in which the drug is used.

Regular use of a drug may lead to tolerance. ***Tolerance*** refers to decreased susceptibility to the same quantity of a drug. A drug user who over time requires more of a drug to achieve the same effect is developing a tolerance to the drug. With continued use, drug users may develop ***dependence***, commonly known as **addiction**. Someone who is **drug dependent** experiences very unpleasant physical and/or emotional symptoms called withdrawal symptoms when not using the drug. **Withdrawal** symptoms are so unpleasant that the user compulsively seeks and uses the drug despite obvious and serious consequences. Psychologists differentiate between psychological dependence and physiological dependence. In **psychological dependence** the user experiences mental or emotional discomfort when not using the drug. In **physiological dependence** the user experiences physical symptoms when not using the drug (i.e., seizures, diarrhea, pain). The physical and psychological withdrawal symptoms are often the direct opposite of the effects of using the drug.

Christian psychologists must reconcile the Christian view of sin and personal responsibility with research indicating a genetic and environmental influence on substance abuse and dependence. Modern psychologists must reconcile their view that substance dependence is a genetic-based disease with research indicating that strong religious beliefs are associated with low levels of substance abuse and dependence.

Psychologists classify psychoactive drugs into four categories:

- Depressants or Sedative-hypnotics.
- Stimulants.
- Opiates or Narcotics.
- Hallucinogens or Psychedelics.

Depressants, also known as sedative-hypnotics or tranquilizers, are a class of drugs that depress neural activity in the brain. There are many types of depressants, and most affect the neurotransmitter **gamma-amino butyric acid (GABA)**. Depressants change brainwave activity from predominately alpha and beta waves, characteristic of wakefulness and alertness, to delta and theta waves, characteristic of rest and sleep. Sluggish movement, slowed motor activity, and a sleepy state of consciousness are characteristic of sedative-hypnotics. As noted earlier, withdrawal effects often are the opposite of the effect of the drug itself. Withdrawal from depressants, which slow brain activity, may cause seizures or out-of-control brain activity.

Alcohol is the most familiar and most widely abused drug in our society. Alcohol is a bulky drug, requiring considerably larger doses than most other drugs. A common misperception of alcohol is that it is a stimulant. Alcohol is a depressant, not a stimulant. Another perception about alcohol is that, in small doses, it reduces inhibitions and enhances social interactions. One reason that alcohol reduces inhibitions is that people expect it to have that effect. Psychologists have shown that people who think they are drinking alcohol, but who really are not, behave as though they were actually drinking alcohol. Subjects were less inhibited and more relaxed. Another reason may be that by depressing the inhibitory functions of the brain, people behave in ways they would not otherwise behave. We may perceive dis-inhibition as stimulating. The perceived social benefits of dis-inhibition stand in contrast to the extreme negative consequences of dis-inhibition (e.g., violence, rape, and a host of risky behaviors).

As the dose of alcohol increases, psychological and physiological functioning declines. The first to decline are the complex cognitive abilities like planning, problem solving, and memory. Next, fine motor skills (e.g., driving, writing, and working with the hands), gross motor skills (e.g., balance and walking), and involuntary motor activity (e.g., reacting to pain and breathing) are disrupted. Alcohol overdose can cause blackouts, amnesia, and ultimately death.

Alcohol **metabolizes** in the liver, and liver disease is the most likely consequence of chronic alcohol use. Chronic alcohol use also contributes to problems with learning, memory, and emotions and has been associated with brain shrinkage, sexual dysfunction, and increased risk for injury.

Stimulants. By mimicking adrenaline, a hormone produced in high-stress situation, stimulants decrease reaction time, increase heart rate, heighten mood, increase vigilance and alertness, and reduce fatigue. Stimulants also may cause nervousness, jittery movements, insomnia, irregular heartbeats, and anxiety or panic.

Caffeine is the most widely used psychoactive drug in the world. Your morning coffee or tea, lunchtime soda, and chocolate snack all contain caffeine. Two cups of coffee, approximately 150 mg of caffeine, generally produce mood-elevating and fatigue-relieving effects. Large doses may produce insomnia, restlessness, and anxiety. Caffeine may raise blood pressure slightly.

College students sometimes take caffeine pills to stay awake to study. Caffeine pills contain a high dose of the drug and may produce symptoms of anxiety, nervousness, fear, and palpitations. If you require high doses of caffeine to experience its effects, you are developing a tolerance to caffeine and if going without caffeine gives you a headache, you are experiencing withdrawal symptoms.

Amphetamine and Methamphetamine. The amphetamine molecule was first synthesized in the late 1800s. American and Japanese pilots used amphetamines extensively during World War II. Low doses of amphetamine increased energy, concentration, alertness, and mood, and decreased the need for sleep. Today, amphetamine and related drugs are used to treat asthma, narcolepsy, obesity, and attention deficit disorder.

Amphetamines were the primary drugs of abuse from the 1940s to the 1970s. Beginning in the 1990s, amphetamine use resurged in the form of methamphetamine and has reached epidemic proportions.

Methamphetamine's **capture ratio**, or the percentage of users who develop dependence, is very high. The feelings of euphoria from methamphetamine are so strong that many methamphetamine users report symptoms of dependence after just one use. Tolerance to methamphetamines builds quickly so users require ever increasing doses to achieve the desired effect.

Symptoms of methamphetamine use include rapid speech, dilated pupils, increased energy and goal directed activity, mood swings, irritability, nervousness, chest pains, palpitations, and sweating. Signs of long-term use include confusion; neglecting school, work, and social activities; aggressiveness and violence; wild mood swings; significant weight loss; sores on face and arms; diarrhea; vomiting; hallucinations; paranoia; tremors; convulsions; long periods of sleeplessness followed by long periods of sleep; and tooth decay from the inside out. Long-term use of methamphetamine produces hallucinations and delusions indistinguishable from schizophrenia.

Cocaine. For centuries, South American Indians used cocoa leaves, the base ingredient in cocaine, to increase endurance, reduce fatigue, and control hunger. Cocaine was first isolated from cocoa leaves in the mid-1800s. After personally testing its effects, Sigmund Freud became an early proponent of the medicinal use of cocaine. Cocaine has been used as a treatment for asthma and colic, and as an anesthetic in eye surgery.

Cocaine is usually inhaled through the nose, but a high-potency crystalline form (**crack cocaine**) is smoked. Initially, cocaine produces feelings of euphoria, increased energy, arousal, alertness, and decreased need for sleep. High doses and repeated use produce irritability, anxiety, and paranoia. Cocaine, like other amphetamines, produces a "rebound effect." When the drug euphoria ends, users may suffer a rebound depression that can lead to suicidal thoughts or attempts. The rebound effect may explain why long-term cocaine users report that they need the drug to "just feel normal." Long-term use is related to hallucinations, severe irritability, damaged social functioning, paranoia, seizures, headaches, and tremors. Recent studies suggest that cocaine use increases the risk for brain aneurysms.

Initially cocaine was thought to be non-addictive, but its capture ratio is near that of methamphetamine – cocaine is highly addictive. Because cocaine acts on the same areas of the brain (the limbic system) that are associated with love, pride, and sex – it provides powerful reinforcement by mimicking those experiences.

Nicotine. Just as cocaine was first administered by chewing cocoa leaves, nicotine was first administered by chewing tobacco leaves. Today people deliver nicotine to their brains by smoking, chewing, or sniffing tobacco. Nicotine has a high capture ratio; one-third to one-half of people who try nicotine become regular users, and most nicotine users begin as adolescents. Today in America, more than 3.5 million teenagers use tobacco. Like the other stimulants, nicotine increases dopamine levels in the limbic system to produce mild euphoria, increased alertness, and increased energy.

Each year nearly half a million Americans die from tobacco-related disease. Tobacco use is strongly associated with cancer, emphysema, heart disease, and stroke. One of every six deaths in the United States is related to smoking tobacco, making tobacco more lethal than all other addictive drugs combined.

Opiates. Opiates, also called **narcotics** are some of the oldest drugs used by humans. Opium is extracted from the poppy plant. Opium derivatives like heroin, morphine, codeine, oxycodone, hydrocodone, and synthetic opiates are powerful painkillers. Opiates mimic **endorphins**, our body's natural painkilling and stress reducing hormone.

Opiates are useful as an anesthetic and to treat pain, to suppress coughs, and to alleviate diarrhea. As a drug of abuse, opiates are ingested orally, smoked, sniffed, or injected. In addition to alleviating pain, opiates produce feelings of euphoria and reduce feelings of anxiety and aggression. Opiate abuse is associated with drowsiness, decreased concentration and motivation, constipation, nausea, vomiting, and decreased respiration. The long-term dangers of opiate abuse include infection, disease, overdose, adulterants in street drugs, and non-sterile administration with used dirty needles.

Opiates are highly addictive, and users may develop a strong tolerance. After months of heavy use, some users may administer many times the dosage that would kill a non-tolerant user. A rebound effect, similar to that of stimulants, requires dependent users to take the drug to "just feel normal." Symptoms of opiate withdrawal are so severe (pain, depression, diarrhea, chills, restlessness, and insomnia) that recovery rates from opiate dependence are low. **Methadone** (a long-acting opiate) allowed many opiate-dependent people to avoid withdrawal symptoms and resume some normal social behavior.

Hallucinogens. **Hallucinogens** are a class of psychoactive drugs that produce hallucinations, depersonalization, thought disturbances, and mood changes. **Hallucinations** are perceptual experiences that occur without any external sensory stimulus. **Depersonalization** is an altered mental state in which one feels detached from oneself or outside of one's body. Common hallucinogens are LSD, MDMA (ecstasy), mescaline, psilocybin, and ketamine.

LSD. Dr. **Albert Hoffman** first synthesized LSD (**lysergic acid diethylamide** or "acid") in 1938. In 1943 he accidentally discovered its psychoactive properties when he absorbed a small amount of the drug through his finger. LSD is the most powerful psychoactive substance known. Thousandths of a gram produce powerful effects.

LSD produces a wide variety of psychological experiences. Users report "deep" religious feelings, sexual feelings, sadness, euphoria, anxiety, and fear. Users experience delusions – bizarre thoughts and beliefs, like believing they can fly or can stop a train by stepping in front of it. Sometimes users report deep new insights into themselves or the nature of the universe. Those so-called "insights" contributed to LSD's reputation as a "mind-expanding" drug. Perceptual disturbances include distortions of vision, sound, taste, smell, touch, and an altered perception of time. Some report **synesthesia**, the experience of a sensation by different sensory process (i.e., "seeing" a smell or "tasting" a sound). Occasionally the experience is extremely frightening (i.e., a "bad trip"). Some users report **flashbacks**, brief episodes similar to the drug-induced state, weeks or months after using the drug. Physical reactions include dilated pupils, low body temperature, nausea, sweating, and increased heart rate.

LSD was used in the early 1950s in research on psychosis, to make patients "more open" to psycho-analysis, and in the treatment of drug dependence. It was even used to treat anxiety and depression in cancer patients. Beginning in the 1960s, the "hippie" counter-culture, led by Dr. Timothy Leary, used LSD to "turn on, tune in, and drop out." The drug became an icon for a new-age worldview that placed great value on self-fulfillment, experimentation with drugs, and a sexual "revolution."

Marijuana. The leaves and buds of the marijuana (**cannabis**) plant have been smoked, brewed, and eaten as an intoxicant and medicinal herb for centuries. Marijuana is in a category by itself because it does not resemble the other classes of drugs in structure or effect. The active ingredient in marijuana is **delta-4-tetrahydrocannabinol (THC)**. **Hashish** is a concentrated form of cannabis resin. Marijuana is the most frequently used illicit drug in the world.

Low doses of marijuana produce a sense of well-being, relaxation, alterations in thinking, enhanced appetite, and altered perceptions of sight, smell, taste, and hearing. Users may perceive colors as brighter, music more vivid, and foolishness as humor. Low doses also increase heart rate, cause "dry mouth," red eyes, and poor concentration called being "stoned." Higher doses produce more significant alterations in cognition, rapidly changing emotions, anxiety and paranoia, impaired memory, and hallucinations. Chronic use is said to lead to **amotivational syndrome** (i.e., apathy, poor judgment, memory and concentration deficits, and a general lack of motivation). Marijuana smoke contains a number of toxins and carcinogens. Chronic users may suffer bronchitis, emphysema, and bronchial asthma.

Chapter Summary.

Consciousness is difficult to define and there is no widely accepted definition of consciousness. Human consciousness is the essence of our God-likeness and is inextricably connected to brain activity. Studying consciousness means understanding our God-given self-awareness in the context of the complexities of the nervous system. Consciousness is not a single constant mental state. Sleep, dreams, hypnosis, meditation, and drug-induced mental states are varieties of consciousness.

We spend about one-third of our lives asleep. While we sleep, our brains continue to work. Our pattern of sleep is part of a set of daily 24-hour circadian rhythm. During rapid eye movement (REM) sleep, we dream and our eyes move rapidly. Brain wave patterns during REM sleep are similar to patterns while awake. In one night's sleep, we pass back and forth through stages of sleep distinguished by differing patterns of brain wave activity. The repair and restoration theory suggests that the purpose of sleep is to allow the brain to repair and restore itself. The information consolidation theory suggests that the purpose of sleep is to allow the brain to consolidate and process the events and experiences of the day.

We dream 4 - 6 times each night. Psychologists explain dreams as:

- the brain's "explanations" for random neural impulses.
- a way the brain eliminates, strengthens, and re-organizes neural connections.
- a safe means for experiencing powerful emotions, resolving psychic conflict, and solving difficult problems.
- a way of interpreting what is going on around us while we sleep.
- a rehearsal strategy to survive in a hostile environment.

Hypnosis is an altered, trance-like state of consciousness in which a person is hyper-suggestible or easily influenced. Meditation is a form of deep concentration in which the mind is focused on a single thing or emptied of thought.

Psychoactive or psychotropic drugs alter consciousness by crossing the blood-brain barrier and altering the way neurotransmitters work. Regular use of a drug may lead to tolerance and dependence, commonly known as addiction. Psychologists classify psychoactive drugs into four categories: depressants (sedative-hypnotics), stimulants, opiates (narcotics), and hallucinogens (psychedelics).

For Review.

1. Describe a Christian perspective of human consciousness.
2. Describe various states of consciousness.
3. Describe sleep, REM sleep, stages of sleep, sleep deprivation, and disorders of sleep.
4. Describe dreams and discuss the meaning of dreams from various worldview perspectives, including a Christian worldview.
5. Describe hypnosis, its history, and worldview issues related to hypnosis.
6. Discuss meditation from various worldview perspectives.
7. Define psychoactive drugs and describe how they generally work.
8. Describe tolerance, dependence, and withdrawal.
9. Describe the four major categories of psychoactive drugs.
10. Describe the effects of alcohol.
11. Describe the effects of sedative-hypnotics.
12. Describe the effects of stimulants.
13. Describe the effects of opiates.
14. Describe the effects of hallucinogens.
15. Describe the effects of marijuana.

Chapter 10

Thinking, Language, and Intelligence

In This Chapter
- Cognition
- Components of Thought
- Schemas and Scripts
- Cognitive Styles
- Problem-solving
- Creative Thinking
- Language
- Theories of Language Development
- Intelligence
- What is intelligence?
- Theories of Intelligence
- Measuring Intelligence
- Types of Intelligence
- Influences on Intelligence

In his letter to the Philippians the apostle Paul wrote, *"Finally, brothers, whatever is true, whatever is noble, whatever is right, whatever is pure, whatever is lovely, whatever is admirable – if anything is excellent or praiseworthy – think about such things* (Philippians 4:8)." The Bible instructs us to guard our thoughts, to think about certain things, and not to think about others. But what does it mean to think? What is a "thought?" What process goes on in the brain when we think? Does the physical brain change when a believer's thoughts are transformed by the renewing of the mind? How is it that spiritual forces (for good or ill) affect our thoughts?

How do we solve problems, make decisions, and think creatively? How do we acquire language, and what is the relationship between thinking and language? This chapter has more questions than answers.

Cognition is the mental processes of thinking, feeling, perceiving, problem-solving, and remembering. Cognition is the way we manipulate and understand information. Cognitions are our thoughts.

When we think and when we use language, we engage in very complex and interdependent mental processes. Language and thought are inextricably intertwined. When we think, specialized areas of the brain perform specific functions that psychologists and neurologists can "see" using brain-imaging technology. Even simple cognitive tasks involve the activation of several specific areas of the brain. To us, thinking feels like a single action, but actually, it is the coordinated effort of different parts of the brain. Although we examine them separately in this chapter, to rigidly distinguish language from thought is an over-simplification. Human thought and language are irreducible parts of our God-likeness.

Components of Thought. When we think, we use mental categories, representations, images, and symbols for objects, actions, events, words, and ideas called concepts. **Concepts** are categories by which we describe the physical world that the brain cannot directly experience. Simple and formal concepts are the basic component of thought. When we think about birds, fishing, death, green, and love, we are using concepts.

Simple, or formal, concepts have a single feature in common. For example, "square" is a **simple concept**; all squares have four sides and four equal angles. A **prototype** is an ideal example of a concept. For example, a robin is prototypical of the concept "bird." Non-flying birds like ostriches and penguins are not prototypical birds.

We build conceptual categories based on common features. **Conjunctive concepts** are classified by the presence of two or more common features. For example, cotton balls and clouds are both fluffy *and* white. We also build conceptual categories based on differences. **Disjunctive concepts** have "either-or" characteristics. The concept of "strike" may mean a work stoppage, a baseball player's swing and miss, or knocking down all ten pins with the first ball in a frame in bowling; but it cannot mean different things at the same time. **Relational concepts** are classified by the relationship between features. Elephants are larger than mice, and Georgia is north of Florida.

Cognitive maps are mental representations of a given place or situation. Your mental representation of your home allows you to find the bathroom at night in the dark without bumping into things.

Schemas and Scripts. The individual way we create and organize concepts is called a schema. **Schema** and worldview are essentially synonymous terms. In terms of thinking, scripts are our usual way of organizing. **Cognitive script** is the term psychologists use to describe our usual way of organizing concepts – a type of cognitive autopilot. Our cognitive script for "throwing a shoe" may bring to mind automatic thoughts about flying sneakers or about a horse who needs a farrier (a specialist in equine hoof care), depending on your cognitive script.

Cognitive Styles. The term "cognitive style" refers to the way in which one usually processes information. Though your specific cognitive style is unique to you, psychologists categorize cognitive styles as field-independent or field dependent. **Field-independent thinkers**, also called **analytic thinkers**, generally break down thinking into component parts and process information in a detailed step-by-step approach. **Field-dependent thinkers**, also called holistic or global thinkers, tend to look at the "big picture" and process information with focus on meaning, connections, and purpose. Your cognitive style

Metacognition refers to thinking about thinking. Though animals "think," thinking about thinking is uniquely human.

An important part of thinking is attention. ***Attention*** refers to our ability to concentrate on one thing while ignoring others. ***Selective attention*** refers the ways to we perceive and process certain pieces of information but exclude others. ***Concentration*** is a much focused form of attention in which we ignore anything that is not related to a particular cognitive task.

also includes your reasoning — the processes you use to make decisions and solve problems. Formal or ***deductive reasoning*** involves using ***algorithms*** and formal rules of ***logic***. Algorithms are rules that, if followed correctly, always lead to a correct result. The written instructions for installing a computer program are a type of algorithm that, if followed correctly lead to a proper installation. Informal or inductive reasoning involves reaching a conclusion based on the information available. Heuristics are a type of informal reasoning. ***Heuristics*** are simple "rules-of-thumb" that serve as cognitive shortcuts to solving complex problems. For example, if we encountered an animal that walks like a duck and quacks like a duck, we would conclude that it must be a duck.

Decision-making and Problem-solving. Decision-making and problem-solving are closely related cognitive processes. They are some of the most complex of all human mental activities. Both involve perception, memories, emotions, attitudes, and reasoning. We spend tremendous mental energy solving problems and making decisions. Some psychologists suggest that all thought is, at some level, problem solving.

Psychologists suggest that problem-solving and decision-making both involve:

- identifying the circumstances — what decision must be made; what problem needs to be solved?
- identifying alternatives.
- evaluating alternatives.
- selecting an alternative.
- evaluating success and making corrections.

A Christian worldview recognizes that there is more to decision-making and problem-solving than identifying and evaluating alternatives. Prayer, biblical direction, Godly counsel, and a commitment to obeying God's will for the believer are crucial.

Barriers to Problem-solving and Decision-making. Just as psychologists have identified strategies for effective decision-making and problem-solving, they have also identified barriers.

- ***Perceptual barriers*** refer to the ways we perceive circumstances. If we perceive a situation incorrectly, the solution/decision may be faulty. For example, if, while dying of thirst in the desert, we follow a mirage (the illusion of water) instead of our map, we will make a bad decision and die.
- ***Fixations*** refer to the tendencies to repeat wrong solutions and bad decisions and to fixate on them to the exclusion of alternatives. "We've always done it that way" and "we tried that once and it didn't work then so it won't work now" are examples of fixations.

- *Mental set* refers to approaching all decisions and problems in similar ways or not using novel approaches. Before the Wright brothers, most people had a mental set that said flying machines, like birds, must flap their wings.
- *Belief bias*, also called *confirmation bias*, refers to our tendency to favor information that confirms existing assumptions. For example, evolutionary psychologists who selectively seek and find evidence of evolution while ignoring evidence to the contrary are exhibiting belief bias.
- *Believe perseverance* refers to our tendency to stick with a decision once we have made it, even in the face of disconfirming evidence.
- *Availability bias* refers to our tendency to make decisions based on available examples that we can remember and to not look for new solutions.
- *Functional fixedness* refers to the inability to see new uses for a familiar object outside of its traditional use.

Creative Thinking. Psychologists define creative thinking, also called *divergent thinking*, as the ability to generate new ideas or concepts, to make new associations, and the ability to act or think in novel ways. The ancient Greeks believed creativity was a gift from the Muses. Evolutionary psychologists believe that creativity evolved to facilitate survival and reproduction. They point to cave-drawings and primitive tool-making as evidence of the dawning of human creativity. A Christian worldview understands that there is nothing new under the sun. Real creativity is the sole purview of God.

Convergent thinkers, in contrast to creative thinkers, are said to think inwardly, solving problems and making decisions via a cognitive process that leads inward to a single "correct" solution. Creative thinkers on the other hand generate many solutions, thinking outwardly by generating several viable solutions for a single problem or decision.

Language. Our ability to communicate using complex systems of communication is one of Mankind's defining characteristics. All normal humans speak, no nonhuman animal does. Children learn this incredibly complex system in a matter of a few years and without formal instruction. Language is part of our design. *Language* is defined as a set of symbols (i.e., sounds, gestures, or written characters) used to represent objects (i.e., actions, events, and ideas) according to a set of rules. Language allows us to describe abstract concepts, objects that are in another place, and events that occurred at a different time.

Psycho linguistics is the term for the study of the mental activity involved in acquiring, using, and understanding language.

Semantics. Semantics is the study of the meaning of language.

> A child who says "I do gooder" is over-generalizing the rule that says adding an –er (tall/taller, big/bigger) indicates one thing is more than another.

Language is organized in a hierarchical structure and composed of phonemes, morphemes, phrases, and sentences. **Phonemes** are the smallest distinguishable sounds in a language. Each sound made by the letter "c" (e.g., cat, reciept) is a single phoneme. There are about 44 phonemes in the English language. Some consonants, all vowels, and some combinations of letters correspond to more than one phoneme. Phonetic reading programs, also called phonics, are based on teaching readers to recognize phonemes. **Morphemes** are the smallest meaningful units in a language. Morphemes are usually whole words but may be parts of words such as prefixes, suffixes, and word stems. **Grammar** and **syntax** describe the system of rules that govern how words form phrases and sentences.

Language Development. Humans in all cultures go through the same stages of language development. Children who have not been exposed to a language make one up. Babies respond to spoken language at birth, but from 0 to 4 months, babies communicate the only way they can – by **crying**. Until they are about 3 months old, babies respond to phonemes from any language. After about 3 months, babies respond better to phonemes from the language they hear most often. At around 3 months, babies begin to produce vocal sounds and at around 6 months, they babble and make sounds that resemble the phonemes of the language they hear. By **babbling**, babies practice the sounds, the intonations, and the rhythms of language, and learn to modulate their voice. Babbling also becomes a new way for the baby to express its needs and wants. Deaf children of hearing and deaf parents babies babble with their hands, even if they have not been exposed to sign language. As babies develop, babbling sounds more like the phonemes from the language the baby hears. Between about 9 and 13 months, children begin to produce simple single word sentences called **holophrases** to express feelings or desires. For example "up!" means "pick me up."

At about two years old, children begin to combine two or three words to make short sentences. The sentences are **telegraphic**, meaning the sentence does not contain articles or prepositions. For example, "truck big" means "that is a big truck." We learn to comprehend language (**receptive language**) faster than we learn to produce it (**expressive language**). As a three year old, you understood far more than you could say. The same is true for learning a second language. Your ability to understand a new language develops faster than your ability to speak it.

By about age three, children begin to use tenses and plurals, but tend to over-generalize the rules of syntax. We continue to develop language ability throughout childhood as we learn the complexities and subtleties of the language. As you probably know from personal experience, language comprehension is complicated by a language's ambiguity. **Ambiguity**, in terms of language, means that the same words can have more than one meaning or can be understood in more than one way. Language acquisition involves learning to merge context and meaning. Research indicates that in the absence of context, we choose the most common or personally relevant meaning for ambiguous term. **Homonyms** and **homophones** are examples of ambiguity in language.

Theories of Language Development. Modern psychologists have described three main theories of how language develops: learning theory, nativist theory, and interactionist theory.

Learning Theory of Language Development. B. F. Skinner applied the principles of behaviorism to language acquisition. Skinner believed that language was just complicated patterns of behavior that we learn through association, reinforcement, and punishment. Skinner argued that children learn language as parents reward grammatically correct "behavior" but do not reward grammatically incorrect "behavior." Similarly, Albert Bandura thought we learned language through observing and imitating the behavior of others.

Nativist Theory. Noam Chomsky (1928 -) believed that the principles of conditioning were insufficient to explain the speed at which children acquire language, the nearly infinite number of ways children combine words into sentences, and the common syntax errors children make (errors that are not modeled or reinforced by parents). Children quickly learn subtle and very complex rules of language without explicit instruction. Chomsky's theory suggested that humans have an inborn mental structure, a type of "organ," called the **language acquisition device**. Chomsky theorized that children are born pre-programmed with a set of rules about language known as **universal grammar**. The pre-programming makes us receptive to the commonalities of all languages allowing us to easily learn any language if it is consistent with the universal grammar. Chomsky believed that language has an evolutionary explanation but struggled to explain the incredibly creative ways we use language.

Psychologists have described interesting accounts of primates acquiring language. **Kanzi**, a chimpanzee at the Great Ape Trust, reportedly has a "vocabulary" of more than 500 words and the ability to comprehend human speech. His comprehension is said to be equal to that of a two-and-a-half-year-old child. Kanzi uses symbols to make requests and is said to "speak" with humans via a keyboard attached to a voice synthesizer. Kanzi's abilities are said to have implications on the understanding of human evolution. Many argue that Kanzi is demonstrating conditioned behaviors that do not constitute language. Others note that primates' use of structure and syntax falls short of that of a two-year-old child.

Interactionist Theory. Today, most psychologists believe that we acquire language through the interplay of innate capacity and environmental influence. Interactionists believe that children have a biological predisposition to acquire a language, but they also stress the importance of parental instruction and social learning in the process.

The Evolution of Language. Evolutionary psychologists struggle to explain how and why the physical structures (e.g., the larynx and vocal chords) and mental processes (e.g., grammar, syntax, and semantics) required for language might have evolved. In an evolutionary worldview, language is nothing more than more complicated versions of the postures, gestures, and vocalizations of animals. Evolutionists suggest that language provided ancient humans a survival advantage by freeing their hands and by allowing groups to better defend themselves from predators.

Intelligence.

To this point we have examined the ways we are all alike. Psychologists propose grand theories describing and explaining similarities in neurology, perception, development, learning, motivation, emotion, memory, thinking, and language. Psychologists are also interested in the ways that each individual is different from everyone else. We turn our attention now, and in the next chapter, to how we differ from one another, or individual differences. Of most interest to psychologists are ways we differ in terms of intelligence and personality.

What is Intelligence? Is intelligence the ability to use reason and logic? Is it the ability to write and speak clearly? Is it a measure of how much knowledge of facts and figures you have? Do Olympic athletes, virtuoso musicians, and fine artists have a type of intelligence? How can we observe intelligence, and how do we measure it? Intelligence is a commonly used term that is extremely difficult for psychologists to define.

Intelligence has been defined as:

- a measure of general mental ability – mental speed, language skills, mathematical ability, knowledge, and creativity.
- the ability to gather and use information.
- the mental abilities that enable one to adapt to, shape, or select one's environment.
- the ability to judge, comprehend, and reason.
- the ability to understand and deal with people, objects, and symbols.
- the global capacities to act purposefully, think rationally, and deal effectively with the environment.
- the capacity for abstract reasoning, problem solving, and the acquisition of knowledge.

Theories of Intelligence. Sir Francis Galton (1822 - 1911) is famous in the history of psychology for his theories of differential psychology, or the variations in human

> ***Differential Psychology*** is interested in the psychological differences between people and not in psychological similarities.

Psychometrics is the study of measuring psychological characteristics, knowledge, abilities, attitudes, and personality traits. Psychometricians specialize in measuring psychological characteristics.

characteristics. Galton, half-cousin of Charles Darwin, proposed that "superior qualities" were passed from generation to generation through heredity. Galton coined the term "nature vs. nurture" and sought to describe the relative strength of each. Galton believed that intelligence was a single, fixed, inborn, and inherited mental characteristic.

Charles Spearman (1863 - 1945) described intelligence in terms of a general mental ability known as **"Spearman's g."** Spearman noted that individuals who performed well on a particular test of mental ability usually also did well on other tests of mental ability. He concluded that intelligence is general ability that can be measured and expressed numerically.

Alfred Binet (1857 - 1911) is famous in the history of psychology for creating the first test of intelligence. Binet identified a variety of cognitive tasks that he thought were representative of "average" children at various ages. A six-year-old child who could perform all the mental tasks of an average six-year-old, but nothing beyond, was said to have a **mental age** of six. A six-year-old child who could perform all the mental tasks of a seven-year-old, but nothing beyond, had a **chronological age** of six, but a mental age of seven. The **intelligence quotient**, or IQ, was calculated as the ratio of mental age to chronological age times 100. A six-year-old child with a mental age of seven had an IQ of 117 (7 ÷ 6 x 100 = 117). A six-year-old with a mental age of five had and IQ of 83 (5 ÷ 6 X 100 = 83). In Binet's test, any person whose mental age and chronological age are the same has an IQ score of 100.

David Wechsler (1896 - 1981) believed that Binet's test over-emphasized verbal skills. The **Wechsler Intelligence Scale for Children** (WISC) measured general intelligence and had sub-tests to measure verbal and non-verbal intelligence. Wechsler also developed a text to measure intelligence of adults called the **Wechsler Adult Intelligence Scale** (WAIS).

Types of Intelligence. Following Spearman's theory of general intelligence, many psychologists suggested that there were as many as 150 different types of intelligence.

Raymond Cattell (1905 - 1998) suggested that general intelligence was composed of two sub-types of intelligence: fluid intelligence and crystallized intelligence. **Fluid intelligence** refers to reasoning, memory, spatial ability, and mental speed. Cattell thought fluid intelligence was hereditary.

Eugenics. Francis Galton coined the term "eugenics." Eugenics means "from good stock and hereditarily endowed with noble qualities." Eugenics led to calls for improving the "stock" of the human species through selective parenthood and to practices such as euthanasia, legally-mandated sterilization, and ultimately Nazi Germany's extermination of "inferior" peoples.

Ranges of intelligence scores. The two extremes of intellectual functioning are known as developmentally disabled and gifted.

Those identified as mentally retarded or developmentally disabled have IQ scores of 70 or below. The gifted usually fall within the upper 2% to 3% of the all scores; between 130 and 145. The highest IQ ever recorded was for **Marilyn vos Savant** with an IQ of 228.

Kim Peek (1951 - 2009) was the inspiration for Dustin Hoffman's character in the movie *Rain Man*. At birth Peek was diagnosed with severe mental retardation. He struggled with ordinary motor skills (e.g., walking) and scored below average on a general IQ test. Despite his disabilities, Peek had tremendous special abilities. He was reading encyclopedias at age four and had near total recall of every book he ever read (over 7,000). He read the right page of a book with his right eye while simultaneously reading the left page with his left eye. Peek was able to instantly tell the day of the week for any date, past or future. He was an expert in world history, geography, sports, movies, literature (including the Bible), and music.

Crystallized intelligence refers to verbal skills, mathematical skills, and the ability to use information to solve problems. Cattell thought that crystallized intelligence was affected by education and experience.

Robert Sternberg (1949 -) described intelligence in terms of three abilities. Sternberg's **triarchic theory of intelligence** describes intelligence as the balance between **analytical**, **creative**, and **practical** abilities.

L. L. Thurstone (1887 - 1955) proposed that intelligence comprises seven different "**primary mental abilities**." Thurstone believed that each ability could be measured separately and that intelligence was the sum of the individual abilities.

- **Verbal Intelligence** is the ability to define and understand words.
- **Word Intelligence** refers to the ability to produce words rapidly.
- **Number Intelligence** refers to the ability to manipulate numbers and solve mathematical problems.
- **Space Intelligence** is the ability to mentally manipulate objects and to visualize relationships.
- **Memory** is the ability to encode and retrieve information.
- **Perception** refers to the ability to recognize and interpret differences and similarities among objects.
- **Reasoning intelligence** is the ability to use logic and rules.

Howard Gardner (1943 -) proposed that instead of a single general intelligence, there were eight distinct intelligences. Gardner based his theory on observations of **savants**, people who have extraordinary abilities in some areas but who lack other basic abilities.

- People with **Logical - Mathematical Intelligence** (number smart) have highly developed logical and mathematical abilities and are adept at understanding and manipulating numbers, quantities, rules of logic, and formulas. Scientists and mathematicians use logical - mathematical intelligence.
- People with **Visual - Spatial Intelligence** (picture smart) have highly developed abilities to mentally represent the physical world. Chess players, architects, and sculptors use visual - spatial intelligence.
- **Verbal - Linguistic Intelligence** (word smart) refers to the capacity to learn, use, express, and understand language. Writers, speakers, teachers and attorneys use verbal - linguistic intelligence.

- *Musical Intelligence* (music smart) is described as a highly developed sensitivity to musical tone, rhythm, and structure.
- *Bodily - Kinesthetic Intelligence* (body smart) is the capacity to expertly use the body (i.e., hands, arms and legs, and fingers). Actors, gymnasts, and craftspeople have high bodily - kinesthetic intelligence.
- *Interpersonal Intelligence* (people smart) refers to the ability to recognize, understand, and respond to the moods, motivations, and attitudes of other people. Counselors, salespeople, pastors, and politicians use interpersonal intelligence.
- *Intrapersonal Intelligence* (self smart) is the capacity to recognize, understand, and respond to one's own moods, emotions, and attitudes.
- *Naturalistic Intelligence* refers to a sensitivity and understanding of plants and animals.
- *Existential Intelligence.* Gardner suggested there may be a ninth intelligence called existential intelligence, said to be a sensitivity to issues involving life and death, philosophy, and religions.

Influences on Intelligence. Today most psychologists agree that heredity and the environment influence intelligence. Studies of twins suggest a genetic component of intelligence. Identical twins' IQ scores are more similar than those of fraternal twins. Also, identical twins raised apart have more similar IQ scores than fraternal twins raised together. Studies of environmental influences suggest that nurturing plays a role in intelligence. Children living in poverty, children with poor nutrition, and children who do not receive mental stimulation generally have lower IQ scores than well-fed children from affluent families who read to and interact with children.

Artificial Intelligence (AI) is a branch of computer science interested in programming computers to use human-like intelligence. In 1997, IBM's computer *Deep Blue* beat chess grand master *Gary Kasparov*. In 2011 another IBM computer called *Watson* defeated two former champions in the game Jeopardy. Watson combined its encyclopedic wealth of knowledge with "understanding" of the subtle verbal complexities of Jeopardy's clues.

Chapter Summary.

Cognition is the mental processes of thinking, feeling, perceiving, problem-solving, and remembering. Cognition is the way we manipulate and understand information. Cognitions are our thoughts. When we think we use concepts – mental categories, representations, images, and symbols for objects, actions, events, words, and ideas. Cognitive maps are mental representations of a place or situation.

The ways we create, organize, and understand concepts are called schemas. Cognitive scripts describe our usual way of organizing concepts – a type of cognitive autopilot. The way that we usually process information is our cognitive style.

Attention means to focus concentration on one thing while ignoring others. Concentration is a focused form of attention in which we ignore anything that is not related to a particular cognitive task. Decision-making and problem-solving are some of the most complex of all human mental activities involving perception, memories, emotions, attitudes, and reasoning.

Our ability to communicate using language is one of Mankind's defining characteristics. All normal humans speak; no nonhuman animal does. Language is a set of symbols used to represent objects according to a set of rules. Semantics is the study of language structure. Humans in all cultures go through the same stages of language development; by crying, babbling, holophrases, telegraphing, and generalizing.

Noam Chomsky suggested that humans have an inborn mental structure called the language acquisition device that is pre-programmed to make us receptive to learning language.

Intelligence is a commonly used term that is difficult to define. Intelligence is a measure of general mental ability, knowledge, and creativity. It is the ability to gather and use information, to adapt, comprehend, and reason. Alfred Binet is famous in the history of psychology for creating the first test of intelligence, the IQ text. Psychologists have suggested there are as many as 150 different types of intelligence. Most psychologists agree that heredity and the environment influence intelligence.

For Review.

1. Describe cognition.
2. Describe simple, conjunctive, disjunctive, and relational concepts.
3. Describe the concept of cognitive style.
4. Compare the processes of decision-making and problem-solving.
5. Describe barriers to decision-making and problem-solving.
6. What is language?
7. Describe semantics and syntax.
8. Describe language development in children.
9. Describe Noam Chomsky's natavist theory of language development.
10. Describe theories of multiple intelligences.

Chapter 11

Personality

In This Chapter

What is personality? In everyday language, we say that someone who is outgoing and charming has "a lot of personality." If we do not get along with someone, we say we have a "personality clash." A person who is seen as unusual may be described as "a real personality." Someone seen as uninteresting is said to have "*no* personality." An important or prominent person is said to be "*a* personality." Some people are even said to have multiple personalities.

In what ways are you "like" your friends and family? How are your moods, preferences, sensitivities, and emotions similar to those of the people around you? How are they different? What are your attitudes, what do you think about, and how do you relate to other people? At your core, who are you and what "kind" of person are you? All of these are questions about personality. These are also questions about worldview, and they are the types of questions that personality psychologists try to answer.

Of the topics in psychology we've explored thus far, none comes closer to the heart of the Bible's message of "what is Man?" than personality psychology. Philosophers throughout history and psychologists from modern psychology's beginning have tried to describe and explain personality. Though they may contain truths about personality, those descriptions and explanations are, at the worldview level, inconsistent with the Bible's message.

A theory of personality that is consistent with a Christian worldview must recognize Mankind's sinful nature; it must acknowledge that our personality changes following our "new birth" in Christ; and it must recognize that only through the supernatural influence of the Holy Spirit can we have a "right" personality. The theories discussed in this chapter do not acknowledge these truths.

Personality. There is no universally accepted definition of personality. It is generally defined as a relatively stable pattern of psychological characteristics called traits. Traits are enduring and consistent patterns of thoughts, feelings, attitudes and behaviors. Shyness is a trait. Peaceful, envious, long-suffering, covetous, kind, prideful, and self-controlled are traits.

Personality Theories. Modern psychologists have developed many personality theories. Each theory reflects the worldview assumptions of the theorist. There is much similarity between modern psychology's theories of personality and its theories of learning, motivation, and development. Is personality learned, either through rewards and punishment or through social interactions? Is personality formed by inborn unconscious forces? Is it the result of cognitive processes, of an inborn drive for self-actualization, or did it evolve as adaptations to environmental forces? Each theory describes the characteristics of personality, explains how those characteristics develop, describes and predicts the relationship between personality and behavior, and prescribes ways to change or repair personality.

Modern psychologists were not the first to describe various personality traits. Astrologers, today and through history, study the putative influence of the planets and stars on personality. ***Astrologers*** believe that personality characteristics are set at birth by the "sign" of the zodiac. People born under the sign of Leo (between July 21 and August 22) are said to be creative, warmhearted, faithful, and loving. Ancient cultures described personality in terms of the elements: water, wood, fire, earth, and metal.

> A ***trait*** is a relatively stable characteristic. A ***state***, however, is by definition short-lived. One who is generally calm (a trait) can, depending on circumstances, be in a very anxious state.

Four hundred years before Christ, the Greek physician Hippocrates believed that personality was comprised of four temperaments. Each temperament was thought to be each associated with a different body fluids, or "humor."

- The ***sanguine*** temperament was said to be extroverted, cheerful, and creative, and was associated with the blood.
- The ***phlegmatic*** temperament was said to be relaxed, slow-moving, and cautions, and was associated with phlegm.
- The ***melancholic*** temperament was said to be introverted, sad, and self-reliant, and was associated with black bile.
- The ***choleric*** temperament was said to be quick-tempered, ambitious, and dominating, and was associated with yellow bile.

Hippocrates' system was accepted through the Renaissance.

Sigmund Freud (1856 - 1939). Freud is famous in the history of psychology for his theory of personality. Like Charles Darwin's impact on the modern study of biology, no one has had more effect on modern psychology than Sigmund Freud. He proposed modern psychology's first comprehensive personality theory. Over 100 years after he proposed his theories, Freud remains the best known and most influential personality theorist.

Somatotype Theory. Another early theory of personality suggested that personality traits were associated with certain somatotypes, or body types. Endomorphs, people with a fat body type, were thought to be friendly and outgoing. Mesomorphs, people with a muscular body type were thought to be confident and assertive. Ectomorphs, people with thin body types, were said to be shy and secretive.

The Unconscious. One of the more revolutionary aspects of Freud's personality theory was his belief that much of our personality operates at the level of the unconscious. According to Freud, the mind operates on three interacting levels of awareness: the conscious, pre-conscious, and unconscious. The *conscious mind* contains mental events of which we are actively aware at the moment. The *pre-conscious* contains aspects of mental life which are not conscious at any moment, but can be easily brought to awareness. The *unconscious* contains thoughts, feelings, and motives which are not available either at the conscious or pre-conscious level. Although we are unaware of the thoughts and feelings stored in the unconscious, Freud believed they were the primary influence of our personalities.

Freud's theory is known as the *psycho-dynamic*, *psycho-analytic*, or *psycho-sexual* personality theory. According to Freud, all mental activity is driven by two competing, universal, and inborn life forces or instincts – the sexual life force called eros and the death force called thantos. *Eros* produces a drive for sensual and sexual gratification called *libido*. *Thantos* produces a drive for aggression, death, and destruction called *destrudo*. Personality, according to Freud, is formed through the psychic warring of libido vs. destrudo.

Id. Freud believed there are three parts of personality. He named them id, ego, and superego. *Id* was said to be an instinctive and unconscious aspect of the personality that seeks immediate gratification. Id operates on the *pleasure principle* – libido's drive to find sexual gratification. Freud described id as primitive, animal-like, irrational, and completely selfish. Very young children were said to be "all id."

Ego. Freud described ego as our *sense of self*, the public and private expression of our personality. Ego is the part of personality that develops as young children experience reality. It is the rational part of our personality that recognizes that immediate sexual gratification is not realistic. It operates on the *reality principle*, which serves to consciously and unconsciously restrain id. Ego's main job is to find satisfaction for id, but in ways that are reasonable and rational. While id stands for untamed passions, ego stands for reason and good sense. Ego restrains impulses, re-directs libido, and defends us against painful thoughts and memories.

Superego. Superego operates like a judge or supervisor of personality. As we are taught morals and values, superego, the last part of personality to develop, internalizes those morals and values and unconsciously applies

It is the id and the libido that got Freud his reputation for being some sort of sex fiend. It was his use of cocaine that got him his reputation for being some sort of cocaine fiend.

them to our behavior. In Freud's theory, it is superego, not the Holy Spirit, which convicts us when we err. Superego is often called the conscience. It operates on the *idealistic principle*. Superego insists that we behave according to the highest ideals taught by society, religion, and most importantly, our parents. Superego demands that we do what we have been taught is right and proper, no matter what the circumstances.

Ego Defense Mechanisms. According to Sigmund Freud and his daughter Anna, the conflicting desires of id, ego, and superego produce anxiety. The ways we cope with anxiety play a major role in forming our personality. Defense mechanisms are the means by which Freud thought we avoid consciously confronting troublesome thoughts, memories, and impulses. Denial, rationalization, intellectualization, projection, displacement, reaction formation, repression, sublimation, and regression are some of the ego defense mechanisms we are said to subconsciously use to lessen anxiety.

- *Denial* is refusing to admit something has happened. Teens who think it ok to use drugs and alcohol are "in denial" about the dangers.
- *Rationalization* is making up good-sounding or over-stated, but wrong, explanations for one's behavior. Explaining that it is o.k. to go fishing instead of going to church because "you don't have to be in church to worship," could be an example of rationalization.
- *Intellectualization* describes taking a detached, rational, and logical approach to emotionally uncomfortable issues. People with severe illnesses who try to learn everything they can about their illness could be said to be intellectualizing, rather than facing the illness.
- *Projection* refers to seeing our own unpleasant/unacceptable impulses in others. We "project" our undesirable traits onto others.
- *Displacement* describes focusing unpleasant emotions somewhere other than where they belong. Kicking the cat instead of yelling at your father is an example of "displaced" anger.
- According to Freud, *reaction formation* occurs when we don't like our initial reaction, so we form another one – we repress an urge to behave in a painful or threatening way by doing the polar opposite of what we really want. Treating someone you strongly dislike in an excessively friendly manner is an example of reaction formation.
- *Repression* refers to pushing uncomfortable memories into the subconscious. Some psychologists specialize in "recovering" repressed memories.
- *Sublimation* refers to channeling primitive sexual and aggressive impulses into socially acceptable activities. Instead of punching your brother when you are angry with him, you sublimate the impulse by going to the gym to punch a punching bag.
- *Regression* describes an unconscious effort to defend ego from stress by reverting to behavior characteristics of a younger age. Adults who, when under extreme stress, behave childishly, are said to have "regressed."

As discussed in Chapter 8, Freud believed that personality develops through *psycho-sexual stages*. He believed that healthy personalities result from successfully moving through each stage. Freud strongly believed that psychological problems were rooted in a failure to move properly through the psycho-sexual stages. Too much or too little sensual gratification during the a development stage interrupts normal personality development. Freud believed that overeating, smoking gum chewers had *"oral personalities"* and were *fixated* on making up for missed oral gratification during the first year of life. Unsuccessful movement through the anal stage resulted in *"anal-retentive"* (e.g., overly fastidious and neat) or *"anal-expulsive"* (e.g., overly messy and disorganized) personalities. Freud thought that during the phallic stage boys have "normal" erotic feelings toward their mothers (the *Oedipal conflict*) and girls toward their fathers (the *Electra conflict*). He believed that little girls had *penis envy* and little boys had *castration anxiety*. The way that we navigate the conflicts and anxieties of the phallic stage are, according to Freud, of major importance in personality formation. Freud suggested that excessively vain and proud adults (*phallic character*), aggressive women (*castrating female*), and homosexuality stemmed from failure to successfully navigate the phallic stage.

You will be taught Darwin's Theory of Evolution in college. You will be taught Freud's personality theory in college too. Please do not forget that understanding the material and accepting the worldview are different. You can do one without the other.

Carl Jung (1875 - 1961). The Swiss Reformed church, in which Carl Jung's (pronounced Yoong) father was a clergyman, affirmed the Bible as the sole and infallible source of God's revelation and Mankind's sin nature (i.e., original sin). In the Jung household, young Carl probably learned that Jesus Christ was the only Savior and that salvation comes by faith in Christ. Jung's theory of personality and psycho-therapy, however, reflects a greater influence of the occult and of his mentor, Sigmund Freud.

Sigmund Freud's atheism was clear. Freud saw God as a universal "obsessional neurosis." To Freud, religion was damaging. Carl Jung, however, viewed religions as *beneficial myths*. Jung's belief in the benefit of religion makes his ideas more acceptable to many in Christendom, but to Jung, Christ and Buddha, as myths, were equal. His denial of the objective truth of the Christian worldview and his use of occultist practices requires Christians to approach his theories with extra discernment.

Freud's theory presumes that God does not exist. It is deterministic and it emphasizes sex and aggression as the prime motivations for human behavior and personality development. With such foundational worldview-level differences of opinion, the criticisms of his theory by Christians and behaviorists are not surprising.

Jung was closely associated with Freud personally and professionally. Although their relationship ended in disagreement over Freud's emphasis on the sexual nature of personality development (they were enemies at the end of their careers), Jung's theory is grounded in Freud's theories. Jung is known as a **neo-Freudian** or "new" Freudian. Whereas Freud focused on the unconscious and sex, Jung emphasized the unconscious and barely mentioned sex.

Carl Jung called his personality theory **analytic psychology**. Jung believed that the psyche (mind) existed in three levels: the **conscious** (comparable to Freud's concept of the ego), the **personal unconscious** (comparable to id), and the **collective unconscious**. Like Freud, Jung thought the most important factors influencing personality were unconscious. The **personal unconscious** contains all of one's life experiences and memories – influential, but inaccessible by the conscious mind. Jung thought that the **collective unconscious** was a storehouse of the collective experiences of all Mankind – a type of genetic memory containing the primitive stories and symbols passed down from our ancestors. Jung believed that we unconsciously experience emotions about the content of our personal and the collective unconscious. The experience of those memories cluster in emotion-laden themes or associations, called **complexes**, that affect our personality and behavior.

Jung was particularly interested in dreams, particularly in the dream themes common to all cultures. Common dream themes led to Jung's description of archetypes. **Archetypes** are universal images and universal ways that people behave and interpret experiences. For example, the **persona** is a universal way of experiencing social situations. According to Jung, we display a persona or mask in social situations. Persona is that part of ourselves that we allow others to see. The **shadow** is an archetypal image of that part of our psyche we do not want others to see. Jung identified several archetypes including **death**, **anima** (our feminine side), **animus** (our masculine side), birth, power, the hero, the child, the wise old man, the earth mother, the demon, the god, and the snake.

Jung described personality in terms of three traits. The sum of personality is in the balance between introversion and extroversion, thinking and feeling, and sensing and intuition. As we will discuss later, Jung's theory is the foundation of the Myers-Briggs personality assessment and a foundation for subsequent trait theories of personality.

Jung communicated with "**spirit guides**", one of whom was named **Philemon**. Jung believed Philemon was real and not the product of his own unconscious. Jung communicated with Philemon much like a medium communicates with the spirit world. Some of Jung's work was the result of **automatic writing**, a **channeling** technique in which a "spiritual being" controls the writer's hand to record information or a message.

Alfred Adler. Alfred Adler is famous in the history of psychology for his approach to personality that he called ***individual psychology***. Freud believed internal sexual and aggressive impulses drove personality development. Jung believed that the collective unconscious shapes personality. Alfred Adler believed that a driving force in personality is ***striving for perfection*** in the context of early relationships. Failing to achieve perfection produces feelings of inferiority that provide the impetus for personality development. According to Adler, compensating for feelings of inferiority shapes our personality. Adler described several terms that have become part of the common language. ***Inferiority complex*** describes paralyzing feelings of inferiority. ***Sibling rivalry*** describes a competition between siblings for parental approval. Adler was an early supporter of the importance of ***birth order*** on personality development. Adler believed that personality was largely formed by about age six.

Behaviorist Perspective on Personality. Where Freudian psycho-dynamic theories explain personality in terms of unconscious drives and forces, the unconscious is of little concern to behaviorists. To behavioral psychologists like B. F. Skinner and John Watson, what we call personality is nothing more than learned patterns of behavior. If we are outgoing, it is because outgoing behavior was reinforced. If we are shy and reserved, it is because outgoing behavior was punished or extinguished. Personality, according to behaviorism, is determined solely by external environmental forces – the result of learning, reinforcement, shaping, and modeling.

Trait Theories. Trait theories are generally more modest than the Freudian, behavioral, and humanist theories. Trait theories focus on ways individual personalities differ. Much of the early research in personality psychology sought to identify the most basic factors of personality, known as traits. ***Traits*** are the mental characteristics that make up our personalities. Traits exist on a continuum or in degrees, so we are able compare people in terms of particular traits. For example, you may be more introverted than your sibling. We can compare ourselves with one another and with others according to each trait. By grouping a number of personality traits, we can describe different personality types. ***Personality types*** are collections of traits that occur together in some individuals.

Gordon Allport (1897 - 1967) wrote extensively about personality and is said to have taught the first college-level personality course in the United States. Allport believed that personality was a collection of specific traits. Allport identified almost 18,000 words in the English language describing personality traits. He thought that ***central*** traits, usually 5 – 10, make up the major characteristics of most personalities. In some people a single trait plays an overarching role in everything they do. Allport called that a ***cardinal*** trait. Allport believed that it was possible to rate an individual on each

Factor Analysis is a statistic technique. Personality psychologists use factor analysis to identify which personality traits are correlated, or occur together. For example, if punctuality, diligence, and neatness are strongly correlated, they may represent a common trait we could call conscientiousness.

personality trait, the sum of which produced a **personality profile**.

Hans Eysenck (1916 - 1997) noted that beginning in infancy, babies interact with others and the environment in stable and predictable manners. Some are fussy, active, curious, and outgoing; others are calm, cuddly, and reserved. Eysenck thought that there were three essential genetic components of personality he called temperaments.

- **Introversion/Extraversion** refers to the extent that we focus on inner experiences. A person with "high introversion" is more quiet and reserved, while an individual with "high extraversion" is more outgoing and social.
- **Neuroticism/Emotional Stability** refers to the extent to which we are moody or even-tempered. A person with "high neuroticism" tends to become upset and emotional. A person with "high emotional stability" tends to be emotionally constant.
- Eysenck called his third dimension of personality psychoticism. **Psychoticism**, not to be confused with psychosis, refers to the extent to which we are impulsive or controlled and self-centered or empathetic. A person with "high psychoticism" tends toward divergent thinking, aggression, manipulation, and impulsivity. A person with "low psychoticism" tends to be empathetic, considerate, social, and less creative.

Raymond Cattell (1905 - 1998) used a statistical method called **factor analysis** to consolidate Allport's thousands of personality traits down to sixteen primary traits, each existing on a continuum from high to low.

- **Warmth**: Reserved, impersonal, and aloof or warm and empathetic?
- **Reasoning**: Less intelligent or more intelligent?
- **Emotional Stability**: Emotionally stable or affected by feelings and emotionally unstable?
- **Dominance**: Accommodating and cooperative or dominant and aggressive?
- **Liveliness**: Serious and restrained or enthusiastic and happy-go-lucky?
- **Rule Consciousness**: Expedient and nonconforming or conscientious and rule-bound?
- **Social Boldness**: Shy and timid or socially bold and uninhibited?
- **Sensitivity**: Tough-minded and unsentimental or tender-minded and sensitive?
- **Vigilance**: Trusting or suspicious and wary?
- **Abstractedness**: More concrete, steady, and practical or more imaginative and abstract?
- **Privateness**: More straightforward and direct or more shrewd and restrained?
- **Apprehension**: More self-assured or more apprehensive?
- **Openness to Change:** Conservative and traditional or radical and flexible?
- **Self-Reliance**: Group-dependent or self-sufficient and individualistic?

- *Perfectionism*: Casual, flexible, and undisciplined or precise, orderly, and self-disciplined?
- *Tension*: Relaxed and composed or tense, impatient, and anxious?

Are there three, sixteen, or sixteen hundred personality traits? Since Allport, Eysenck, and Cattell, a number of psychologists, in several separate studies, have identified five fundamental personality traits. Today, most psychologists believe that personality can be well-described in terms of the *"Big Five"* personality traits. The Big Five personality traits are:

- Extroverted or introverted
- Agreeable or antagonistic
- Conscientious or negligent
- Emotionally stable or emotionally unstable
- Open to new experiences/ideas or closed to new experiences/ideas

Biologic Theories. Trait theories do a good job describing the factors that make up personality. They do not, however, explain why the factors are present. Biologic theories, including evolution, suggest that genes, body type, and body chemistry explain why the factors are present. The common denominator of biologic theories of personality is a naturalistic presupposition. The explanation for why we think, feel, and behave must natural; it cannot be supernatural.

Eysenck suggested that individual differences in extraversion and introversion are strongly determined by genetic differences in the nervous system. Extraverts are "wired" in a way that enables them to tolerate a high degree of stimulation from the environment. Neurologically, according to Eysenck, introverts have "weak" nervous systems that cannot tolerate as much stimulation. Twin studies and studies using adopted children support Eysenck's idea that genetics, at some level, are a factor in personality.

Evolution and Personality. Evolutionary psychologists have yet to develop a model explaining how variation and natural selection produced the variety of personality traits and types we see in people. They are confident, however, that the principles of natural selection are sufficient to explain personality. Beginning from an assumption that physical characteristics evolve as survival adaptations, evolutionists believe that behavioral variations that were adaptive for survival were passed on from generation to generation. Some suggest that variations in personalities are the result of evolution endowing our species with multiple strategies for surviving in a variety of environments and circumstances.

Twins Studies. There was a time when social service agencies routinely placed identical twins for adoption in separate families. Twins separated at birth and raised in different families and cultures provided psychologists a way to compare the effects of heredity and environment. One large study found that although identical twins differ in many ways (intelligence skills, abilities, preferences, thinking styles), personalities were strikingly similar.

Cognitive Theories. Cognitive theories, also known as *information-processing models*, suggest that personality is a result of the way we think. Cognitive personality theories explain personality in terms of the different ways people process information about the world. *George Kelly* (1905 - 1967) believed that personality is a habitual way of interacting with the world. We develop our ways of interacting based on the meaning we give to past events and the results we anticipate from future behaviors. If we interpret our past interactions with others to mean that people are friendly and helpful, we will behave accordingly in future interactions. If we anticipate that a particular behavior will bring a desired outcome, we are likely to repeatedly behave that way.

Locus of Control refers to the extent to which individuals perceive they have control over the events in life. An *external locus of control* refers to the perception that chance or outside forces determine one's "fate." An *internal locus of control* refers to the perception that one controls one's own fate.

Cognitive-behavioral Theories. *Albert Bandura* believed that personality develops through an interaction of behavior, the environment, and cognitive processes. Bandura suggested that we learn our personality by observing and modeling. Whereas the psycho-analytic personality theories viewed Mankind as passive and unconscious recipients of experiences, cognitive theories emphasize active mental processes. Bandura believed that we consciously regulate our behavior and develop personality through a number of cognitive processes including self-observation, judgment, attention, memory, motivation, self-regulation, expectation, and self-concept in a reciprocal relationship with our environment. He labeled this concept *reciprocal determinism*.

Humanistic Theories. *Carl Rogers* (1902 - 1987) and *Abraham Maslow* (1908- 1970) are famous in the history of psychology for their humanistic theories of personality. The humanistic, or *person-centered,* personality theory was, in part, a response to the deterministic nature of Freudian and behavioral theories. Humanists believe that Mankind is innately good and able to choose, through the exercise of free-will, to determine our destinies and rise above genetic and environmental influences. Humanistic personality theories suggest that a tendency toward personal fulfillment and *self-actualization* is the primary force driving personality development. According to humanistic theories, all people have an inborn drive to achieve self-actualization.

Is Personality Stable? *William James* (1842 - 1910) in 1887 wrote, *"In most of us, by the age of 30, the character has set like plaster, and will never soften again."* Since James, psychologists have sought to discover the extent to which personality changes during adulthood. Psychologist *Jack Block* (1924 - 2010) tracked 500 children from birth through adulthood. Block concluded

The Third Force. Humanistic psychology is known as the third force because it stood in opposition to the determinism of behavioral and Freudian psychology.

that individuals' personalities reach final adult levels at about age 30. Personality traits, especially introversion and extraversion, found in teens were very likely to be present in adulthood.

Assessing Personality. Assessing personality is difficult and imprecise. Not surprisingly, psychologists' perspectives about the nature of personality affect the methods by which they measure and assess personality.

Self-report inventories are a type of questionnaire in which people provide information about themselves by answering questions. Psychologists correlate responses with known personality traits and types. One well-known self-report inventory is the ***Minnesota Multiphasic Personality Inventory*** (MMPI). The MMPI was designed to make predictions about mental disorders. People with known mental conditions were given a large battery of true/false questions. Their responses were compared to "normal" people. Questions that discriminated between people with mental disorders and those without mental disorders were included in the MMPI. A score above a certain level on a particular scale indicated a response pattern like that of people with known mental problems and perhaps indicated a need for treatment. Today the MMPI-2 has 10 clinical scales that psychologists use to identify emotional, personal, social, or behavioral problems and to aid in treatment planning. The MMPI contains five validity scales that gauge the accuracy of the clinical scales by "catching" test-takers who lie or try to fool the examiner.

The Myers-Briggs Type Indicator (MBTI) is the most popular self-report personality inventory in use today. Many companies today use the MBTI in their hiring decisions. The MBTI's premise is that we usually think and act according to our personality type. The MBTI describes ways of thinking and acting in terms of 16 possible combinations of four dichotomous preferences. The four dichotomies are:

- ***Extraversion*** (E) vs. ***Introversion*** (I). The extraversion/introversion scale indicates whether you prefer to focus your energy on the outer world of people and things or on your own inner world of ideas and beliefs.
- ***Sensing*** (S) vs. ***Intuition*** (N). The sensing/intuition scale indicates how you prefer to process information. Do you prefer to focus clearly on basic factual information (S) or do you prefer ideas, interpretation, and meaning (N)?
- ***Thinking*** (T) vs. ***Feeling*** (F). The thinking/feeling scale indicates how you prefer to make decisions. A "T" indicates a preference for objective logic and consistency. An "F" reflects a preference for emotions and circumstances.
- ***Judging*** (J) vs. ***Perceiving*** (P). The judging/perceiving scale indicates how you structure and organize information. Do you prefer to plan and make decisions (J) or to be flexible and open to changes (P)?

Projective Personality Assessments. Psycho-dynamic personality theories led to personality tests intended to reveal the content of the unconscious mind. Projective tests ask subjects to interpret ambiguous images or scenes. Psychologists believe that because the images are ambiguous, people "project" unconscious thoughts into their interpretations. An early projective personality assessment was the famous Rorschach inkblot test. In the ***Rorschach inkblot test***, subjects are shown a series of inkblots and asked to interpret the "scene."

The Thematic Apperception Test (TAT) is a projective personality assessment in which people are thought to project unconscious thoughts and feelings to describe the theme of an ambiguous scene.

A typical inkblot used in projective personality assessments. What do you see?

Today there are literally thousands of tests on the Internet and in popular literature that claim to provide information about your personality. Your favorite color, your favorite action-adventure hero, and the way you draw a pig are all said to shed light on your personality. Please review Chapter 15 (Research Methods) to help you evaluate such tests.

Chapter Summary.

There is no universally accepted definition of personality. It is generally defined as the relatively stable pattern of psychological characteristics called traits. Traits are enduring and consistent patterns of thoughts, feelings, attitudes and behaviors.

Modern psychologists have developed many personality theories. Each theory reflects the worldview assumptions of the theorist. Sigmund Freud is famous in the history of psychology for his psycho-dynamic theory of personality. One of the more revolutionary aspects of Freud's theory was his belief that personality operates on three interacting levels of awareness; the conscious, preconscious, and unconscious. According to Freud, personality is comprised of the id, ego, and superego. Id was said to be an instinctive and unconscious aspect of the personality that seeks immediate gratification. Ego is our "sense of self," and superego operates like a judge or supervisor of personality. Freud believed that personality develops through psycho-sexual stages. Psychological problems are the result of failing to successfully move through a psycho-sexual stage.

Carl Jung called his personality theory analytic psychology. Like Freud, Jung thought the most important factors influencing personality were unconscious. Jung believed that unconsciousness was comprised of the personal unconscious and the collective unconscious. Jung was particularly interested in dreams. Archetypes are common dream themes that Jung thought was a part of Mankind's collective unconscious memories.

Alfred Adler is famous in the history of psychology for his theory of personality called individual psychology. Adler believed that striving for perfection, feeling inferior, birth order, and sibling rivalry shapes our personality.

Traits are the mental characteristics that make up our personalities. Gordon Allport believed that "central" traits make up the major characteristics of most personalities. Raymond Cattell used a statistical method called factor analysis to identify sixteen primary traits. Hans Eysenck thought there were essential genetic components of personality he called temperaments.

Today, most psychologists believe that personality can be well-described in terms of the Big Five personality traits. The Big Five personality traits are:

• Extroverted or introverted.
• Agreeable or antagonistic.
• Conscientious or negligent.
• Emotionally stable or emotionally unstable.
• Open to new experiences and ideas or closed to new experiences and ideas.

Cognitive personality theories explain personality in terms of the ways people process information about the world. Albert Bandura believed that we learn our personality by observing and modeling in a process involving the interaction of behavior, the environment, and cognitive processes.

One well-know self-report personality inventory is the Minnesota Multiphasic Personality Inventory (MMPI). The MMPI was designed to make predictions about mental disorders. Projective personality assessments are said to reveal the content of the unconscious mind by asking subjects to interpret ambiguous images or scenes. The famous Rorschach inkblot and the thematic apperception tests are types of projective personality assessment techniques.

For Review.

1. Define personality, traits, and personality types.
2. Describe tests that psychologists use to assess personality.
3. Describe the personality theory of Sigmund Freud.
4. Describe the personality theory of Carl Jung.
5. Describe the personality theory of Alfred Adler.
6. Describe the personality theory of Albert Bandura.
7. Describe the personality theory of Carl Rogers.
8. Describe personality development from a behaviorist's perspective.
9. Describe the "Big Five" factors of personality.
10. Describe the MMPI and Myers-Briggs Type Indicator.

Chapter 12

Abnormal Psychology

In This Chapter

- What is Abnormal?
- What is Mental Illness?
- What Causes Abnormal Thoughts and Feelings?
- Behaviorist Perspective
- Cognitive Perspective
- Psycho-dynamic Perspective
- Evolutionary Perspective
- The Medical Model
- Classifying Mental Illnesses
- Prevalence
- Social-Cognitive-Behavioral Approach
- Classification of Mental Illness

For many people, abnormal or *clinical psychology* is what psychology is about. Learning about the abnormal is often what attracts students to the study of psychology, but few topics in psychology are as controversial among Christians as abnormal psychology.

Some topics that psychologists study are more worldview-dependent than others. Topics like the nervous system and sensory processes are far from the "core" of our humanity and are not the focus of the Bible's message. Others, like personality, development, and consciousness define us. Few topics in psychology come closer to the "core" aspects of the human condition – our sin nature, salvation, restoration, and sanctification, than "abnormal" psychology. One's perspective on sin, personal responsibility, and moral absolutes has huge implications on one's view of the causes of abnormal thoughts, feelings, and behaviors. As you might predict, the gravity of the subject matter contributes to disagreements among Christians about the nature and causes of abnormal thoughts, feelings, and behaviors. For the Christian studying psychology, the nature and importance of these issues require great caution. For the Christian who plans to serve God in a career in mental health care, an in-depth and Holy Spirit-informed Christian worldview is crucial.

Some of the key worldview questions with which Christians who are psychologists, pastoral counselors, and theologians wrestle are:

- Is the experience of abnormal thoughts, feelings, and behaviors a mental illness?
- Are mental disorders best understood as the result of disunity with God, chemical imbalances, brain illness, trauma and life experiences, or some combination?

- Are mental disorders best treated from a spiritual or a medical perspective?
- Can the techniques developed by modern psychology contribute to a Christian approach to counseling?
- Can Christians safely borrow techniques from modern psychology to help those in mental pain?
- Can modern therapeutic techniques be detached from their underlying worldview assumptions?
- Has the Church lost confidence in the power of the Gospel and God's ability to heal?
- How do we explain that medication and secular therapeutic techniques help Christians and non-Christians alike?

What is Abnormal? What does the word "abnormal" mean to you? We all have a personal sense of what is normal and what is abnormal, but defining it is more difficult. Normal and abnormal can be described from different perspectives and in varying degrees. Are people who are a "little odd" abnormal? Is reading the Bible, praying daily, and remaining sexually abstinent until marriage abnormal? Is communicating with God abnormal? Is it abnormal to communicate with the dead? These questions are meaningless outside of the context of worldviews.

Are pain, difficulty, hardship, and suffering normal? A Christian worldview believes that God uses trials and difficulties as tools to strengthen and refine us. Modern psychology's worldview is that pain, difficulty, and hardship are abnormal, absurd, and to be avoided at all costs. Statistically, something is abnormal if it varies sufficiently from the average, the usual, or the customary. Many people define abnormal in terms of ***variance from culturally accepted standards*** (i.e., political correctness). Some define abnormal subjectively (i.e., "If I believe that my feelings are abnormal, they are abnormal"). Some people believe that normal and abnormal are no more than ***value judgments***, and that to label another's thoughts and behaviors as abnormal is to exercise power inappropriately. Some people define abnormal in terms of ***dysfunctions in biological processes***, some in terms of ***sin*** and ***disunity with God***, and others describe abnormality as a ***failure to live according to moral rules***.

Thoughts, emotions, and behaviors are generally considered abnormal if they are:
- *Maladaptive*, meaning that they are harmful to the individual or make it difficult or impossible to function "normally."
- *Disturbing*, either to the individual or to others.
- *Unusual* and not shared by many other people.
- *Irrational*, meaning that it just does not make sense to most people.

What is Mental Illness?
It is more difficult to define mental illness, in a way that is respectful of various worldviews, than it is to define abnormal. Abnormality is a part of mental illnesses, but

---

> ***Rosenhan Experiment.*** In 1973 David Rosenhan published a research article titled *On Being Sane in Insane Places*. In his experiment, eight pseudo-patients falsely gained admission to twelve psychiatric hospitals by claiming to be hearing voices. Among the pseudo-patients were three psychologists, a pediatrician, a psychiatrist, a painter, and a housewife. Three were women and five were men. Immediately upon admission to the psychiatric ward, the pseudo-patients stopped simulating any symptoms and when asked, reported feeling fine and experiencing no symptoms. They were friendly, cooperative, and, to the best of their ability, exhibited no signs of abnormality. Despite appearing normal, none of the pseudo-patients were detected. Their hospitalizations ranged from 7 to 52 days with an average of 19 days.

the terms are not synonymous. ***Mental illness*** literally means ***disease of the mind***. Such a definition fits some conditions (e.g., schizophrenia) better than others (e.g., generalized anxiety and post-traumatic stress disorders). However, describing all mental conditions as "illnesses" eliminates, by definition, sin, unconscious psychic conflict, trauma and abuse, learning, the demonic, and bad parenting from consideration as possible causes or contributing factors.

For this reason, this text uses the terms "mental illness" and "abnormal thoughts, feelings, and behaviors" purposefully. "Mental illness," to many people, is synonymous with "abnormal thoughts feelings, and behaviors." All mental illnesses involve abnormal thoughts, feelings, and/or behaviors, but not all thoughts, feelings, and behaviors are mental illnesses. Mental illness is one possible cause of abnormal thoughts, feelings, and behaviors – a literal brain disease. A Christian worldview believes that sin, at least in part, is a cause of some abnormal thoughts, feeling, and behavior."

Understanding mental illness is made more difficult by the fact that over time, psychologists' beliefs about what constitutes a mental illness have changed. For example, prior to the 1970s the American Psychiatric Association (APA) included homosexuality in its listing of mental illnesses. Today, homosexuality is not a recognized mental illness. During the 1800s dementia paralytica, commonly called general paralysis of the insane, accounted for more than 10% of admissions to mental hospitals. ***Dementia paralytica*** is characterized by loss of personality and memories, mania, poor judgment, apathy, violence, and convulsions. It was eventually fatal. Today dementia paralytica accounts for no admissions to mental hospitals, and it is not included in the APA's list of mental illness. What was called dementia paralytica and thought to be a mental illness was actually the symptoms of third stage syphilis. Modern antibiotics "cured" dementia paralytica. Similarly, ***drapetomania*** was the name given to the "mental illness" that caused slaves in the American south to run away from their masters. Draptomania is not a recognized mental illness today.

> ***Schizophrenogenic mothers.*** From the late 1940s to the early 1970s, schizophrenia was believed to be caused by a mother's behavior toward her child in early childhood. A schizophrenogenic mother was said to be dominant and overprotective, but emotionally rejecting of the her children. Few psychologists today accept this explanation.

What Causes Abnormal Thoughts, Feelings, and Behaviors? A Christian worldview holds that the ultimate cause for all abnormal thoughts, feelings, and behaviors is sin, in the same way that cancer, plague, and chicken pox are ultimately caused by the effect of sin on all of creation, but describing the proximate cause for a particular condition in individuals, however, is not so clear.

What causes someone to be depressed and anxious? What causes people to hear voices, to experience mood swings, or to be dependent on drugs and alcohol? Is it individual sin, unconscious psychic conflict, chemical imbalances, demonic activity, or some combination of causes?

> Mental illness is also referred to as psychopathology. ***Psychopathology*** is any pattern of emotions, behavior, or thoughts inappropriate to the situation and leading to personal distress or the inability to achieve important goals.

Supernatural Explanations. As has been the case for centuries, many people explain abnormal thoughts, feelings, and behaviors in terms of the supernatural influences of gods, demons, witchcraft, sorcery, and "spirits." In ancient cultures, abnormal thoughts and behavior were believed to be the result of supernatural beings taking possession of a person's mind and body. Performing rituals and offering sacrifices to placate the supernatural beings was part of one's daily routine. In the Middle Ages, like today, many people explained all abnormal thoughts, feelings, and behaviors in terms of character flaws and sinfulness.

Each of modern psychology's major schools of thought has proposed explanations for abnormal thoughts, feelings, and behaviors according to its worldview of the nature of Mankind. ***Behaviorists*** suggested that abnormal thoughts and behaviors are learned by association, punishment, and reinforcement. The ***cognitive perspective*** suggested that distorted patterns of understanding and interpreting experiences and relationships are responsible. ***Freudian psycho-dynamic*** theories explained psychological disorders in terms of unconscious psychic conflicts. The ***humanist perspective*** explained that mental illness developed when circumstances blocked one's progress toward self-actualization. The ***evolutionary perspective*** suggested that mental disorders can be explained using the same evolutionary principles that have been applied to other aspects of psychology and physiology. From this

> ***Insanity.*** Insanity, once the accepted term for mental illness, is a legal concept. One is judged, according to law, to be insane. The judgment is based on the person's ability to know or understand right from wrong, to control their actions, and to participate in a legal defense.

The purpose of this chapter is not to settle any arguments between Christians about the existence and nature of mental illnesses. The purpose of this text is to expose you to the issues, so that when you are taught that "all mental illnesses are the result of chemical imbalances in the brain" or that "all mental illnesses are the result of sinful behavior and disunity with God," you will know that it just might not be that simple.

perspective, patterns of thought and behavior that today are detrimental must have served an adaptive survival purpose for ancient humans. You will be taught the various perspectives on mental illness in college. Please do not forget that understanding the perspective and accepting their underlying worldview assumptions are different. You can do one without the other.

The Biological Perspective of Abnormal Thoughts, Feelings, and Behaviors. The Greek physician Hippocrates is credited with offering the earliest natural biological explanation of mental illness around 400 B. C. He theorized that mental disorders were caused by imbalances in the four body fluids called "***humors.***" In the late 18th century, this ***disease view***, also called the ***medical model,*** re-emerged. From this perspective, abnormal thoughts, feelings, and behaviors are diseases of the brain, like every other physical disease, with discrete physical causes.

Classifying Mental Illnesses. Setting aside questions about whether mental illnesses exist and what causes them, we can turn our attention to describing and classifying them.

In 1952 the American Psychiatric Association (APA) published the first edition of ***The Diagnostic and Statistical Manual of Mental Disorders (DSM)***. The DSM categorizes various mental conditions and describes the characteristic symptoms of each condition.

The DSM is used by practically every psychologist and mental health worker in the world. It provides checklists of symptoms serving as diagnostic rules, and it provides a standard vocabulary for describing mental disorders. There are no laboratory tests for most mental illness, so the DSM provides a standard language, diagnostic criteria, and nomenclature for psychiatrists, insurance companies, and pharmaceutical companies.

Labels, diagnoses, and categories describe, but do not explain, mental disorders nor do they offer treatment suggestions. Determining what is a disorder and what is not a disorder is not exact. The DSM categories and diagnoses do not have clear boundaries dividing one mental disorder from another or from no mental disorder. A label, like "schizophrenia," does not explain, but only describes, abnormal patterns of thoughts, feelings, and behaviors.

The first edition of the DSM described 106 disorders. There are 185 disorders in the 2nd edition, 265 in the 3rd, and 365 disorders in the DSM-IV-TR. The DSM-5, published in May 2013 is the first major revision of the manual in twenty years. The DSM-5 contains new and revised categories and diagnoses. DSM-5 contains 19 categories of mental disorders:

Stigma. In addition to troubling thoughts, feelings, and behaviors, people with mental illness often experience stigma. Stigma refers to a stereotype that having a mental illness is a reflection of one's character.

Neurodevelopmental Disorders are disorders of the growth and development of the brain or nervous system. The Neurodevelopmental Disorders include Intellectual Disabilities -- previously called Mental Retardation, Communication Disorders, ADHD, Specific Learning Disorder, Motor Disorder, and a new diagnosis called Autism Spectrum Disorder.

Neurodevelopmental Disorders interfere with normal cognitive and social development in learning, communication, judgment, and/or social interactions.

Intellectual Developmental Disorders – previously called Mental Retardation -- impact both cognitive ability (IQ) and adaptive functioning.

Down Syndrome is the most common form of intellectual disability. It is caused by a common genetic problem that can be diagnosed while a baby is still in the womb. Normally, the nucleus of each cell contains 23 pairs of chromosomes, half of which are inherited from each parent. Down syndrome occurs when some or all of a person's cells have an extra copy of chromosome 21.

Communication Disorders, including Language and Speech Disorders describe defi cits in verbal and nonverbal communication. Specific Learning Disorder describes deficits in reading, mathemati cs, and writt en expression.

Hyperactive and inattentive children are not a new phenomenon. In 1800, the symptoms that today are known as ADHD were known as "mental restlessness." Since that time, it has been called "minimal brain damage," "minimal brain dysfunction," and "hyperkinetic reaction of childhood." In 1987 the DSM-III included attention-deficit disorder as an "official" disorder. Since then millions of children and adults have been diagnosed with ADHD.

Children with learning disorders may do well in all

but one area of learning and may aff ect informati on input, informati on organization and manipulaiton, memory, or informati on output. The most commonly diagnosed learning disorder is *dyslexia*, a reading disorder where lett ers, words, and numbers are perceived out of order, upside down, or completely incomprehensible.

Motor Disorders are characterized by significant impairment in the normal development of motor abilities.

Autism Spectrum Disorder is a new diagnosis for a group of neurodevelopmental disorders that can cause significant social, communicati on and behavioral challenges. In previous editi ons of the DSM, children could be diagnosed with *Autistic Disorder, Asperger's disorder, Childhood Disintegrative Disorder*, or *Pervasive Developmental Disorder*. Autism Spectrum Disorder describes a continuum of communication deficits, responding inappropriately in social situations, dependence on routines, sensitivity to changes in their environment, or intense focused on inappropriate items.

Attention-deficit/hyperactivity disorder (ADHD) is the single most common problem that brings children to the attention of psychologists and psychiatrists. The definition of ADHD has been updated in the DSM-5 to include the experience of ADHD in adulthood. ADHD is characterized as a persistent pattern of inattention and/or hyperactivity-impulsivity that is more frequent and severe than is typically observed in individuals at a comparable level of development. People with ADHD typically are inattentive, easily distracted, have difficulty concentrating, are impulsive, and are hyperactive. *Stimulants* (like Ritalin and Adderall) often have a paradoxical effect on people with ADHD. Paradoxical refers to the fact that for many with ADHD, a stimulant serves to slow them down and help them focus.

Schizophrenia Spectrum and Other Psychotic Disorders. The word *psychosis* stems from the Greek "psyche," meaning soul or mind, and "osis," meaning diseased or abnormal condition. In a general sense, psychosis means a "break from reality." Psychosis has come to be understood more generally as a severe disturbance in perception (hallucinations), thought (paranoia and delusions), speech, emotion, mood, orientation, organization, or serious disturbance in daily functioning. Psychosis is the main characteristic of schizophrenia and all psychotic disorders. Though other disorders may include psychotic symptoms, psychosis is the defining characteristic of these disorders.

Hallucinations are perceptual experiences of stimuli that do not exist. A hallucination may be a sound, sight, touch, taste, or smell. The most common type is auditory hallucinations. A person experiencing auditory hallucinations "hears" sounds (e.g., humming, whistles, or clicking) or voices that are not really there. The voices may or may not be comprehensible, recognizable, or meaningful. The voice may be perceived as the voice of someone the person knows (e.g., friends, family, or even "God") and may seem to originate from anywhere (e.g., the walls, the radio, from heaven). The message may be gibberish, threatening and demeaning, or commanding. Hallucinations are often relentless and usually very unpleasant.

Delusions are beliefs that are clearly false but that are firmly and persistently believed to be true. People with delusions are convinced that their beliefs are true and they will hold firmly to the beliefs regardless of evidence to the contrary.

Ideas of reference are a type of delusion in which one believes that common events, remarks, or objects in the environment have special and personal meaning, like "the television news sends me special information about how to save the world." *Delusions of grandeur* are exaggerated beliefs in one's importance or a belief that one has special powers, talents, or abilities. Believing that one is invincible, famous, and magical is a grandiose delusion. *Persecutory delusions* could be beliefs that one is being controlled, persecuted, followed, watched, cheated, drugged, spied on, or poisoned (e.g., "The CIA put listening devices in my apartment.").

The most common is psychotic disorder is Schizophrenia. *Schizophrenia* describes a chronic, severe, and disabling condition that affects about 1% of the population worldwide and accounts for over 50% of admissions to psychiatric hospitals in the United States. The set of symptoms known as schizophrenia is described in ancient literature, but the word "schizophrenia" is less than 100 years old. In modern psychology, the condition was first called *dementia praecox* (the dementia of youth) because the symptoms and behaviors generally appear in older teenagers and young adults. The word "schizophrenia"

> *Affect.* Earlier we defined psychology as the study of human affect, cognition, and behavior. Affect, in that context, referred to the experience of emotions. In the context of the symptoms of psychosis, however, affect refers to the outward expression of emotions. If you feel sad, your affect (emotion) is sad. If you look sad, your affect (the outward expression) is also sad. For people with psychosis, the outward expression of emotions may be blunted, absent, exaggerated, or inappropriate for the situation. A person with flat affect seems emotionless. A person with inappropriate affect may weep uncontrollably at something that seems harmless, or laugh hysterically at nothing in particular.

comes from the Greek roots schizo (split) and phrene (mind), describing the fragmented thinking of people with the condition or their split from reality. Schizophrenia does not mean "split personality." A better understand of schizophrenia is that it is a split from reality.

Schizophrenia is characterized by the presence of positive and negative symptoms. In this case, positive and negative do not mean "good" and "bad;" both are debilitating.

Positive symptoms are added to one's mind; they include hallucinations, delusions, and disorganized thinking and speech. Some people may babble, jump from idea to idea in a seemingly random manner, and make up words. Negative symptoms are more difficult to evaluate because they are not as grossly abnormal as positive symptoms.

Negative symptoms are cognitive abilities and experiences that are subtracted from people with schizophrenia. People with schizophrenia (sometimes stigmatized as "schizophrenics") may have blunted and impoverished thinking, a limited range of emotional expression, little motivation, and bizarre behavior. People suffering from schizophrenia may be unable to experience pleasure (*anhedonia)* and may have difficulty performing simple cognitive tasks like reading, planning, and remembering.

Bipolar disorders are characterized by symptoms of both depression and mania.

A *Major Depressive* Episode is characterized by a depressed mood most of the day nearly every day, decreased interest in activities, significant weight change, too much or too little sleep, fatigue, feelings of worthlessness or guilt, poor concentration or indecisiveness, and thoughts of death and suicide.

A *Manic Episode* is described as an abnormally and persistently elevated, expansive, or irritable mood. Manic episodes are characterized by inflated self-esteem or grandiosity; decreased need for sleep; pressured, loud, and rapid speech; flight of ideas; distractibility; increased goal-directed activities; restlessness; and excessive involvement in pleasurable activities with a high potential for painful consequences (e.g., sky-diving, drug use, impulsive and risky relationships, and impulsively spending money).

Bipolar disorder, formerly known as *manic-depressive disorder*, describes moods that may alternate between major depressive episodes and manic episodes. People with bipolar disorder may have rapidly changing moods, sleep difficulty, anxiety, and thoughts of suicide, agitation, impaired judgment, depressed mood, and difficulty concentrating.

Panic attack symptoms include:

- Rapid heart rate
- Sweating
- Trembling
- Shortness of breath
- Hyperventilation
- Chills
- Hot flashes
- Nausea
- Abdominal cramping
- Chest pain
- Headache
- Dizziness
- Faintness
- Trouble swallowing
- A sense of impending death

Depressive disorders. The DSM-5 contains new depressive disorders, including disruptive mood dysregulation for children up to age 18 years who are persistently irritable and have frequent episodes of extreme misbehavior.

Depressive disorders, as the name suggests, are characterized by symptoms of depression -- a depressed mood most of the day nearly every day, less interest in usual activities, significant weight change, too much or too little sleep, fatigue, feelings of worthlessness or guilt, poor concentration or indecisiveness, and thoughts of death and suicide. Interestingly, the DSM-5 removes makes it easier to diagnose a major depressive episode. In the DSM-IV depressive symptoms lasting less than 2 months following the death of a loved one did not quality as a disorder. The bereavement exclusion has been removed from DSM-5.

Anxiety Disorders. Anxiety is sometimes called angst, dread, fear, or worry. Anxiety may be a fear of something specific or just a generalized groundless feeling for no identifiable reason. Anxiety produces physiological responses. *Panic* is extreme anxiety and intense fear with severe physiological reactions. Panic is the essential feature of most anxiety disorders.

A *panic attack* describes the sudden onset of intense fear, apprehension, an urge to escape, and a sense of impending danger, doom, or death. Palpitations, sweating, trembling, shortness of breath, chest pain, nausea, dizziness, numbness, or chills accompany the feeling of panic.

Evolution theory suggests that phobias are remnants of behaviors that were adaptive for ancient humans. Phobias about spiders and snakes are common across cultures. The theory is ancient humans who feared spiders and snakes had a survival advantage over humans who did not fear them. The ancient humans who feared spiders and snakes survived to pass along that tendency to future generations.

A *phobia* – or "morbid fear" -- is a persistent and irrational fear of an object or situation that is disproportional to the actual danger with causing distress and impairment in social or occupational activities.

Agoraphobia characterized by anxiety due to an environment's openness or crowdedness. Social Anxiety Disorder, previously called Social Phobia is characterized by intense fear, distress, and impaired functioning in social situations.

Obsessive-compulsive and related disorders. *Obsessions* are recurrent, unwanted, and intrusive thoughts. *Compulsions* are unwanted and irrational urges to repeat certain behaviors. Obsessive-compulsive and related disorders are characterized by a recurrent preoccupation with orderliness, perfectionism, and control at the expense of flexibility, openness, and efficiency

Common obsessions and compulsions are about germs and dirt, leading to repetitive behaviors like hand washing and cleaning. Some people are filled with doubt and feel the need to check things over and over again or to ritualistically perform some task in exactly the same way each time.

Trauma and Stressor-related Disorders. *Post-traumatic stress disorder (PTSD)* is a severe disorder resulting from exposure to an extremely traumatic event that involved, or could have caused, death or serious injury. PTSD-like symptoms have been described in battlefield soldiers for centuries and have been called shell shock, battle fatigue, and traumatic war neurosis. PTSD is characterized by reliving the trauma over and over, nightmares about the trauma, avoidance of places and events that are remindful of the trauma, emotional numbness, guilt, depression, hyper-vigilance, angry outbursts, and difficulty sleeping.

Reactive-attachment disorder (RAD) describes disturbed and inappropriate social behavior in most contexts and is characterized by serious problems in emotional attachments. Some children with reactive attachment disorder may also be overly or inappropriately social or familiar with strangers. The cause of reactive attachment disorder is not known, but most children with RAD had severe problems or disruptions in their early relationships. Many have been physically or emotionally abused or neglected. Many have experienced inadequate care in institutional settings. Even after being adopted into loving and attentive homes, children with RAD still struggle to establish normal emotional attachments.

Dissociative Disorders. Dissociative disorders are characterized by changes in personality or consciousness. Though from time to time we all "zone-out," the word dissociate refers to a "split" or dis-association of one's consciousness, memory, identity, or perception. Dissociative disorders are extremely rare and many psychologists disagree about whether dissociative disorders are "real."

Dissociative identity disorder, formerly known as multiple personality disorder, is said to be the existence of two or more distinct identities or personality states that take control of an individual's behavior. Dissociative disorders involve "fragmentation" of the personality. While most episodes last only a few hours or days, they can last longer.

Feeding and Eating Disorders describe severe disturbances in eating.

Anorexia Nervosa is characterized by a refusal to maintain a minimally normal body weight, an intense fear of gaining weight, and a disturbance in the perception of body size or shape.

Bulimia Nervosa is characterized by binge eating followed by inappropriate compensatory behavior (e.g., vomiting and using laxatives). ***Bing-Eating Disorder***, new to the DSM-5, is characterized by binge eating at least once weekly over the last 3 months.
functioning.

Sleep-wake Disorders are characterized by disturbed sleep that causes distress and im¬pairment in daytime functioning. Sleep-wake disorders disturb the amount, quality, or timing of sleep and include ***insomnia*** (not enough sleep), ***hypersomnia*** (too much sleep), ***narcolepsy*** (sleep when you least expect it), and ***sleep apnea*** (sleep interrupted by breathing difficulties).

Sexual dysfunctions are characterized by a severe and persistent disturbance of sexual desire or in the sexual response cycle.

Gender Dysphoria is a new diagnostic category in DSM-5 that reflects a change in beliefs about gender and sexuality. Gender dysphoria is characterized by cross-gender identification, aversion toward one's gender, and a strong desire to be the other gender.

Disruptive, Impulse-control, and Conduct Disorders are characterized by problems in the self-control of emotions and behaviors that violate the rights of others or that conflict with societal norms or authority figures.

Oppositional Defiant Disorder (ODD) describes children with a pattern of negativistic, hostile, and defiant behavior, who often lose their temper, argue with adults, defy or refuse to comply with requests or rules, deliberately annoy people, blame others for own mistakes, or who are irritable, angry; resentful, spiteful, or vindictive.

Conduct Disorder describes repetitive and persistent patterns of behavior in which the basic rights of others or societal norms or rules are violated. Children with conduct disorder are characterized by aggression to people and property.

Intermittent Explosive Disorder is characterized by the inability to resist aggressive impulses leading to serious assaultive acts or property destruction The degree of aggressiveness is grossly out of proportion to any provocation.

Kleptomania is characterized by a recurrent failure to resist impulses to steal objects that are not needed for personal use or for their monetary value. ***Pyromania*** is characterized by deliberate and purposeful fire setting to relieve tension and for self-gratification.

Substance Related and Addictive Disorders are characterized by recurrent substance use that results in failure to fulfill major obligations, use in hazardous situations (e.g., drinking and driving), legal problems, and continued use despite social or interpersonal problems. Substance related and addictive disorders are characterized by tolerance and withdrawal.

Tolerance refers to a decreased reaction to a substance so that larger doses are required to achieve the same effect. ***Withdrawal*** refers to distressing physical and/or psychological symptoms when no longer using the substance.

The substance-related disorders in DSM-5 have been expanded to include ***Gambling Disorder***, reflecting a belief that behaviors like gambling activate the brain's reward system similarly to drugs.

Neurocognitive disorders are a category of conditions that involve disturbances in thinking, memory, language, and awareness of surroundings.

Delirium describes a disorder of consciousness that develops over a short period of time. Delirium is characterized by rambling and incoherent speech, disorientation, hallucinations, and memory impairment. Delirium is usually short-lived (one week to one month) and is caused by infection, injury, metabolic disturbances, and drug or alcohol intoxication or withdrawal.

The neurocognitive disorders include symptoms of dementia and amnesia. *Dementia* also describes impaired memory and cognitive functioning, but whereas delirium has a quick onset and is short-lived, dementia is a slow, gradual, and persistent decline in mental functioning. *Amnesia* is characterized by an impaired ability to create new memories or to retrieve past memories. Some people with amnesia confabulate, which means that they fill in memory gaps with false information that they believe to be true.

Personality Disorders describe enduring, pervasive, and inflexible patterns of thinking, feeling, and behaving that deviate substantially from the expectations of the culture. Personality disorders are characterized by disturbances in cognition, affect, interpersonal functioning, and impulse control. Personality disorders are inflexible and maladaptive exaggerations of normal personality traits. The DSM 5 describes ten personality disorders.

The *Paranoid Personality Disorder* is characterized by a pattern of suspicion and distrust. Unlike paranoid schizophrenia, people with paranoid personality disorders are not delusional. They do not hear voices.

Voluntary detachment from social relationships and a restricted range of emotional expression characterize the *Schizoid Personality Disorder*.

The *Schizotypal Personality Disorder* is characterized by acute discomfort in close relationships, cognitive or perceptual distortions, and eccentric behavior. People with this disorder often misinterpret casual incidents as having special and personal meaning and are often superstitious and preoccupied with paranormal phenomena.

Of the personality disorders, perhaps the most noteworthy is the *Anti-social Personality*, sometimes referred to as psychopath or sociopath. Anti-social personality disorder is characterized by disregard for and violation of the rights of others. Deceit and manipulation are central features of this disorder, and the person with this disorder is guiltless, lacks a sense of moral responsibility or conscience, and feels no remorse about hurting other people or violating social norms. People with this disorder often appear charming, intelligent, poised, and calm. Some suggest that anti-social personality disorder is practically synonymous with criminal behavior.

Borderline Personality Disorder (BPD) is characterized by pervasive instability in interpersonal relationships, self-image, mood, and extreme impulsivity. People with this disorder have a pattern of unstable and intense relationships and a persistently unstable self-image.

Excessive emotionality and attention seeking characterize the ***Histrionic Personality Disorder***. People with this disorder are uncomfortable or feel unappreciated when they are not the center of attention and are often inappropriately sexually seductive or provocative.

The ***Narcissistic Personality Disorder*** is characterized by a grandiose self-image, exaggerated sense of self-worth, and lack of empathy for others. People with this disorder care mostly about themselves, believe they are special or superior, and may be preoccupied with dreams of fame, success, or power.

The ***Avoidant Personality Disorder*** is characterized by social inhibition, feelings of inadequacy, and extreme sensitivity to negative comments. People with this disorder view themselves as unappealing and inferior and may be unwilling to get involved with people unless they are certain of being liked.

A persistent and excessive need to be taken care of characterizes the ***Dependent Personality Disorder***. People with this disorder may have trouble making simple decisions without advice and reassurance and may want others to take responsibility for most areas of their lives.

Paraphilic Disorders. A paraphilia, also called a fetish, is an atypical sexual urge, fantasy, or behavior that involves unusual objects, activities, or situations. In the past, atypical sexual interests were by definition disordered. In the DSM-5, a paraphilia is not necessarily a disorder – to make a diagnosis requires that people with these urges feel personal distress about them -- not merely distress from society's disapproval. Behavior involving another's distress, injury, or death or sexual behaviors involving unwilling persons or persons unable to give legal consent is still considered a disorder.

Costs of Mental Illness. The National Institue of Mental Health estimates that 26.2 percent of Americans ages 18 and older -- about 58 million people -- have a diagnosable mental disorder. The impact of mental illness on health throughout the world is staggering. The World Health Organization estimates that mental illness ranks second worldwide in the burden of disease, behind cardiovascular diseases. Mental illness and substance abuse have tragic effects on people's health, life-expectancy, ability to earn a living, and on their families and relationships. What can be done?

In the next chapter we will look a current and historical approaches to caring for people with psychological disorders illness and examine the reasons that a Christian worldview provides the best context for caring for those disorders.

Chapter Summary.

We all have a sense of what is normal and what is abnormal, but defining abnormality is difficult. Normal and abnormal can be described from different perspectives and in varying degrees. Generally, thoughts, emotions, and behaviors are considered abnormal if they are maladaptive, disturbing, uncommon, and irrational.

The term "mental illness," also called psychopathology, is more difficult to define than the word "abnormal." Abnormality is a part of mental illnesses, but the terms are not synonymous. Mental illness literally means "disease of the mind" and is characterized by severe disturbances in thinking, feeling, acting, and relating with the world and with others. Over time psychologists' beliefs about what constitutes a mental illness have changed. As has been the case for centuries, many people explain abnormal thoughts, feelings, and behaviors in terms of the supernatural influences of gods, demons, witchcraft, sorcery, and "spirits." Today, abnormal thoughts, feelings, and behaviors are generally explained in terms of brain disorders called mental illnesses.

Behaviorists suggested that abnormal thoughts and behaviors are learned by association, punishment, and reinforcement. The cognitive perspective suggested that distorted patterns of understanding and interpreting experiences and relationships are responsible. Freudian psycho-dynamic theories explained mental illness in terms of unconscious psychic conflicts. The humanist perspective explained that abnormal thoughts, feelings, and behaviors developed when circumstances blocked one's progress toward self-actualization. The evolutionary perspective suggested that mental disorders, though detrimental today, must have served an adaptive survival purpose for ancient humans. A biological perspective, also called the medical model, described mental illnesses like other physical diseases, with discrete physical causes.

The American Psychiatric Association (APA) publishes the The Diagnostic and Statistical Manual of Mental Disorders (DSM). The DSM categorizes various mental conditions and describes the characteristic symptoms of each condition. The DSM is used by practically every psychologist and mental health worker in the world.

- Developmental disorders interrupt or interfere with normal mental development and affect social and cognitive development.
- Cognitive disorders involve disturbances in thinking, memory, language, and awareness of surroundings.
- Mental disorders due to medical conditions are characterized by changes in mental functioning directly attributed to general medical conditions.
- Substance-related disorders are characterized by drug use that results in failure to fulfill obligations and in social or interpersonal problems.
- Psychotic disorders involve disturbances in perception, thought, and serious dysfunction in daily functioning. Hallucinations are perceptual experiences of stimuli that do not exist.
- Mood disorders are characterized by symptoms of depression and/or mania.
- Worry, fear, dread, or panic are characteristic of the anxiety disorders.
- Somatic disorders are psychological conditions characterized by physical symptoms that are not explained by a medical condition.
- Factitious disorders are conditions in which a person acts as if he or she has an illness by deliberately producing, feigning, or exaggerating symptoms.
- Dissociative disorders are characterized by changes in personality or consciousness.
- Sexual dysfunctions are characterized by a disturbance of sexual desire or disturbance in the sexual response cycle. Gender identity disorders are characterized by strong and persistent cross-gender identification.
- Eating disorders describe severe disturbances in eating.
- Sleep disorders describe disorders of the amount, quality, or timing of sleep.
- Impulse-control disorders are characterized by episodes of failure to resist aggressive or dangerous impulses.
- Adjustment disorders describe the symptoms that appear in response to an identifiable stress.
- Personality disorders describe patterns of thinking, feeling, and behaving that deviate markedly from the expectations of the culture.

For Review.

1. How does worldview impact one's beliefs about the causes of abnormal thoughts, feelings, and behaviors?
2. Describe supernatural explanations of abnormal thoughts, feelings, and behaviors.
3. Describe various approaches toward defining what is abnormal.
4. What is mental illness?
5. Describe the causes of mental illness from the behaviorist perspective.
6. Describe the causes of mental illness from the Freudian psychodynamic perspective.
7. Describe the causes of mental illness from the humanistic perspective.
8. Describe the causes of mental illness from the cognitive perspective.
9. Describe the causes of mental illness from the evolutionary perspective.
10. Describe the Diagnostic and Statistical Manual of Mental Disorders (DSM).

Chapter 13

Treatment

In This Chapter

In the previous chapter, we examined the worldview issues that shaped the various theories about the causes of abnormal thoughts, feelings, and behaviors. This chapter examines various models of treatment for people with psychological problems, with an emphasis on the link between the model and its underlying worldview assumptions. Your worldview about what causes abnormal thoughts, feelings, and behaviors greatly influences your beliefs about treatment.

If your worldview belief is that abnormal thoughts, feelings, and behaviors are the result of *sin*; *unconscious psychic conflicts*; *trauma and abuse*; *demonic influences*; *biological malfunctions*; *chemical imbalances in the brain*; *bad parenting*; *blocked self-actualization*; or a *combination of causes*, your beliefs about treatment will reflect that worldview. Every approach to caring for people with abnormal thoughts, feelings, and behaviors brings with it underlying beliefs about the cause of the conditions. You will be taught a number of approaches to treatment in college. Please do not forget that understanding an approach to a treatment and accepting its underlying explanation of the cause of the problem are different. You can do one without the other.

Historical Approaches to Treatment. Throughout history there have been a number of widely varying treatments for psychological disorders. Both physical illnesses and abnormal thoughts and behaviors were understood in terms of religion or magic. Shamans cast healing spells, offered sacrifices, and cast out evil spirits. Some cultures practiced ***trephination***, a primitive type of brain surgery.

Benjamin Rush (1745-1813) is known as the father of American psychiatry. Rush believed that mental diseases were caused by irritation of the blood vessels in the brain. His treatment methods included inducing seizures, blood-letting, ice baths, and doses of a number of different chemical compounds.

Cornelius Celsus, a Roman physician who lived around the time of Christ, recorded that treatment for mental illness consisted of starvation, chains, and flogging.

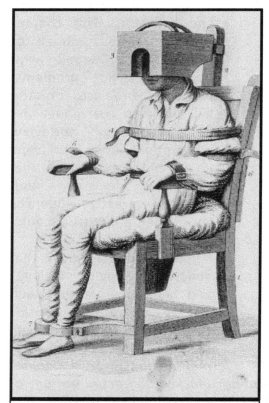

Tranquilizing Chair.

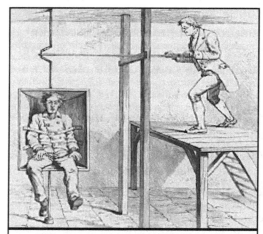

The gyrator was intended to use centrifugal force to send more blood to the brain to relieve "brain congestion."

From the Middle Ages through the Renaissance, mental illnesses were often understood as demon possession. Treatment consisted of exorcism. Abnormal behavior was interpreted as evidence of witchcraft or of moral weakness and was "treated" with punishment intended to drive the evil from its victim and the patient toward repentance.

In 1247 the ***Bethlem Royal Hospital***, the first asylum for the mentally ill in England, was founded. The hospital came to be known as Bedlam, and the word ***"bedlam"*** came to be used generically for all psychiatric hospitals, and eventually bedlam entered the general language as a term to describe uproar and disorder. For a time, Bethlem hospital was infamous for its brutal treatment of its patients.

In colonial America people with psychological disorders were usually cared for at home. With the increase in urbanization, state governments built institutions for the care of the mentally ill. The first ***asylum*** for the mentally ill was built in Virginia in the mid-18th century.

Through the 17th and 18th centuries the mentally ill, known as ***lunatics***, were kept in hospitals, asylums, and madhouses. Patient rooms often contained only a mattress, a chamber pot, and an iron ring in the wall to which the patient was chained. The mentally ill were viewed as less than human and were locked away like animals, caged, chained, and beaten, and put on display.

Beginning in the 19th century, public attitudes about the care of the mentally ill began to change. ***Moral management,*** as it was known, saw patients not as immoral possessed animals, but as people who were "sick" and

In 1808 Philippe Pinel released the first mental patients from confinement in the first massive movement for more humane treatment of the mentally ill.

Dorothea Dix (1802 - 1887) is famous in the history of psychology for her work as an advocate for the humane treatment of the mentally ill. Dix's efforts led to the establishment of 32 psychiatric hospitals and to the elimination of housing the mentally ill in jail.

in need of treatment. The mentally ill were unchained and treated in more home-like facilities, they were given structured work activities, and punishment was eliminated as a treatment.

Following the American Civil War a large number of veterans were admitted to mental hospitals and asylums. This created an overcrowding crisis that lasted well into the 20th century until the discovery of effective psychiatric medications.

Lobotomy. Around the end of the 1800s, knowledge of the relationship between brain structure and behavior was increasing. Psychologists discovered that dogs that had parts of their brain removed were more tame and calm. This and similar discoveries led to the surgical procedure known as lobotomy. A lobotomy was first performed on humans in the 1890s. Early procedures were time-consuming and delicate and involved drilling holes in patients' skulls to allow surgeons to destroy brain tissue. In 1945, ***Walter Freeman*** developed a quick and easy ten-minute procedure using an ice pick to sever neural connections in the frontal lobe of the brain. Freeman later replaced the ice pick with a flat cutting tool that he inserted into the brain through the eye socket. Sweeping the tool from side to side, Freeman cut neural connections in the frontal lobe. The result was calmer, less agitated patients; many of whom were able to leave institutions and return home. Though after surgery patients were calmer, they were not cured, in fact, the surgery did irreversible damage. Lobotomy's side effects included blunting of the personality, apathy, childishness, and irresponsibility. Initially limited to patients with schizophrenia and severe depression, lobotomies were eventually performed on thousands of people including children and

The ***trans-orbital lobotomy*** was touted by some as a miracle cure for mental illness. Walter Freeman, who was called the "traveling lobotomist," personally performed over 3,000 procedures and trained psychiatrists across the country to perform the procedure. In the 1940s and '50s, the lobotomy was performed on about 40,000 patients in the United States. As barbaric as the procedure sounds, it was popular because there was no better alternative treatment for the hundreds of thousands of patients in overcrowded institutions.

criminals and as a treatment for chronic headaches.

Convulsive Therapies. Psychologists had long observed that following high fever and seizures, the mentally ill were often symptom-free. That observation led to the 20th century development of techniques including ***insulin overdose***, ***chemicals***, ***microwaves***, ***oxygen deprivation***, and ***electric currents*** to induce brain seizures. The most commonly used technique was called ***electroconvulsive therapy*** (ECT). In the 1940s and 1950s ECT was misused as a behavior control technique for patients in mental institutions. The convulsions that accompanied the seizures were so intense that patients would often suffer broken bones.

Psychopharmacology. In 1952, a surgeon in Paris looking for a way to reduce surgical shock in his patients, made an accidental discovery that started a revolution in the care and treatment of the mentally ill. When patients facing surgery were given a dose of a strong drug called ***thorazine***, they were calm and less anxious. When tested on patients in psychiatric hospitals, thorazine had a powerful calming and sedating effect there, too. Patients who had been restrained because of violent behavior could be unchained, and patients who stood without moving or speaking began to walk and talk normally.

In 1954, Thorazine was approved by the U.S. Food and Drug Administration, and in the ten years that followed, 50 million people around the world had taken the drug. Thorazine and related ***major tranquilizers*** had a calming effect, alleviated hallucinations and delusions, and allowed many patients to live outside of mental institutions. Some psychologists compare the development of anti-psychotic drugs for mental illnesses to

> A modern version of electroconvulsive therapy is used today for the treatment of chronic and severe depression. Today patients receive an anesthetic and a muscle relaxer to prevent painful convulsions. The treatment involves passing a carefully controlled electrical current through a patient's brain to trigger a seizure. Despite studies suggesting its effectiveness, ECT remains a very controversial treatment.

the discovery of antibiotics for infectious diseases, anti-convulsants for epilepsy, and anti-hypertensive drugs for cardiovascular disease.

Though there were serious side effects and drawbacks to thorazine, its discovery started what has been called the ***pharmacological revolution***, a search for new psychoactive drugs to treat a variety of psychological disorders. Following the discovery of thorazine, many new drugs were developed to treat psychological disorders. In 1954, ***miltown*** (meprobamate) was approved as the first ***anxiolytic*** (anxiety reducer). In 1957, ***iproniazid*** was approved for the treatment of depression, and in 1970, ***lithium*** was approved for the treatment of manic symptoms. Today Americans spend tens of billions of dollars annually on psychiatric drugs.

> ***Classification of Psychiatric Medications***. Psychiatric medications are typically classified by the disorder for which they are most usually employed.
>
> - ***Anti-psychotics***, also called neuroleptics, are used to treat psychotic symptoms by blocking dopamine receptors.
> - ***Anti-depressants*** treat depression by increasing the availability of norepinephrine and/or serotonin at neural receptor sites.
> - ***Anxiolytics*** are used to treat anxiety symptoms and sleep difficulties by enhancing the activity of the neurotransmitter GABA. GABA has an inhibitory effect on motor neurons, so enhancing its activity effectively slows nerve impulses throughout the body.
> - ***Mood stabilizers*** have anti-mania qualities and anti-depressant effects and are often used in the treatment of bipolar disorder.

Psychiatric drugs are designed to alter the way neurotransmitters work. Psychologists have associated certain neurotransmitters with particular mental functions and mental illnesses. Psychiatric drugs are intended to correct the "chemical imbalances" that cause mental illnesses by making more or less of a particular neurotransmitter available in the brain. For example, too little of the neurotransmitter serotonin is thought to be associated with depression and anxiety. Too much dopamine has been associated with psychotic symptoms and schizophrenia. Anti-depressants and anti-anxiety medications increase serotonin and dopamine levels in the brain.

From a worldview perspective, psychiatric drugs reflect the belief that psychological disorders are **biological problems**. From the perspective of naturalism, good psychological health and bad psychological health are both reducible to electrochemical brain activity. From that perspective, it is logical to look to science to produce chemical solutions to chemical problems. Critics of the biological (medication) approach to treatment suggest that the emphasis on medications provides a false hope that a "magic pill" will "fix" all of our problems. Critics suggest that the emphasis on alleviating symptoms with medications ignores underlying spiritual and social problems. Other people suggest that by treating the symptoms of psychological problems with medications, it allows people to then focus on their spiritual and social problems.

Christians disagree with other Christians about the role, if any, that psychiatric medications should play in the treatment of psychological problems. Many Christians believe that because the brain is a physical organ, it can have physical defects that are not qualitatively different than bad eyesight, diabetes, or cancer. From this perspective, psychiatric medications are a gift from God. But other Christians believe that abnormal thoughts, feelings, and behaviors are not the manifestation of defects in the physical brain, believing instead that they are manifestations of sin and disunity with God on the non-physical soul. From this perspective, psychiatric medications provide false hope and divert people from seeking God's healing (or His comfort, should He choose not to heal).

De-institutionalization of the Mentally Ill. The discovery of psychotropic medications allowed many patients to leave psychiatric institutions to live at home in the community. From 1955 to 1980, the population of psychiatric hospitals fell from over 500,000 to around 50,000 in a social movement that came to be called de-institutionalization. **De-institutionalization** refers to the wide-spread release of the mentally ill from mental hospitals to community-based treatment centers. Today people with mental illness cannot be hospitalized against their will unless they are an obvious threat to themselves or others. Deinstitutionalization, however, led to **unintended**

The **Community Mental Health Act of 1963** provided grants to states for the creation of local mental health centers as an alternative to institutionalization.

> ***Free Association***. Freud believed that accessing the unconscious was crucial to treating psychological disorders. Freud developed a technique called "free association" to access unconscious thoughts and feelings. Freud asked patients to speak anything that came to mind, regardless of how irrelevant it seemed to be. He believed that by using this technique, important unconscious mental content would eventually come to the surface.

consequences. The mentally ill were released to communities that were not prepared to care for them. The result was a rise in the number of homeless mentally ill in the 1970s and 1980s. There was also an increase in the number of mentally ill people in jails and prisons. Today, jails and homeless shelters serve as ***de facto mental institutions***. The U. S. Justice Department estimates that over 200,000 people with severe mental illnesses are held in jails and prisons at any given time.

Freudian Psycho-therapy. Sigmund Freud is famous in the history of psychology, among other things, as the father of psycho-therapy. As noted earlier, Freud believed that the source of psychological disorders was unconscious psychic conflict. His approach to treating disorders, known as ***the talking cure***, involved talking to patients while they reclined on his famous couch. Freudian psycho-analytic or psycho-dynamic therapies, still popular today, look to the unconscious to discover and treat psychological problems. Psycho-dynamic therapists help patients to bring unconscious motivations and conflicts to light, to confront beliefs and actions, and to examine memories, events, and feeling from the past for clues to current problems. Although there is a current trend toward ***brief therapy***, Freudian psycho-analytic therapy typically lasted for several years.

Following Freud, psychologists proposed other models of treatment according to their worldview beliefs about the nature of Mankind and the causes of mental illness. Behaviorists proposed behavioral models. Cognitivists developed cognitive therapies, and humanists developed humanistic therapies. Though each model is different at the worldview level, each is similar in that all therapies offer reassurance and support, minimize distress, encourage adaptive functioning, and offer understanding and insight.

Counseling, therapy, psycho-therapy, talk therapy, and analysis are general terms that describe countless techniques by which therapists enter into relationships with a patient for the purpose of helping the patient with symptoms of mental illness, behavioral problems, or personal growth. Therapists meet patients face-to-face, over the telephone, or over the Internet. Therapy may be brief or extend over months or years. ***Clinical psychologists***, ***social workers***, ***marriage-family therapists***, ***expressive therapists***, ***trained nurses***, ***psychiatrists***, ***psycho-analysts***, ***mental health counselors***, ***school counselors***, and the ***clergy*** may provide therapy.

Therapy is used to help people with symptoms of serious mental illness, to help people choose a career path, to solve relationship problems, or to deal with trauma, abuse, neglect, grief, disappointment, anger, and stress. Therapy can help repair self-concept, ease fears and anxiety, resolve conflict, improve communication, or seek "the meaning of life."

Behavior therapy (also called *behavior modification*) refers to the systematic application of behavioral techniques to the treatment of psychological disorders. Behavior therapy presumes that psychological disorders are collections of learned responses. Behavior therapy establishes *rewards* and *reinforcements* to change unwanted thoughts, feelings, and behavior. Behavior therapy focuses on current behavior and does not address underlying or unconscious issues or conflicts. *Exposure therapy* is a form of behavior therapy in which one is deliberately exposed to disturbing situations in order to learn to cope with them effectively. *Systematic desensitization* is a form of behavior therapy for people with fears of specific objects or situations. In systematic desensitization, the patient is taught relaxation techniques, and is then gradually exposed to the source of their fear over time.

Examples of irrational or distorted thinking:

- *Emotional Reasoning*: Using emotion alone to determine truth. "I feel ugly, so I am ugly."
- *Dichotomous Thinking* (All or Nothing): Interpreting situations only in extremes without considering the possibility of alternate interpretations.
- *Catastrophizing* (Magnification): Expecting and looking for the worst.
- *Filtering*: Focusing on the negative, magnifying the negative, and ignoring or minimizing the positive.
- *Personalization*: A tendency to believe that "it is all about me" and take responsibility for negative events even if there is no reason to do so.
- *Mind-reading*: Assuming that we know what others are thinking or feeling, and why they behave the way they do.

Cognitive therapy seeks to correct distorted thinking patterns that lead to unwanted feelings, and behaviors. Cognitive therapy presumes that irrational thoughts and beliefs underlie emotional and behavioral problems. The therapist helps a patient identify and change the way they think about things, their beliefs, and their expectations. Though Christians, like anyone else, may hold irrational beliefs, it is crucial that the identification of "rational" and "irrational" be examined in terms of underlying worldview. Many cognitive therapists define "belief in God" as an irrational belief. Like behavior therapy, cognitive therapy focuses on current thinking and not on underlying or past issues.

Cognitive-behavioral therapy (CBT) combines a cognitive and behavioral approach to recognize and change distorted thought patterns and unwanted behaviors. It is based on the premise that the way we think about a situation and the way we behave in a situation are more important than the situation itself. CBT is one of the most commonly used approaches to therapy today and research suggests it is an effective approach to treating many problems.

Humanistic therapy, also called *person-centered therapy*, seeks to help patients achieve self-actualization and high self-esteem. Humanistic therapy emphasizes Mankind's inborn "goodness" and potential. Humanistic counselors presume that in an accepting, non-judgmental, and non-directive environment of unconditional positive regard, the innate goodness in all Mankind will propel us toward our full potential.

Family therapy, also called *systemic therapy* and *family systems therapy*, focuses on relationships between people. Where other therapies focus on individuals, family therapists deal with interaction patterns within a family system. This approach emphasizes the importance of family relationships to mental health. From this perspective, abnormal thoughts, feelings, and behaviors in individuals are the expression of problems in the family system. By adjusting interactions within the family, the family functions more effectively, and the individual members experience symptom relief.

Spiritual treatments, in a broad sense, are treatments that rely on spiritual or religious means to treat psychological disorders. In that broad sense, there are probably hundreds of spiritual treatments for a number of conditions.

- In *past life therapy*, the clues to solving the problems in "this" life are found in "past" lives.
- In *polarity therapy*, the therapist is said to adjust the patient's energy field in order to improve the functioning of the mind and body.
- In *therapeutic touch*, therapists are said to smooth-out irregularities in the patient's "energy field," divert excess energy back into the environment, and channel some of the limitless energy of the universe to "jump start" the weakened energies of the patient.
- In *organic process therapy* patients are taught to how to return to their "unobstructed and unfractured organic self."

These "spiritual" approaches are clearly inconsistent with a Christian worldview.

Christian Counseling. Obviously, a Christian "spiritual" approach to therapy is consistent with a Christian worldview. There is, however, no agreement among Christian psychologists as to what constitutes Christian therapy. As mentioned before, there is no topic in psychology more controversial among Christians than counseling psychology. The controversy is a result of differing worldview beliefs among Christians. Some Christian psychologists believe that modern psychology's counseling techniques are a helpful enhancement to the Bible's guidelines for living. Other Christians believe that the Bible is the sole and sufficient counseling tool. Through the ages, Christians have struggled to relate the Bible to other academic disciplines. How do Christians studying or working in biology, physics, or sports medicine "connect" their worldview with science, without compromising either one? Christian psychologists face a similar challenge – connecting effective secular counseling techniques with a Christian worldview.

Anti-psychology refers to a belief among some Christians that modern psychology, especially counseling psychology, is spiritually dangerous, that it is not a science, or that it is invalid because it relies on knowledge derived from sources other than the Bible. Christians studying psychology, especially those considering a career in counseling, should carefully consider this belief.

Many Christians denounce counseling psychology as idolatrous, heretical, and an ungodly rival "religion" that places Christians at risk of spiritual deception and demonic attack. Some Christians refer to counseling psychology as "psycho-babble," as "psycho-quackery," and as Satan's substitute for biblical remedies. Christians holding this position believe that there is nothing that modern psychology can contribute to our understanding about the nature of Mankind, about the nature of abnormal thoughts, feelings, and behaviors, or about the process of becoming psychologically "whole." According to this position, modern psychology's underlying atheism, naturalism, and reductionism deny God's central and pervasive role in life, making it wholly irreconcilable with a Christian worldview. From this perspective, it is impossible to reject modern counseling psychology's non-biblical presuppositions while adopting the techniques born of those presuppositions. From this perspective, counseling psychology is seen as an attempt to free people from responsibility for their actions. From this perspective, a good seminary education, not a degree in clinical psychology, is the most fitting background for a counselor.

Biblical Counseling. While many Christians who are counselors consider their approach to counseling to be "biblical," the *biblical counseling movement* rejects the use of any extra-biblical sources to understand or to care for abnormal thoughts, feelings, and behaviors. Biblical counseling, also known as *nouthetic counseling*, emphasizes the redemptive and healing aspects of biblical admonition and instruction. A key characteristic of biblical counseling is the belief that an individual's psychological problems are caused by that individual's sinfulness, wrong patterns of thinking and living, and disunity with God. This approach sees the Bible as completely sufficient for dealing with all problems of living, including those described as mental illnesses. Nouthetic counselors discern sin and wrong patterns of thinking and living in the counselee, and use the Bible to admonish, confront, motivate, and provide spiritual direction. The goals of nouthetic counseling are confession, repentance, reconciliation and restoration, and support for the counselee's walk with God in order to produce maturity and Godly living in their life. Many biblical counselors believe that to use any technique, model, approach, theory, or method from modern psychology is compromise (at best) or heresy (at worst).

The word *nouthetic* comes from the Greek word *noutheteō* , which refers to reasoning with someone through instruction and admonition; to admonish through instruction.

Integration. Many Christians believe that God reveals truths through the Bible and through psychological research. This approach, known as integration, presumes that valid findings of psychology and accurate interpretations of the Bible will not ultimately contradict – that psychological discoveries are not inherently anti-Christian, and that psychology can contribute, it its own way, to a comprehensive understanding of Mankind and to solutions to psychological disorders. From this perspective, the motto *"all truth is God's truth"* applies to counseling psychology, too. Integration presupposes truth in biblical revelation and in the "essential correctness" of scientific psychology. If all truth is God's truth, then a truth discovered by psychology can be translated for understanding and use by Christians. Integration means finding an approach to counseling psychology applying the unified truths of both psychology and the Bible. Integration requires that Christians planning further studies or a career in psychology have excellent preparation in theology, biblical interpretation, the principles of Christian discipleship, and in the rich history of Christian psychology stretching from the early Church. Though most Christians who study psychology understand that the Bible ought to influence their scholarship and career, too many Christians know far more about psychology than they do about their own religious traditions.

Many Christians believe that integration has improved Christians' attitudes toward psychology, helped distinguish between spiritual and physiological problems, decreased the stigma of seeking psychological help, increased insight into human behavior, encouraged ministers and theologians to attend to the whole person, and encouraged Christians both young and old to view psychology as a potential field of Christian service.

Popular Psychology. In addition to the models of treatment described in this chapter, there are hundred, perhaps thousands of good-sounding "popular" approaches described in books, magazines, tabloids, talk radio, and the internet. Some are supported by quality research, but many are not. Popular psychology offers the promise of happiness, a good marriage, perfect children, and advice for overcoming every imaginable problem of living. However, popular psychology titles generally avoid academic and technical terms and any reference to theory or underlying assumptions.

Each year, Christians spend millions of dollars on Christian popular psychology books, CDs, and DVDs. Some are supported by quality research and good theology, but many are not. Some Christian titles offer sound biblical solutions to problems of living, but sometimes, Christian "pop psychology" uncritically presents anti-Christian worldview assumptions and disguises them by sprinkling in Jesus' name and a few verses of the New Testament. Though these "Christianized" works may contain truths, they are likely to dangerously distort important biblical doctrines. Truths from popular psychology are only discernible from error at the worldview level.

Chapter Summary.

Abnormal thoughts, feelings, and behaviors are the result of chemical imbalances in the brain, biological malfunctioning, sin, unconscious psychic conflict, trauma and abuse, the demonic, moral weakness, bad parenting, learning, blocked self-actualization, or the result of a combination of causes. Each model of treatment reflects underlying beliefs about the causes of the conditions.

Through the 17th and 18th centuries the mentally ill, known as lunatics, were caged, chained, and beaten and housed in hospitals, asylums, and madhouses. Beginning in the 19th century, public attitudes about the care of the mentally ill began to change. "Moral management" as it was known, saw the mentally ill not as immoral possessed animals, but as people who were sick and in need of treatment. The lobotomy, involving cutting neural connections in the frontal lobe, was touted by some as a miracle cure for mental illness. Convulsive therapies used insulin overdose, microwaves, oxygen deprivation, and electric currents to induce brain seizures.

In 1954 Thorazine was approved by the Food and Drug Administration and in the ten years that followed, 50 million people around the world had taken the drug. Thorazine and related major tranquilizers had a calming effect, alleviated hallucinations and delusions, and allowed many patients to live outside of mental institutions. Following the discovery of Thorazine, many new drugs were developed to treat psychological disorders.

Psychiatric medications (also called psychotropic medications) are typically classified by the disorder for which they are most usually employed.

• Anti-psychotics, also called neuroleptics, are used to treat psychotic symptoms.
• Anti-depressants treat depression.
• Anxiolytics are used to treat anxiety symptoms and sleep difficulties.
• Mood stabilizers have anti-mania and anti-depressant effects and are often used in the treatment of bipolar disorder.

The discovery of psychiatric medications allowed many patients to leave psychiatric institutions and return to their home communities. From 1955 to 1980, the population of psychiatric hospitals fell from over 500,000 to around 50,000. Deinstitutionalization led to unintended consequences, including a rise in the number of jailed and homeless mentally ill in the 1970s and 1980s.

Therapy, psycho-therapy, talk therapy, analysis, and counseling are general terms that describe countless techniques by which therapists enter into relationships with patients for the purpose of helping the patient overcome abnormal thoughts, feelings, and behaviors, or for the patient's personal growth.

Sigmund Freud is famous in the history of psychology as the father of psycho-therapy. His approach to treating disorders, known as "the talking cure," involved talking to patients to help bring unconscious motivations and conflicts to light, to confront beliefs and attitudes, and to examine memories, events and feelings from the past for clues to current problems. Behavior therapy refers to the systematic application of behavioral techniques to the treatment of psychological disorders. Cognitive therapy seeks to correct distorted thinking patterns that lead to unwanted thoughts, feelings and behaviors. Cognitive-behavioral therapy (CBT) combines a cognitive and behavioral approach to recognize and change distorted thought patterns and unwanted behaviors. Humanistic therapies help patients achieve self actualization and high self-esteem. Family therapy, also called systemic therapy and family systems therapy, focuses on relationships between people. Spiritual treatments, in a broad sense, rely on spiritual or religious means to treat psychological disorders. Many Christians integrate biblical and secular techniques into their counseling. Other Christians rejects the use of any extra-biblical sources in favor of biblical admonition, confession, repentance, and reconciliation.

For Review.

1. Describe some of the historical approaches to treating abnormal thoughts, feelings, and behaviors, including the worldview assumptions underlying the approach.
2. Describe how attitudes toward the mentally ill changed in the 19th century.
3. Describe the history of lobotomy and electroconvulsive therapy.
4. Describe the discovery of thorazine and the pharmacological revolution.
5. Describe the classification of psychiatric medications.
6. Explain the phrase "chemical imbalance of the brain.
7. Describe psychopharmacology.
8. Describe the de-institutionalization of the mentally ill.
9. Describe the unintended consequences of de-institutionalization.
10. Define therapy.
11. Describe Freudian psycho-therapy.
12. Describe behavior therapy.
13. Describe cognitive therapies.
14. Describe humanistic therapy.
15. Describe family therapy.
16. Describe "spiritual" treatments.
17. Describe Christian anti-psychology.
18. Describe "integration."
19. Describe biblical counseling.
20. Describe popular psychology.

Chapter 14

Social Psychology

In This Chapter
- Social Influences on Communication
- Social Influences on Cognition
- Social Influences on Feelings
- Social Influences on Behavior
- Social Influences of Groups

In Luke 10:30-37 Jesus tells the parable of the *Good Samaritan*. In the parable, Jesus tells us of one man's social interactions with a robber, a priest, a Levite, and a "good" Samaritan. Social psychologists are interested in such stories. In 1973 social psychologists **John Darley** and **Daniel Batson** at Princeton Theological Seminary put subjects to the test in a fascinating experimental re-creation of the parable of the Good Samaritan. They wanted to know what factors influenced **helping behavior** or **altruism** – actions we take to help other people.

In their experiment, Darley and Batson recruited seminary students to be subjects in what was supposedly a study on religious education. They divided the subjects into two groups; one group was asked to prepare a sermon based on the story of the Good Samaritan. The second group was asked to prepare a presentation about seminary jobs. In an alley along the way to deliver their presentations, the subjects would encounter a man; slumped over, coughing, and groaning in obvious distress. The real purpose of the experiment was to find out whether thinking about helping increased helping behavior. Would the subjects who had been thinking about the moral imperatives communicated in the parable of the Good Samaritan be more likely to offer assistance to someone in need than subjects who were thinking about more "earthly" matters? Darley and Batson also wondered if **hurriedness** affected helping behavior. To find out, when the subjects arrived at the appointed time and place to deliver their message, they were told that the location for the presentation had been changed at the last minute. The researchers assigned the subjects in the two groups, the seminary jobs presentation or good Samaritan sermon group, into one of three conditions:

- In the **high pressure** condition, subjects were told that they were late and had hurry to the new location.
- In the **moderate pressure** condition, subjects were told that they had just enough time to get to the new location.
- In the **low pressure** condition, subjects were told that they were early and could take their time going to the new location.

What do you think happened? What tendencies did the subjects display, what factors influenced their responses, and what general conclusions can we draw from the results? These are the types of questions social psychologists ask.

In Darley and Batson's recreation of the Good Samaritan, the researchers found that the students were not particularly helpful. Overall, only 40% of the subject offered some help to the victim. The single largest factor in their subjects' helping behavior was hurriedness. Of the subjects in the low pressure condition, 63% offered assistance, and of the subjects in the high pressure condition, only 10% offered to help. Thinking about the Good Samaritan had an effect on helping behavior too. Of the subjects delivering the message on the Good Samaritan, 53% offered to help, but of those giving the talk on seminary jobs, only 29% offered to help.

Social psychology is the study of how the presence of other people influences the ways we think, feel, and behave. Because we spend our lives in a series of social interactions, our thoughts, behavior, and emotions are constantly under some type of social influence. Technology that allows instant and constant communication and social networks like Facebook have opened up whole new areas of study for social psychologists.

Worldview Check. The Bible has quite a lot to say about social influences and social interactions. Social psychologists describe what factors *do* influence social behavior. A Christian worldview describes what factors *should* influence social behavior. A Christian worldview believes that sin affects all areas of life – including social interactions. Part of Christian spiritual growth is developing biblical social interactions and rising above the world's social influences.

Sometimes the study of social psychology seems to students to be like learning a list of Mankind's carnal characteristics. That is because most social psychologists approach their research and theories from a naturalistic perspective. Without referencing God's supernatural influence on social behaviors, a naturalistic worldview assumes that human interactions are reducible to social determinants. In other words, social psychologists approach social behavior much like behavioral psychologists approach individual behavior – individual behavior is determined by environmental influences and social behavior is determined by social influences. A naturalistic worldview presumes that complex social interactions evolved from simpler social interactions. Social interactions, in an evolutionary perspective, evolved to facilitate survival and reproduction. To strict naturalistic social psychologists, there is nothing special about human social behavior.

Underlying social psychology's concepts and theories is the worldview question *"what is the nature of Mankind?"* Why, in social interactions, do we do the things we do? A Christian worldview provides the best answer. A Christian worldview sees human societies, nations, and cultures as part of God's created order and subject to His dominion. A Christian worldview includes the expectation that we individually are to be *salt and light* in the world and that we

Social psychology and *sociology* are related fields of study. While social psychologists study human behavior *in* groups, *sociologists* study the behavior *of* groups and whole societies. Sociologists study humans collectively and are concerned with the economic, social, political, and religious aspects of groups.

should oppose, not just study, *racism*, *greed*, and *violence*. In college, you will be taught naturalistic descriptions of Mankind's social nature. Please do not forget that understanding the concepts and accepting the worldview are different. You can do one without the other.

Social Influences on Communication. The most basic human social interaction is interpersonal communication. We may take it for granted, but ***interpersonal communication***, simple communication between two or more people, involves complex and uniquely human psychological process.

The Shannon-Weaver Model of Communication. While Claude Shannon and Warren Weaver were telephone engineers and not psychologists, their communication model has been adopted and used by psychologists because it shows the basic communication process in easy-to-understand "telephone" terms.

Communication takes place between a source and a receiver. The ***source*** initiates the message and the ***receiver*** receives it. The message is sent from the source to the receiver via some ***channel***. Speech is a channel of communication. Channels are the media through which messages pass – the connection between the source and the receiver. Speech communication occurs via the ***vocal-auditory channel***. The words you are reading are a channel of communication. A mime communicates through movement, without words. Artists communicate through paintings and dancers through movement. Text messages, Tweets, E-mails, and Facebook posts are channels of communication.

Because we cannot read each others' minds, messages must be encoded and decoded. The process of converting ideas into a form suitable for the channel is called ***encoding***. The receiver must ***decode*** the message to understand the meaning that the sender intended. ***Noise*** refers to anything that disrupts or interferes with the message accurately getting from source to receiver. Noise can be ***physical*** (i.e., interference in a telephone connection or loud background sounds), ***psychological*** (i.e., the attitudes and emotions we bring to communication), or ***semantic*** (i.e., the receiver cannot clearly understand the sender's language or grammar).

Communication can occur ***verbally, non-verbally, intentionally, and unintentionally.*** If you have ever gotten bad news from someone face-to-face, you probably knew that it was going to be bad news by non-verbal messages. The message (the bad news) was encoded and sent ahead via non-verbal channels. The messenger's ***facial expressions***, ***tone of voice***, ***gestures***, ***body position,*** and ***movement*** are powerful tools in communication. Psychologists believe that much of what gets communicated in social conversation is communicated non-verbally. Similarly, your dress and appearance, manner of speaking, and even smell may unintentionally affect communication. Wearing jeans and a t-shirt to a job interview sends a strong unintentional negative message.

Social work is a professional and academic discipline interested in sociology and social psychology. ***Social workers*** pursue social welfare, social change, and social justice. Social workers also seek to improve that quality of life for individuals in the context of their social relationships.

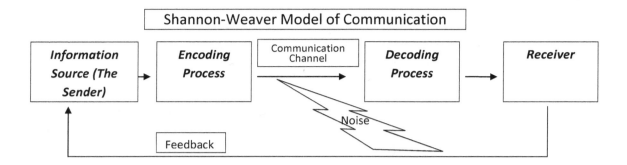

Communication is not a one-way process. The receiver provides feedback in response to the message. **Positive feedback** (e.g., nods and "uh huhs") provides an indication that the message is getting through. **Negative feedback** (e.g., puzzled looks and folded arms) provides clues that the message is not getting through.

Social Influences on Cognition. Social psychologists are interested in mental processes in the context of social interactions, or social contexts. In Chapter 5 we learned about the mental process called sensory perception. We learned that sensory perception is the mental process by which we organize, interpret, and understand raw sensory inputs like sound waves or airborne molecules. Similarly, **social perception** refers to the ways we organize, interpret, and understand social inputs. Just as our sensory schemas guide the way we understand sensory input, we have a number of **social schemas**, or "mental short cuts" that we use in social interactions. For example, when we form **first impressions** of the people we meet, we tend to assume a great deal about someone based on very little information. If someone we meet has one characteristic that we like or is similar to ourselves, we tend to assume that all their characteristics will be similarly favorable. First impressions are formed quickly, but they change slowly – especially negative first impressions. Our thoughts are affected by social context. **Social context** refers to the characteristics of the situations in which social interactions occur. The social context of a church service is very different from the context of hanging out with friends, and both are different from the social context of a funeral.

Characteristics of a Good Listener:

- Uses eye contact appropriately
- Is attentive and alert to a speaker's verbal and non-verbal behavior
- Is patient and doesn't interrupt
- Is responsive and provides verbal and non-verbal feedback
- Asks questions in a non-threatening tone
- Paraphrases, restates, and summarizes the speaker's message
- Is empathic, caring, and seeks to understand the speaker's emotional context

---

Characteristics of a Bad Listener:

- Impatiently interrupts the speaker
- Makes poor eye contact
- Is distracted, inattentive, and uninterested
- Provides little or no verbal or non-verbal feedback
- Changes the subject

Proxemics is the study of personal space. Things that are close are said to be **proximal** or **proximate**. Psychologists observing the physical distance, or space, that we maintain while communicating in various relationships and social situations have identified three types of "social "distance."

- **Intimate distance** – about 18 inches or closer – is reserved for special intimate conversations and displays of affections. It is uncomfortable for people to be closer than 18 inches to someone with whom they are not intimate.
- **Personal distance** – from about 18 inches to 4 feet – is used for day-to-day interactions with acquaintances and friends.
- **Social distance** – from about 4 to 12 feet – is a comfortable distance for social interactions with people we do not know well.

Social psychologists are interested in the effect other people has on our self-identity. **Self-identity** is the way we understand ourselves in relation to others. **Social comparison** refers to our tendency to compare ourselves to other people. Psychologists have observed what a Christian worldview understands – that comparing ourselves to others affects how we think and feel about ourselves – our self-identity and our self-esteem. Christians are not immune from the tendency to compare oneself to other people instead of measuring one's worth in terms of biblical standards.

Attribution Theory. Social psychologists are interested in how we interact with the world, make sense out of what goes on around us, and understand ourselves and others. **Attribution theories** and **biases** describe some of the factors that influence how we think about and make sense and understand ourselves and others – our **predispositions** and the inferences and explanations we give ourselves to explain why people do what they do, and why we do the things that we do. If you see a man picking up garbage along the road, what assumptions do you make about why he is doing it and what inferences do you make about his character and personality? Is he picking up trash because he is civic-minded and environmentally concerned or because he is a scoundrel under a community-service sentence for committing a crime? If a friend fails to send you a birthday card, do you attribute the failure to thoughtlessness, an internal characteristic, or do you attribute the oversight to some emergency circumstance? If you fail to send your friend a birthday card, do you attribute the failure to thoughtlessness, an internal characteristic, or do you attribute it to environmental circumstances? If you get a bad score on a test, do you blame yourself or the teacher and the test?

Attributions are the quick cognitive processes that happen outside of our conscious awareness. Attributions are explanations we form for the circumstances, thoughts, feelings, and behaviors of others. Attributions are also the explanations we form for the things that happen to us and for our own thoughts, feelings and behaviors. Attributions may be dispositional, based on our assumptions about internal personal characteristics, or situational, based on our observations and assumptions about external events and circumstances.

Internal attribution refers to an inference that a person is behaving in a certain way because of something about, or from inside the person, such as attitude, disposition, or personality trait. Internal attribution refers to

Fill in the blank. I am a(n) _____. Your answer is a reflection of your social identity, your attitudes and beliefs about yourself and the groups with which you identify. If you answer with terms like "hard worker," "good student," or "loyal friend," you have described a part of your ***personal identity***. Answers like "Christian," "African-American," and "male/female" are descriptions of your ***social identity***. Together they describe how you "see" yourself – your ***self-identity***.

the inference that we behave the way we do because of our internal characteristics. ***External attribution*** refers to an inference that a person is behaving a certain way because of something about the situation and circumstance the person is in. External attribution refers to the inference that we behave the way we do because of external forces and circumstances.

If the man we thought was picking up trash because he was a scoundrel turns out to be a civic-minded volunteer, we made an ***cognitive error*** – an attribution error. An ***attribution error*** is an incorrect or distorted understanding of what happens around us. The ***fundamental attribution error*** refers to the tendency to overestimate internal dispositional influences and underestimate external situational influences upon others' behavior. The fundamental attribution error predicts that if a friend fails to send you a birthday card, you are more likely to attribute the failure to your friend's internal characteristic than to circumstances. Interestingly, the fundamental attribution error predicts that if you fail to send your friend a birthday card, you will attribute the failure to circumstances (e.g., "I was too busy studying for the psychology test") and not to your internal characteristics. The ***ultimate attribution error***, a type of extension of the fundamental attribution error, describes the tendency to apply the negative behavior of a member of a group member to all the members of the group. For example, the statement "she is a Christian and she is being hypocritical which just proves that all Christians are hypocrites" reflects the ultimate attribution error. The ultimate attribution error is thought to underlie racism, religious persecution, and genocide. A Christian worldview sees those things as sin.

Attribution errors and biases can lead to ***stereotyping***, ***prejudice***, and ***discrimination***. ***Stereotypes*** are a type of biased schema; a mental shortcut used to characterize whole groups of people based on a false assumption that all members of a group share the same characteristics. Your answer to the question, "*all Christians are (fill in the blank)*" is a stereotype. Stereotypes can be positive (e.g., "*all Asians are smart*"), but they are usually made up of negative characteristics (e.g., "*white men can't jump*"). ***Prejudice*** is an attitude, positive or negative, about an individual based their membership in a group. When one's behavior is affected by stereotyping or prejudice, the result is ***discrimination*** – treating someone differently because of their membership a group. "*All Christians are closed-minded*" is a stereotype. "*He is a Christian so I don't like him,*" is a prejudice. "*We do not hire Christians*" is discrimination.

A ***bias*** is a predisposition toward a particular attribution. The ***self-serving bias*** refers to tendency to use a double standard when attributing meaning to our own circumstances. When things go well for us, we attribute it our internal personal characteristics like motivation, talent, or skill. When things go poorly, we tend to attribute it to external factors like bad luck, the devil, or unreasonable expectations. We tend to use different standards to attribute meaning to our own circumstances than we do to attribute meaning to other people's circumstances. The ***actor-observer bias*** refers to our predisposition to make an external attribution to explain our own bad circumstances, but to make an internal attribution to explain the bad circumstances of others. The ***just-world bias***, or the ***just-world hypothesis***, refers to the tendency to believe that bad things happen to bad people – that people get what they deserve. We tend to attribute people's bad circumstances to their bad character. Presuming that someone is unemployed because he or she is shiftless and lazy is an example of the just-world bias in action. Though some people are sometimes unemployed because they are lazy, it is a bias to presume they are. A Christian worldview recognizes that the world is not "just," but God is. A Christian worldview balances God's sovereignty and his grace with Mankind's sinfulness in a fallen world.

In-group and Out-group Bias. One explanation for stereotypes, prejudice, and discrimination is that they are attribution errors grounded in a "in-group/out-group bias." ***In-group bias*** refers to the tendency to have positive attitudes and give preferential treatment to people in the group to which we belong. The opposite of in-group bias is out-group bias. ***Out-group bias*** refers to the tendency to view negatively people who are not part of a group to which we belong. So we tend to accept some people and reject others, based on their group membership and our own.

Muzafer Sherif (1906 – 1988) is famous in the history of psychology for his studies of in-group and out-group bias, prejudice, group conflict, and discrimination. In his famous experiment known as the ***Robbers Cave study***, Sherif demonstrated how easily out-group bias can be created, even among boys at summer camp.

Sherif randomly assigned twenty-two 11-year-old boys into two groups that he took to a summer camp in Robbers Cave State Park, Oklahoma. Initially, neither group knew of the other group's presence at the camp. For the first week the groups hiked, swam, ate, and slept apart from and unaware of the other group of boys. One group adopted the name Eagles; the other, the Rattlers. When Sherif allowed the groups to find out about each other, the signs of out-group bias and ***between-group conflict*** soon appeared. The groups name-called and taunted each other and eventually refused to eat in the same room together.

To find out if the groups could be reconciled, Sherif created a ***super-ordinate goal***. A super-ordinate goal is a goal that benefited all and required the participation of both groups to achieve. Sherif told the groups that the drinking water supply had been attacked by vandals. By successfully working together to repair the water supply, the members of both groups were soon eating together again. Sherif suggested that groups of boys, like countries, cultures, and races, draw boundaries and create rules and norms to differentiate in-group from out-group members. In those structures, according to Sherif, are the roots of conflict between groups of boys and between nations.

Social Influences on Feelings. Have you ever known someone who had a "bad attitude?" How about someone with a really "positive mental attitude (PMA)?" A "bad attitude" to most people means disagreeableness – a personality trait or characteristic. Likewise, a "positive attitude" to most people means having an overall sense of optimism. Social psychologists, however, define attitude differently.

As said before, social psychology is the study of social influences on our thoughts, feelings, and behaviors. When social psychologists study and describe attitudes, they are describing the affective, or feeling, characteristics of social interactions. ***Attitudes*** are defined by social psychologists as pre-dispositions, positive or negative, toward someone or something. Attitudes are feelings, value judgments, evaluations, or opinions about something. An attitude requires an object – something or someone about which we have feelings (e.g., broccoli, rap music, homosexuality). Attitudes are comprised of cognitive, emotional, and behavioral components. The ***cognitive component*** of attitudes refers to perceptions, beliefs, thoughts, and memories about the object. The ***emotional component*** includes our feelings about the object, and the ***behavioral component*** of attitudes refers to our actions toward the object.

How are attitudes formed? Most psychologists believe that attitudes are primarily learned. Psychologists believe that as parents teach their children about objects (i.e., *"this is a pig"*), they also teach attitudes about those objects (i.e., *"this is a pig – stinky!"*). The entire advertising industry is devoted to forming and changing attitudes in hopes of increasing sales. Advertisers and psychologists both understand mere-exposure effects. The ***mere-exposure effect*** describes our tendency to have a positive attitude toward familiar things. The more we are simply exposed to an object, the more likely we are to have a positive attitude toward that object. If we repeatedly see and hear advertising for a particular brand of clothing, all other things being equal, we are more likely to have a favorable attitude toward that brand.

How do attitudes affect behavior? Psychologists suggest that our attitudes do not influence our behavior as much as we might think. Each of the subjects in the Darley and Batson's recreation of the Good Samaritan probably had a very positive attitude towards helping people in need, but for most of them, their behavior did not reflect that attitude. Psychologists believe that ***attitudes influence behavior,*** but that ***behavior more powerfully influences attitudes***.

Psychologist ***Leon Festinger*** (1919 - 1989) defined ***cognitive dissonance*** as the discomfort caused by when our behavior and attitudes conflict. Festinger suggested that the discomfort motivates us to achieve **consistency** between attitudes and behaviors by changing behavior or changing attitudes. The classic example of cognitive dissonance is the example of the conflict experienced by many cigarette smokers. Smoking (a behavior) and a positive attitude toward living a long life are in conflict. Cognitive dissonance motivates the smoker to quit smoking or to change their attitude. The smoker may deny that smoking is dangerous or rationalize that *"if smoking does not kill me, something else will."* Later in this chapter we will examine the social influences on obedience, conformity, and altruism – other situations in which social influences affect behavior more so than personal attitudes.

How do attitudes change? A Christian worldview understands that God can supernaturally change attitudes (i.e., a change of "heart"). Social psychologists, however, are interested in the interpersonal or ***social pressures*** that influence attitude changes. As mentioned previously, social context, roles, and norms create implicit social pressure on attitudes. A large part of all interpersonal communication is explicitly intended to change someone's mind or attitude about something by persuasion. ***Persuasion*** is a communication process, a social interaction, by which attitude change. Persuasive messages take two forms: ***rational-logical*** (the ***central route***) or ***emotional*** (the ***peripheral route***). ***Central route persuasion*** uses data, pros and cons, or other logical reasons in order to change someone's attitude. In the case of clothing brands, central-route persuasion emphasizes the reasons why the brand is best (e.g., it costs less and lasts longer). Central route persuasion relies on thinking. ***Peripheral route persuasion*** uses fear, love, guilt, envy, affiliation, authority, or other emotional appeals. Clothing brands featuring athletes and celebrities are sending peripheral-route messages to change attitudes about the product. Peripheral route persuasion relies on feeling.

> Psychologists and direct marketing companies have identified a number of strategies and techniques to change people's attitudes (for good or ill).
>
> - The *foot-in-the-door phenomenon* refers to our tendency to comply with a large request after first complying with a small one. For example, people are more likely to make a donation to a charity if they have first agreed to sign a petition in support of that charity.
> - The *door-in-the-face phenomenon* refers to our tendency to grant a small request after first refusing a large one. Teenagers who first make an unreasonable request (*"May I go with my friends to the Bahamas?"*) are more likely to get consent for a smaller subsequent request (*"May I go with my friend to the mall?"*).
> - The *norm of reciprocity* refers to our tendency to think that when we do something nice to someone, they should do something nice in return. Charities that send "free" return address labels hope that the norm of reciprocity will cause you to send a donation in return.

What are the characteristics of effective persuasion? Psychologists suggest that the most important factors in persuasion are the characteristics of the communicator. Someone who is credible, respected, believable, or an expert is generally more persuasive than someone who is not. The characteristics of the message; the logic, facts, and emotional power of the argument, and the circumstances are also important factors in persuasive messages. The powers of persuasion, however, are often used to manipulate other people. Cult leaders, false prophets, and charlatans use their persuasiveness to manipulate and control people. A Christian worldview sees persuasion in terms of "salt and light," not manipulation and control.

Interpersonal Attraction. Earlier you learned that an attitude is a positive or negative opinion toward someone or something. Social psychologists are interested in the factors that contribute to very positive attitudes, or attractions, toward other people. What is it that attracts us to some people but not to others? *Attraction* is defined as a powerful favorable attitude toward another person. Attraction theory refers to the ways we form attractions and the factors that affect attraction. The strongest factor influencing the chance that people will like one another is *physical proximity*. Although folk wisdom suggests that "absence makes the heart grow fonder," in another example of the mere-exposure effect, the more time we spend with someone; the more likely we are to like that person. Folk wisdom says that "opposites attract," but research suggests that *similarity* – the extent to which people are like us in terms of attitudes, values, personality, and physical qualities – is a most important factor in attraction. *Reciprocity* refers to the tendency to be attracted to people who are nice to us and who we believe are attracted to us. We tend to like those who like us and dislike those who dislike us. Another factor influencing attraction is *self-disclosure*. We tend to be more attracted to people about whom we have personal knowledge. Sharing personal information about yourself increases the likelihood that you will be found attractive by others, but good relationships require both parties to self-disclose.

Social Influences on Behavior. *Philip Zimbardo* (1933 -) is famous in the history of psychology for his 1971 study of social influences on behavior. In the *Stanford Prison Experiment*, Zimbardo set up a mock prison and selected 24 college students to play the roles of prisoners and guards. The students were randomly assigned to play the role of prisoner or prison guard. Prisoners stayed in the mock prison twenty-four hours a day and guards rotated eight-hour shifts. Zimbardo observed the guards and prisoners using hidden cameras and microphones. In the role of a prison guard, normal college students quickly began to interact with the prisoners in aggressive, brutal, sadistic, and dehumanizing ways. The prisoners, also normal students, became passive, withdrawn, and depressed. One prisoner had to be released after just 36 hours because of uncontrollable bursts of screaming, crying and anger. Over the next few days three other prisoners had to be released early after showing signs of serious depression and the guards' behavior became more demeaning. The experiment, scheduled to last fourteen days, had to be stopped after just six days.

Social Pressure. In an illustration of the power of social influence over attitudes on behavior, in Mark 14: 29 and 31, Peter expressed his strong positive attitude toward Jesus – assuring Him that he would never fall away. In Mark 14:66-72, under intense social pressure, Peter denied Jesus.

Zimbardo's experiment was one example of the many ways by which social psychologists examine the affects of social roles and social norms on behavior. *Social roles* refer to the different patterns of behavior appropriate to various social situations. Each social situation carries with it a set of expectations about the proper way to think, feel, and behave. Our thoughts, behaviors, and emotions change as we "play" the role of son, daughter, brother, sister, friend, student, teammate, or prison guard. The roles we are given and the roles we assume may be the result of our interests and abilities or by cultural, economic or biological conditions. Though you may never be a prison guard, Zimbardo's experiment demonstrated the power of social roles in influencing behavior. *Role conflict* refers to situations in which two or more roles make conflicting demands on behavior. For example, serving as a tutor for your best friend requires you to think and behave both as a teacher and a best friend – roles that may conflict.

Social norms refer to unwritten, but generally accepted rules of appropriate behavior in various social situations or contexts. Social norms can be very subtle, but they have a powerful influence on behavior. The social norms in the context of a prison (even a mock prison) are very different than the social norms in the context of a church service. Social norms not only differ from situation to situation – they differ from family to family, culture to culture, time period to time period, and worldview to worldview. Norms, as defined by biblical standards however, do not change. A Christian worldview recognizes that we tend to conform with social norms and that sometimes norms have a greater impact on our behavior than our beliefs and attitudes, but it acknowledges the biblical requirement that we not conform to the patterns, or social norms, of the world (i.e., Romans 12:2).

Social facilitation, another type of social influence, refers to the influence the presence of other people has on how well we perform various tasks. Do you work well when other people are watching, or does the presence of other people make it harder to do your work? Psychologists have shown that when other people are around, we are more aroused and perform better on simple or familiar tasks. On the other hand, when we are performing difficult or unfamiliar tasks, we tend to perform more poorly in the presence of others. This phenomenon is known as *social impairment* and it should serve as a reminder that we should learn tasks especially well if we are going to perform them in the presence of others.

Roles, norms, and context create social pressure. *Social pressure*, explicit or implicit, can be a powerful influence on behavior, and left unchecked, can lead to prejudice, discrimination, blind obedience, and violence.

Conformity. Social psychologists describe the factors that influence our tendency to adapt our thoughts, emotions, and behaviors of other members of a group; to conform. **Conformity** refers to perceived pressure to change one's thoughts, feelings, or behavior to match those of the group. We have a tendency to feel anxiety when we stand out from other people and we feel strong pressure to conform and fit in. The pressure to conform is commonly known as **peer pressure**. If you ever complained to your parents that "everyone else is doing it," you were experiencing social pressure to conform. Though a Christian worldview understands that God does not want us to conform to this world, the pressure to conform is very strong – on Christians and non-Christians alike.

The **Asch conformity experiment** is famous in the history of psychology for its demonstration of the power of social pressure to conform. Social psychologist **Solomon Asch** (1907 – 1996) asked under what conditions would people, when faced with a strong group consensus, go along with the group even if they think the others are wrong?

Asch's experiment involved one test subject and a number of confederates. **Confederates** are actors playing roles in an experiment, unbeknownst to the "real" experimental subject. In the Asch's experiment, the test subjects were asked to judge the length of lines, when presented with lines of different lengths, after hearing the confederates give answers that were clearly wrong. Only 29% of the subjects resisted the pressure to conform and refused to join with the majority judgment. In other words, 71% of the subjects gave answers they knew to be wrong in order to conform with the group. Asch found that it was unlikely for subjects to resist conforming when the rest of the group was unanimous in its opinion. If one other confederate disagreed with the group, however, it was much easier for subjects to not conform. The tendency to conform is powerful. Christian students are well-advised to keep that in mind and constantly ask, *"am I conforming to the group or conforming to Christ?"*

Obedience. Stanley Milgram (1933 - 1984) is famous in the history of psychology for his research on obedience to authority. Obedience refers to changing one's behavior in response to a directive from an authority figure. In his famous experiment, a person in a position of authority ordered subjects to deliver progressively more intense, ultimately potentially fatal, electric shocks to another person. What the subject didn't know was that the shocks were not real.

Milgram built a bogus shock generator with a series of switches labeled from 30 volts to 450 volts. The last three switches were marked "XXX." The study participant served as the "teacher" and a confederate played the role of "student." The teacher was instructed to deliver progressively stronger shocks to the "student" for each incorrect answer. Milgram took elaborate steps to make the teacher believe that he was delivering real shocks to the student. As the experiment progressed, the teacher heard the student complain about the pain, demand to be released, and eventually fall silent. When the teachers questioned whether to continue the shocks, the "authority" issued a series of four commands.

- *"Please continue."*
- *"The experiment requires that you continue."*
- *"It is absolutely essential that you continue."*
- *"You have no other choice; you must go on."*

Sixty-five percent of the participants in Milgram's study continued and delivered the maximum shock. Why?

In the almost 40 years since Milgram's study, psychologists have struggled to reconcile the results with their worldview. The results, like real-life examples of evil and human atrocities (i.e., Nazi Germany's extermination of Jews), do not fit well with evolutionary and humanistic worldviews. Modern psychology can describe evil behavior, but it cannot make sense of it. A humanistic worldview would suggest that because Mankind is inherently "good," people should not inflict lethal shocks on other people. A Christian worldview, balancing free-will, obedience to authority, and moral absolutes, provides the best context for explaining why people do evil things. "Good" and "evil" are very difficult concepts for naturalistic modern psychologists to explain. Interestingly, one of Milgram's subjects was a professor of Old Testament theology. This subject disobeyed authority and stopped giving the victim shocks shortly after the first protest. The professor explained his actions saying, "***If one had as one's ultimate authority, God, then it trivializes human authority***."

Milgram identified several factors that affect subjects' willingness to deliver painful shocks. Teachers were less likely to obey if they were in the same room with the student. They were even less likely to obey if they had physical contact with the student – directly, not remotely, administering the shock. The physical qualities of the "authority figure" played a factor. Professorial-looking authorities dressed in white lab coats were obeyed more readily than regular-looking, plainly dressed authorities. Obedience rates were lower when two "teachers" were present and when two authority figures appeared to disagree whether the shocks should continue.

Altruism (Helping Behavior). In 1964, 28-year-old ***Kitty Genovese*** was returning home from work late one night when she was attacked in front of her apartment building. Miss Genovese ran screaming for help. Many apartment residents, at least 38 people, heard her screams. One resident shouted "leave that girl alone," but no one called the police. The attacker fled only to return minutes later to continue his assault and ultimately to kill Miss Genovese. No one called the police until it was too late. Police received the first call 30 minutes after the attack began, from a caller who said that he did not want to "get involved."

The ***bystander effect***, also called the ***Genovese syndrome***, suggests that an individual's likelihood of helping someone in need is related to the number of other people present at the time. Why didn't Kitty Genovese's neighbors call for help? Why didn't the seminary students in the Good Samaritan experiment offer to help a man in need? Why do fire fighters, police officers, soldiers, and civilian heroes risk their lives for others? Social psychologists seek answers to these kinds of questions.

Psychologists suggest that we are less likely to engage in helping behavior if there is diffusion of responsibility. ***Diffusion of responsibility*** refers to the spreading of responsibility for a task across all members of the group. With responsibility spread across a group, individual members perceive less personal accountability. The larger the group the more responsibility gets diffused across group members. Diffusion of responsibility, in the extreme, can lead to ***de-individualization*** – a loss of one's individual self-awareness, self-restraint, and moral values when in group situations that foster anonymity.

From a naturalistic evolutionary perspective, not engaging in helping behavior makes sense. Why would I risk my DNA to save your DNA? A naturalistic worldview struggles, however to explain why we do engage in altruistic behavior. For example, Darley and Batson suggested that thinking about moral imperatives influenced helping behavior. That explanation is meaningless from an evolutionary perspective. Christians may explain our social behavior in terms of moral imperatives, but from an evolutionary perspective, helping behavior is just another adaptive behavior. From a morality-free evolutionary perspective, it makes no sense for us to help other people. From an evolutionary perspective, it seems ludicrous that anyone to ever willingly suffer harm or even die to help another person. The kin selection theory is evolutionary psychology's leading theory of to explain the "problem" of altruism. The ***kin selection theory of altruism*** suggests that from an evolutionary standpoint, helping behavior is determined by the extent to which one perceives a genetic similarity between oneself and the person in need of help. You are more likely to help someone if they share your genetic material. You may give up your life for someone else's if the genetic calculations are favorable. If survival of your genetic code is what is really important, it might make more genetic sense for you to give up your life to save the lives of two brothers and a first cousin than to live yourself. In order to explain altruism, evolutionists must give genes the capacity to cause us to act based on a cold-blooded calculation that from the standpoint of the genes, there really is no hard and fast difference between us and our kin.

Social Influences of Groups. Social psychologists are interested in understanding the thoughts, feelings, and behaviors of people in group settings or ***group dynamics.*** How do groups form, how do groups relate with other groups, and what factors influence group membership, identification, leadership, cooperation, and conflict? A group is any gathering of people in some sort of relationship. Without some relationship, a group is just a gathering of people. Groups can be for *socialization* or *education*, like support groups and Bible study groups, or for the purpose of *completing some task*, like a party planning committee. Generally, groups are characterized by the *purpose* of the group, its *roles* and its *norms*, and its *cohesiveness*. *Primary groups* are close and personal, like family and close church groups. In *secondary group* relationships there is a sense of purpose, but not strong emotional attachment with the members (i.e., sports teams, working groups, and committees).

Secondary, or task-oriented groups, generally progress through four predictable stages:

- When the group is new, known as the *forming stage*, group members are polite and focused on being accepted in the group. Members generally do not voice strong opinions during the forming stage.
- During the *storming stage* the group begins its work in earnest. During this stage the group establishes its goals, members express opinions, group leaders come forward, and there is often competition and conflict.
- During the *performing stage* the group members are focused on and working toward the agreed-on goals.
- During the *adjourning stage*, with the goals accomplished (or not), the group disbands and the members go their separate ways.

Group Roles and Norms. There is a social pressure that groups exert on its members to follow the group's rules of behavior and the roles that its members fill. *Group cohesion* refers to the strength of the relationships between group members, agreement about group goals, and adherence to group norms. A characteristic of excessive group cohesiveness is known as Groupthink. *Groupthink* refers to a group decision-making process in which the group norms of harmony and cohesion actually override a realistic view of the alternatives. In groupthink, reaching a consensus trumps careful consideration of differing perspective. Groups suffering from groupthink are over confident, they rationalize away or avoid alternative perspectives, and they may pressure members to conform to the majority or leadership position. Groups that are isolated, groups with strong directive leaders, groups comprised of members with homogenous backgrounds, and groups under stress are at risk for groupthink. In these groups, members must find a way to establish new norms of creativity and openness to differing perspectives.

Group Decision-making. Western cultures generally value group decision-making over individual decisions. Groups benefit from the collective memories and experiences of its members. Groups also generally recognize incorrect solutions to problems more quickly, but groups do not always function effectively or efficiently. *Group polarization* refers to a tendency of groups to drift toward and strengthen extreme positions – positions very different than group members would have taken individually.

This chapter began by drawing a distinction between how people actually behave in social situations and the biblical mandates about how we should live in social situations. Social psychology provides a type of warning for Christians – a type of "heads up" about and a confirmation of the biblical description of fallen Mankind. Social psychology also provides an opportunity for Christian psychologists to demonstrate and illustrate the biblical anthropology of the redeemed – that God changes hearts, He changes patterns of responses in social interactions, and He replaces social determinism with with Spirit-filled living.

Chapter Summary.

Social psychologists are interested in psychological concepts as they relate to the interactions between individuals and small groups. Social psychology is the study of how people think about, influence, and relate to one another. Social psychologists study social cognition, the ways that thoughts, feelings, behaviors, perceptions, decisions, motivation, and personality are influenced by the presence of others and by different situations.

Interpersonal communication is a complex psychological process that takes place between two or more people. The Shannon-Weaver model of communication is a basic visual representation of interpersonal communication. Communication takes place between a source and a receiver. The message is sent via a communication channel. Channels are the media through which messages pass. Communications must be encoded and decoded. The process of converting ideas into a form suitable for the channel is called encoding. The receiver decodes and interprets the message and provides feedback to the sender. All interpersonal communication takes place in a social context (environment), and for a purpose. Communication can be verbal or non-verbal and can be intentional or unintentional. Proxemics is the study of personal space in interpersonal communication.

Social influence refers to the effect the presence of other people has on the ways we think, feel, and behave. Social comparison refers to the tendency to compare oneself to others. Social facilitation refers to the influence the presence of other people has on how well we perform tasks. Social role-playing refers to patterns of behavior appropriate to various social situations. Role conflict refers to situations in which two or more roles make conflicting demands on behavior. Social norms refer to generally accepted rules of appropriate behavior in various social situations or contexts. Roles, norms, and context create social pressure. The norm of reciprocity refers to the tendency of people to respond to each other in kind. Social perception refers to the ways we organize, interpret, and give meaning to social experiences.

Attribution theory is about meaning. It describes the factors that influence the meaning we give to why other people do what they do, and our explanations for why we do the things that we do. Attributions are the quick mental explanations we form to explain the thoughts, feelings, or actions of ourselves and others.

Internal attribution refers to the inference that a person is behaving in a certain way because of something about the person – such as attitude, disposition, or personality. External attribution refers to the inference that a person is behaving a certain way because of something about the situation and circumstances the person is in. An attribution error is an incorrect or distorted understanding of what happens around us. The actor-observer bias refers to a predisposition to attribute our own behavior to external forces, but to attribute the behavior of others to their internal characteristics. The self-serving bias refers to the tendency to make favorable attributions for one's own behavior. The fundamental attribution error refers to the tendency to overestimate internal dispositional influences and underestimate external situational influences upon others' behavior.

An attitude is a pre-disposition, positive or negative, toward someone or some thing. Most psychologists believe that attitudes are largely learned. The mere-exposure effect describes our tendency to have a positive attitude toward familiar things. Cognitive dissonance is the discomfort caused by inconsistencies between attitudes and behavior. Persuasion is a process through which attitudes are changed. Persuasive messages can be categorized as emotional or rational-logical.

Attraction is a powerful favorable attitude toward another person. Attraction theory refers to the ways we form attractions and the factors that affect attraction. The strongest factor influencing the chance that people will like one another is physical proximity. Another factor influencing attraction is similarity – the extent to which people are like us in terms of attitudes, values, personality, and physical qualities. Reciprocity refers to the tendency to be attracted to people who are nice to us.

Social psychologists are also interested in people in group settings. A group is any gathering of people in some sort of relationship. Groups are characterized by their the purpose, roles and norms, and cohesiveness. Groups generally progress through four stages called forming, storming, performing, and adjourning. Western cultures are said to value group decision-making over individual decisions. Social loafing refers to the tendency of some people in groups to exert less effort when working in a group. Diffusion of responsibility refers to a diluting of individuals' feeling of responsibility when a task is assigned to a group and not to the individual. Diffusion of responsibility can lead to de-individualization. Groupthink is an ineffective decision-making process in which group harmony overrides a realistic view of the alternatives. Group polarization refers to a tendency of groups to drift toward and strengthening of more extreme positions. Conformity refers to perceived pressure to change one's thoughts, feelings, or behavior to match those of the group.

Solomon Asch is famous in the history of social psychology for his research on conformity. Stanley Milgram is famous in the history of psychology for his research on obedience to authority. The principles behind schema, attitudes, attribution, attraction, conformity, and group dynamics come together in understanding and explaining stereotypes, prejudice, and discrimination.

Stereotypes are the attitudes and beliefs one has about a group of people. Prejudice is a attitude, positive or negative, about an individual based on their membership in a group. When one's behavior is affected by prejudice the result is discrimination – treating someone differently because of their membership in a group. In-group bias refers to the tendency to have positive attitudes and give preferential treatment to people in the group to which we belong. Out-group bias refers to the tendency have negative attitudes toward people from other groups. The ultimate attribution error describes the tendency to interpret the negative behavior of a group member in terms of negative characteristics of the entire group. Muzafer Sherif's Robbers Cave study is famous in the history of psychology for its contributions to understanding in-group/out-group bias, prejudice, group conflict and discrimination.

For Review.

1. Describe interpersonal communication.
2. Describe the Shannon-Weaver model of communication.
3. Describe feedback, non-verbal communication, and proxemics.
4. Describe the characteristics of good listeners.
5. Describe social influence, social comparison, and social norms.
6. Describe attitudes, attitude formation, and attitude change.
7. Describe interpersonal attraction.
8. Describe group dynamics, group roles, and group norms, and group decision-making.
9. Describe groupthink.
10. Describe the Stanford Prison experiment.
11. Describe the Asch conformity study.
12. Describe Milgram's obedience study.
13. Describe Sherif's Robbers Cave study.
14. Describe conformity and obedience.
15. Discuss stereotypes, prejudice, and discrimination.

Chapter 15

Research Methods

In This Chapter

The Christian worldview and true science cannot ultimately conflict – there is no inherent faith/science dichotomy. Science developed in the context of worldview beliefs about God's orderliness and Man's dominion. Modern science, properly understood, is consistent with a Christian worldview.

You learned earlier that many of the founders of modern psychology wanted it to be a "hard" science like physics and chemistry, so they adopted controlled empirical, or scientific methods for their research and limited their study to the "physics" of mental life. Many of psychology's important interests (e.g., emotions, personality, and cognitions) were thought to be outside of the realm of scientific study because they could not be observed directly, measured, or controlled. How to you measure a thought? How do you quantify emotions? A common criticism, therefore, of early modern psychology was that it was sterile and meaningless.

Today there is little about the mind that has not been subject to some kind of "scientific" investigation. Controlled empirical investigation is, however, still better-suited to disciplines like chemistry and physics than psychology, sociology, and anthropology. Also, some of psychology's subfields (e.g., neuro-psychology and sensory psychology) are better-suited to controlled empirical investigation than others (e.g., personality and consciousness). A common criticism of psychology today is that it is not a "real" science – that modern psychologists' methods are not "scientific" methods.

Students should understand the limits of science and should be able to distinguish quality research from "junk" science. Often psychologists

A *confounding variable* is any factor that corrupts or distorts research results. Unlike variables scientists control or measure on purpose, these are variable to be avoided. We will discuss several types of confounding variable throughout this chapter.

make grand claims about psychological discoveries based on very flimsy or scant research. It is very difficult, especially in psychology research, to faithfully apply scientific methods. Research psychologists must be very careful, perhaps impossibly careful, to prevent bias and other confounding variables from influencing their research. As consumers of research, we must be very careful to critically evaluate psychologists' methods and their research conclusions.

Often, under the banner of "science," psychologists promote philosophies and worldview positions. A Christian worldview recognizes that some things (e.g., values, morality, and God) are outside the realm of scientific study. Modern psychology's dominant worldview, *empiricism* (also called *logical positivism*), in its extreme, is a belief that the empirical method is the only valid source for any knowledge, including psychological knowledge. From this perspective, the only "things" we can know are "things" that can be observed with one of the senses. As you learned earlier, empiricism is part of a naturalistic worldview. Naturalism excludes the possibility of the supernatural. Ultimately, with better technology, everything about being human can be measured, observed directly, and subjected to empirical study. A Christian worldview recognizes the importance of empirical research, but it rejects that science is the only way of knowing. Christians should not shy away from the scientific study of Mankind, but we should insist that the limits of science be respected.

Research methods refer to the *design*, *execution*, and *evaluation* of psychological research and psychological tests. How do we evaluate the quality of psychological research methods and conclusions? What conclusions can we draw from a study finding that 90% of seminary students in a big hurry did not stop to aid a person in distress? Can we *generalize*, or extend the conclusion to other groups; would non-seminary students, Buddhists, or atheists in a hurry be more or less likely to be helpful? What does it mean when a toothpaste company makes a claim like *"9 out of 10 dentists agree, Aqua Clean toothpaste is best at cleaning stubborn plaque?"* Can we trust claims like that?

The Empirical Method. We learned in Chapter 1 that one of the main purposes for psychological research is to formulate and test hypotheses in a systematic and standard way. Though there is no "official" empirical method, the term refers to systematic and standard ways of defining research questions, forming and testing hypotheses, analyzing and interpreting data, drawing conclusions, and publishing the results. The scientific method prescribes a basic process, or cycle, despite the particulars of the specific research question(s) at hand.

The Empirical Method

- Define the Question.
- Form a Hypothesis.
- Test the Hypothesis.
- Analyze and Interpret Data.
- Draw Conclusion.
- Publish Results.

Define The Question. Psychological research begins with questions. Some are applied research questions and some are basic research questions. **Applied research** is designed to solve a particular problem. **Basic research** seeks to expand our knowledge and understanding for its own sake. Basic psychological research asks basic questions like *"how do neurons communicate?"* or *"how do people form attitudes?"* B. F. Skinner's operant conditioning experiments represent basic research into how animals learn. Developing behavior management techniques, based on Skinner's research, to manage student behavior in the classroom is an example of applied research. Applied research seeks solutions to problems like *"how can we help people quit smoking?"* or *"what are the best methods for teaching science?"*

Hypothesis. An hypothesis is a restatement of the research question in a way that can be tested. The hypothesis suggests that one variable causes or is related to some other variable. An hypothesis is a testable prediction about a relationship between things. Some examples are:

- Students thinking about the Good Samaritan are more likely to help a person in distress.
- Students who receive a Christian education achieve higher SAT scores.
- Children who play violent computer games behave more violently.

A hypothesis must be stated in a way that makes it possible to find it false; it must be **falsifiable**. Hypotheses can be relational or causal. A **relational hypothesis** predicts that two variable are related. The hypothesis that students thinking about the Good Samaritan are more likely to help a person in distress is a relational hypothesis. A **causal hypothesis** predicts that one variable causes or leads to the other. The hypothesis that children who play violent computer games will behave more violently is a causal hypothesis.

Every aspect of a good psychology experiment should be standardized. **Standardization** is the process of assuring that experimental procedures and measurements are precisely defined and carefully controlled. Standardization minimizes the effects of that confounding variable. Standardization is a challenge in experiments in every science, but it is particularly difficult for psychologists. The problem of standardization is even greater when psychologists study subjective mental processes like emotions, attitudes, personality, and consciousness — concepts that are difficult to define, much less standardize. **Operationalizing** refers to precisely defining key

Examples of Research Questions

- Is there a relationship between being in a hurry and exhibiting "helping behavior?"
- Is there a relationship between Christian education and high SAT scores?
- Is there a relationship between playing violent computer games and exhibiting violent behavior?

concepts, processes, and measurements. A good experiment, in psychology and elsewhere, is **operationalized**, or described in such detail that subsequent researchers can replicate the experiment in every meaningful way to confirm its findings. Good experiments are **replicable**.

Variables. All research seeks to determine the relationship between variables. A variable is any event, condition, or behavior that researchers can measure. Gender can be measured as male or female. Age, test scores, time, intelligence, experience, education, grades, skills, and attitudes can all be measured.

Independent and Dependent Variables. In experiments there are three types of variables: independent variables, dependent variables, and everything else, or the confounding variables. In the Good Samaritan experiment the researchers manipulated certain variables or conditions and measured other variables. Some students were manipulated into thinking about helping

---

Psychologists measure four types of variables.

- **Nominal variables** classify data according to category. Nominal variable differ qualitatively but not quantitatively. Gender, hair color, race, and religion are nominal variable.
- **Ordinal variables** can be classified quantitatively in rankings. With ordinal data we can know who finished the race 1st, 2nd, and 3rd, but we do not know the time difference between 1st place and 3rd place.
- **Interval variables** can be ranked in order, and the difference between intervals is known and fixed. For example, temperature is an interval measurement. The difference between 70° and 80° is equal to the difference between 20° and 10°. Interval measurements can be added or subtracted but not multiplied or divided. We can say that 70° is 10° cooler than 80°, but we cannot say that 20° is twice as warm as 10°.
- **Ratio variables**, like rational numbers, can be counted, and it is meaningful to say that there is an absolute zero level of the variable. Ratio measures can be ranked in order, the intervals are known and fixed, the measurements can be added or subtracted, and multiplication and division make sense. For example, we can count bullying behaviors before and after an experimental treatment and know in which condition there was more bullying, how much more, and the ratio between the two conditions.

---

people in distress and others into thinking about seminary jobs. The variable that the researcher manipulates is called the **independent variable**. The students' thought content (thinking about helping versus not thinking about helping) is the independent variable. The researcher also manipulated the students' level of hurriedness (low, moderate, or high hurriedness). Hurriedness is also an independent variable. Independent variables are also known as experimental treatments. The independent variable is the cause in cause-and-effect relationships.

The **dependent variable** is the "effect" in cause-and-effect relationships — it is the result of the experimental treatment. Does helping behavior (the dependent variable) depend on hurriedness (an independent variable)? Does helping behavior (the dependent variable) depend on thinking about helping (an independent variable)? The dependent variable is what the researcher measures; it is the answer to the research question.

In the hypothesis that students who receive a Christian education achieve higher SAT scores, the method of education is the independent variable. SAT score is the dependent variable. In the example of the hypothesis that

---

children who play violent computer games will behave more violently, the amount of violent play time is the independent variable. Violent behavior is the dependent variable.

Reliability and Validity. Remember that variables are anything that we can measure. Some variables, like eye color, gender, and age, can be measured very accurately. Other variables are much more difficult to measure (e.g., attitudes, personalities, aptitudes). If the measurements are not reliable and valid, the research conclusions are not valuable. ***Reliability*** refers to the extent to which a measurement tool gives the same result when administered to the same people at different times. ***Validity*** refers to the extent to which the measurement measures what it is supposed to measure. The SAT is a valid test of scholastic achievement. The SAT test is also a pretty reliable measure too. Test results vary little in retests. A bathroom scale in not a valid measure of scholastic achievement. A bathroom scale provides a very valid measure of weight, however. A bathroom scale that says you weigh 125 lbs. one day and 250 lbs. the next is not reliable. Good research has variables that are both reliable and valid.

Representative Sample. Consider the hypothesis that students who receive a Christian education achieve higher SAT scores. Ideally, researchers would compare the SAT score of *every* student in Christian education to the score of *every* student not in Christian education. Because psychologists rarely have access to an entire population, they select representative samples from the entire population. A ***representative sample*** is a relatively small group of participants selected from the population of all possible participants. If the representative sample closely matches the characteristics of the population as a whole, the research results can be generalized to the population. An experiment has ***sample bias*** if the sample is not representative of the larger population for some characteristic.

Experimental and Control Groups. Pharmaceutical companies conduct hundreds of research studies called drug trials each year examining the effectiveness of psychiatric medications. In drug trials subjects are divided into two groups. One group receives the experimental treatment (the new medication), and the other does not. The ***experimental group*** receives the experimental treatment, and the ***control group*** does not.

Confounding Variables. Psychologists take careful precautions to control for confounding variable. Confounding means "mixed up" or confused. A confounding variable, also called an ***extraneous variable***, is any influence on the dependent variable other than the independent variable. Did some variable other than hurriedness or thought content influence the helping behavior of seminary students? Are there variables other than Christian education that influence SAT scores, and are there other factors in violent behavior besides

Extraneous Variables – The Hawthorne Effect. An extraneous variable is a variable that is not being studied but that influences the outcome of an experiment. Between 1927 and 1932 researchers at the Western Electric Company's Hawthorne Plant tried to discover the relationship of working conditions to worker productivity. The researchers manipulated the lighting, humidity, work hours, break schedules, and a number of other factors in hopes of discovering which factors were associated with higher worker productivity. They were surprised to find that worker productivity improved with every change in the environment. In fact, the change in worker productivity was associated with the presence of the researchers and not with the specific environmental changes the researchers made. Workers worked faster when they were being watched. The researchers' presence was an extraneous variable.

computer games? If so, those are confounding variable that jeopardize the integrity of the research conclusions.

Random Selection and Random Assignment. The single most important control psychologists take in designing experiments is randomization. True ***random selection*** means that every member of a population has the exact same chance of being selected to be part of the study sample as every other member. ***Random assignment*** means that each member of the sample has the same chance of being placed in the experimental as the control group. Random assignment helps assure that the control and experimental groups are equal in every way possible. Random assignment helps control for bias by spreading any differences that subjects "bring with them" evenly between groups. If groups are equal before an experimental treatment, any differences between groups after the treatment may be caused by or correlated with the treatment.

Subject Bias. Psychological experiments are by necessity somewhat artificial. Subject bias occurs when subjects know what the experiment is about. People behave differently when they know they are being studied in an experiment. Subjects' knowledge, beliefs, and expectations about the experiment influence the outcome. Psychologists design experiments to control for subject bias. In a ***single-blind*** design, the subjects do not know the true purpose of the experiment or whether they are in the experimental or the control group. It may seem surprising, but the experimenter's knowledge, beliefs, and expectations about the experiment can also subtly and unintentionally influence the research results. ***Experimenter bias*** describes anything the experimenter does that influences the results. To control for experimenter bias, researchers create a ***double-blind*** procedure in which neither the experimenter nor the subject knows which subjects receive the treatment and which do not.

The placebo effect is a one example of subject bias. In drug trials both groups take pills. The experimental group's pills contain the active ingredient. The control group's pills are chemically inert placebos with no active ingredients. (sugar pills). Placebos are not, however, psychologically inert. The placebo effect is real and measurable. The active ingredient in the medication is effective only to the extent that its effect exceeds that of the placebo. The placebo effect has come to describe the mental process by which believing or expecting that something is going to happen tends to make it happen.

Research Designs. In order to study the wide variety of human thoughts, emotions, and behaviors, psychologists employ a number of techniques, or research designs. The dozens and dozens of research designs psychologists use are generally divided in two categories: qualitative designs and quantitative or experimental designs. ***Qualitative research*** is descriptive; it describes the qualities and characteristics of psychological phenomena. ***Quantitative research*** seeks to discover cause-and-effect relationships and to measure the strength of relationships among psychological variables.

Qualitative research is a generic term for a number of non-experimental research techniques. Qualitative research observes and describes phenomena in the context of the "real world" or natural circumstances. Qualitative research lacks careful controls, random assignment, control groups, and/ or researcher-manipulated variables; it cannot determine establish cause-and-effect relationships. Instead it focuses on psychological phenomena in their "real-life" complexity and context. Qualitative research is descriptive, not experimental; it generates new questions, not answers; and it creates a narrative of information about a topic. Because of the subjective quality of qualitative research, it is viewed as an inferior source of knowledge by strict empirical psychologists. But in many ways, qualitative research is better-suited for psychological research than is quantitative research.

Observation designs encompass a number of qualitative research designs for learning about human behavior by watching human behavior. ***Naturalistic observation*** is observational research conducted in natural settings. A psychologist might observe and record teenage behavior at school, at church, or while hanging out with friends. Naturalistic observation tries to minimizing the observer's impact by observing or recording from a hidden vantage point. ***Ethnologies*** are naturalist observations of entire cultures. In ***clinical observation***, psychologists interact with people in laboratories and offices and record their observations about those interactions. Psychiatric and mental health evaluations are types of clinical observations.

Case studies are a type of observation in which psychologists study a single subject, program, or event in depth to provide a detailed analysis of the "case." Case studies are phenomenological, meaning they provide psychologists with knowledge and understanding about a particular situation or event from one's personal perspective. A number of case studies describe the impact of the terrorist attacks of September 11, 2001.

Other types of observational research includes ***standardized tests*** (e.g., the SAT), ***personality inventories*** (e.g., the Myers-Briggs Personality Type Indicator), and ***aptitude tests*** (e.g., the U.S. Military's Armed Services Vocational Aptitude Battery – ASVAB).

The ASVAB is a timed multi-aptitude test, developed by the Department of Defense and used to determine qualifications to enlist in the military.

Surveys and *polls* are types of observational research used to gather data about attitudes and opinions. Surveys and polls allow researchers to gather data from large numbers of subjects. A survey can be about anything. A poll usually asks for opinions or value judgments. While case studies provide in-depth information about a single subject, surveys provide minimal information about many subjects.

Quantitative Research Designs. The goal of experimental or quantitative research is to systematically identify cause-and-effect relationships. In simple quantitative research designs, a single independent variable is manipulated and a single dependent variable is measured. The ideal quantitative design involves two groups of subjects that are equal in every relevant characteristic. Both groups are measured on some variable. One group receives the experimental treatment and the other does not. Both groups are measured again on the same variable. Results from the two groups are statistically analyzed to determine if the observed difference between the groups is significant – if it was unlikely to have occurred by chance. If the dependent variable changes in the experimental treatment but not in the control group, we can conclude, all other things being equal, that the treatment caused that change. The challenge of quantitative research is in assuring that all other things are truly equal.

Quasi-experimental Design. Unlike experimental designs which randomly assigns subjects and carefully controls for extraneous variables, quasi-experimental designs lack some or many of those characteristics. Quasi-experimental designs may lack random assignment, the participants may not be "blind," a control group may not be possible, or other controls may be missing. For example, a psychologist interested in the affect of poverty on school performance cannot ethically or feasibly randomly assign children to poverty. Because quasi-experimental design lack important controls, they are subject to numerous interpretation difficulties.

Interpreting Research Results. *Statistics* help psychologists describe, organize, summarize, interpret, and draw inferences from research data. Statistics are tools to help understand data. *Descriptive statistics* organize, describe, and summarize data. Psychologists use *inferential statistics* to interpret and draw inferences from the research data. Statistical analyses can provide evidence that measurements were valid and reliable and that the effect of the experimental treatment was statistically significant and not likely to have occurred by chance. Statistics cannot, however, prove anything.

Correlation. Human thoughts, emotions, and behaviors are incredibly complex. It is not always reasonable to expect to identify direct cause-and-effect relationships between psychological variables. The human mind consists of a great number of variables existing in complex interdependent

Psychologists have reported a positive correlation between Christian beliefs and practices and:

- Hope and optimism.
- Better coping with loss.
- Less depression and fewer suicides.
- Greater marital satisfaction and stability.

relationships. The interdependent relationships between variables are called correlations (think "co-relations"). Not being in a hurry and thinking about the Good Samaritan are correlated with helping behavior, but does may not cause it. Correlations are things that occur together. Correlations make it possible to use the value of one variable to predict the value of another. For example, we could now predict that a student in a hurry to deliver a talk on seminary jobs will probably not stop to help someone along the way.

Psychologists measure the strength of correlation on a scale from negative one (-1) to positive one (+1) using a *correlation coefficient*. Correlation coefficients close to -1 or +1 both indicate strong relationships between variables. A correlation coefficient of zero indicates no relationship between the variables. A positive coefficient means that as one variable increases, so does the other. A negative correlation reflect and inverse relationship between variable.

- There is a strong positive correlation between high education level and high lifetime income (so go to college!)
- There is a strong negative correlation between high levels of absenteeism in school and good grades (so go to class!)
- There is no correlation between shoe size and income or good grades (so wear whatever size shoes you want!)

Descriptive Statistics. Psychologists use descriptive statistics to describe how members of a sample are similar and how they differ according to some variable. Measures of *central tendency* include the mean, median, and mode.

- The *mean* is the arithmetic average.
- The *median* is the measurement in the exact middle of an ordered range of measures.
- The *mode* is the value that occurs most often. A population set can have more than one mode.

Measures of variability or dispersion examine how a variable is distributed and how it varies in a sample or population. The *range* describes the difference

Eight psychologists took a psychological test.

Sigmund scored 100.	Wilhelm scored 80.
Carl scored 85.	B. F. scored 83.
Ivan scored 87.	Stanly scored 90.
John scored 85.	Albert scored 30.

Mean = 80
Median = 85
Mode = 85

between the lowest and highest values. In our sample psychological test results, the range is 70, the difference between Sigmund's score (100) and Albert's score (30). The size of the range tells whether scores are are close together

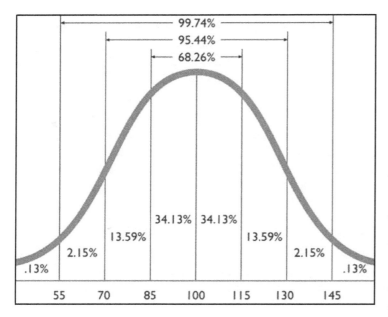

or spread out. Comparing individual measurements to the mean produces a measure of **variance**. Wilhem's score (80) does not vary from the mean (80). Albert's score (30) varies from the mean by 50 units. In fact, this score is so far from the mean, psychologists call Albert's score an **outlier**.

The **standard deviation** is a statistical tool psychologists use to describe the **total variation** in a set of measures. The standard deviation is an indication of how the measures are spread out from the mean. If all the measures are the same, the standard deviation would be zero. If measures vary greatly, the standard deviation will be greater.

Many psychological characteristics are thought to be normally distributed. A **normal distribution** is often shown graphically by a normal or bell curve. If we could measure the entire population according to some normally distributed variable (e.g., height), we would expect that the mean (average height), median (middle point in the range of heights), and mode (most frequently occurring height) would all be the same. We would expect to find equal numbers above the mean (tall people) and below the mean (short people). We would expect to find few people who varied greatly above or below the mean (really tall or really short people).

Inferential Statistics. Psychologists use inferential statistics to make generalizations and draw conclusions about a population based on data obtained from samples. A major concern of inferential statistics is determining the likelihood that the results occurred by chance. Psychologists calculate the **statistical significance**, or the **confidence level**, that the results did not occur by chance. Psychologists also use inferential statistics to determine if the difference between control and experimental groups is due to the experimental treatment or to chance.

Historical Examples of Unethical Research

- In 1961, Stanley Milgram tested the limits of human obedience and willingness to inflict pain on another person.
- In 1920, John Watson conditioned a nine-month-old baby, Little Albert, to fear furry animals.
- In 1924, Carney Landis was interested in discovering whether specific emotions produced unique and universal facial expressions. In order to observe the facial expressions associated with disgust, Landis asked subjects to decapitate a live rat. Landis filmed the subjects' facial expressions while they, sometimes clumsily, followed his instructions. For the one-third of the subjects that refused to decapitate the rat, Landis did it for them, while recording their reactions.

Ethics in Research with Humans and Animals. Psychology's history contains many examples of experiments that were harmful to its subjects. Today psychologists conducting research using humans or animals must follow ethical standards established by the American Psychological Association (APA). The APA provides ethical guidelines and a code of conduct for psychologists in clinical and research practice. Colleges and universities conducting psychological research must have an ***Institutional Review Board*** (IRB) to review and approve all research proposals in advance.

The APA prohibits coercion and placing human subjects at risk of physical or psychological harm. Human subjects must voluntarily consent and must be informed of any risks associated with participating in the study. The APA permits deceiving subjects if it is justified by the research's scientific value and if non-deceptive alternatives are not feasible. Research participants must be debriefed and provided with ways to contact the researchers about the results. The APA requires that animals used in research be treated humanely, with minimal discomfort and pain.

The Limits of Psychology. Worldviews define the limits of scientific psychology. Through much of history, there was no scientific psychology, so psychology was pretty limited. Early modern psychologists limited their research to the physics of mental life, believing that the "higher" mental experiences (e.g., morality, faith, aesthetics, and consciousness) were non-material and beyond the limits of scientific psychology. Later, as a naturalistic worldview developed in psychology, psychologists came to believe that all mental experiences were material and all mental life was reducible, quantifiable, and subject to scientific investigation. Today, using non-scientific and quasi-scientific techniques, nothing is outside of psychology's limits. Naturalistic psychology is limited only by naturalism – if a phenomenon is not natural, like Mankind's soul, it is outside of psychology's limits, because it not considered to exist.

To support "scientific" research in evolutionary psychology, the limits and methods of psychology are changing again. Scientific methods in evolutionary psychology are very different than the methods described earlier in this chapter. The scientific method, from an evolutionary worldview perspective, includes:

- Identifying the environmental conditions faced by early humans – *"what was life on earth like a million years or so ago?"*
- Identifying the adaptive problem presented by the environmental conditions faced by early humans – *"what things on earth were dangerous a million or so years ago?"*
- Identifying the psychological characteristics that would have solved the adaptive problems presented by the environmental conditions faced by early humans – *"what psychological characteristics do humans have today that would have helped humans survive a million or so years ago?"*

Worldview Check. In college you will be taught that science has proven, shown, or indicated many things about human psychology. From a traditional and historical understanding of what constitutes "science," many of those claims are exaggerated at best, and spurious at worst.

The study of psychology is about more than research methods. Psychology is more than the brain, personality theories, mental illnesses, psychiatric drugs, and counseling techniques. It is more than learning to analyze, manipulate, or control people. You do not need to surrender your worldview in order to study psychology nor do you need to compartmentalize your faith. To study psychology, you do not need to adopt anti-Christian assumptions about the nature of God, Mankind, knowledge, right and wrong, psychopathology, or anything else.

You can learn about the wonders of the human brain and behavior while maintaining respect for the complete inspiration and authority of the Scriptures. Conversations and debates with classmates and professors about the Christian perspective on psychology represent evangelistic opportunities. Your study of psychology can prepare you to think Christianly about psychology's influence in academia, the culture, and society. Your studies in psychology can help reduce the Church's misunderstanding and fear of psychology and help the Church fulfill its duty to minister to the world's psychological needs. In your study, you join others in physics, biology, history, the arts, sociology, theology, and many other fields seeking a deeper understanding of all of God's creation. Christ is Lord of all, indeed.

Chapter Summary.

Research psychologists are interested in the design, execution, and evaluation of psychological research and psychological tests. The scientific method, properly understood, is consistent with a Christian worldview. Empiricism, also called logical positivism, is a worldview position and an approach to science. Empiricism, in its extreme, is a belief that the empirical method is the only valid source of psychological knowledge. Empirical methods are systematic and standard ways of defining research questions, forming and testing hypotheses, analyzing and interpreting data, drawing conclusions, and publishing the results.

Applied research is designed to solve a particular problem. Basic research seeks to expand our knowledge and understanding for its own sake. A hypothesis is a restatement of the research question in a way that can be tested. A hypothesis is a testable prediction about a relationship between variables. Standardization is the process of assuring that experimental procedures and measurements are precisely defined and carefully controlled. Good psychological research should be replicable – designed, executed, and documented in a way that allows other researchers to re-create the experiment.

A variable is any event, condition, or behavior than researchers can measure. Nominal variables classify data according to category. Ordinal variables can be classified in rankings. Interval variables can be ranked in order and the difference between intervals is known and fixed. Ratio variables can be ranked, the intervals between measures are consistent, and they can be expressed as ratios.

In experiments there are two types of variables; independent and dependent variables. The variable that the researcher manipulates is called the independent variable. The dependent variable is the "effect" in cause-and-effect relationships – it is the result of the experimental treatment. Reliability refers to the extent to which a measurement tool gives the same result when administered to the same people at different times. Validity refers to the extent to which the measurement measures that which it is supposed to. A representative sample is a relatively small group of participants selected from the entire population of all possible participants. An experiment has sample bias if the sample is not representative of the larger population. The most important control psychologists take in designing experiments is randomization.

Qualitative research designs describe the "qualities" of psychological phenomena. Quantitative research seeks to discover cause-and-effect relationships and to measure or quantify the strength of relationships between psychological variables. Experimental designs that lack random assignment or some other control are called quasi-experimental designs.

Descriptive statistics organize, describe, and summarize data. Inferential statistics allow for interpreting data and drawing inferences from the data. Measures of central tendency include the mean, median, and mode. Measures of variability describe how a variable is distributed and how it varies in a sample. Many psychological characteristics are thought to be normally distributed.

Psychologists conducting research using humans or animals must follow ethical standards established by the American Psychological Association (APA). Colleges and universities conducting psychological research must have an Institutional Review Board (IRB) to review and approve all research proposals prior to conducting the research.

For Review.

1. Respond to the assertion that a Christian worldview is anti-science.
2. Describe empiricism as a worldview and an approach to science.
3. Describe the steps in the empirical method.
4. Why is standardization important in psychological research?
5. Describe nominal, ordinal, interval, and ratio variables.
6. Explain independent and dependent variables.
7. Explain why reliability and validity are important in psychological research.
8. Explain bias in research. Describe subject and experimenter bias and research designs to control for subject and experimenter bias.
9. Describe the Hawthorne effect.
10. Describe qualitative and quantitative research.
11. Describe correlation research and the correlation coefficient.
12. Describe the placebo effect.
13. Describe descriptive and inferential statistics.
14. Describe a normal distribution.
15. Describe ethical considerations of research using human and animal subjects.

Index

Bibliography

Chapter 1 – What is Psychology?

Astin, A. (1993). *What matters in college?* San Francisco: Jossey-Bass.

Bobgan, M. & Bobgan, D. (1979). *The Psychological Way/The Spiritual Way.* Minneapolis, MN: Bethany Fellowship.

Bobgan, M. & Bobgan, D. (1987). *Psychoheresy: The psychological seduction of Christianity.* Santa Barbara: Eastgate Publishers.

Carter, J. D. (1977). Secular and sacred models of psychology and religion. *Journal of Psychology and Theology, (5),* 197-208.

Collins, G. R (1975). Popular Christian Psychologies: Some Reflections. In Fleck, J. R., & Carter, J. D. (Eds.), (1981). *Psychology and Christianity: Integrative Readings.* Nashville: Abingdon.

Collins, G. R. (1975). The Pulpit and the Couch. In Fleck, J. R., & Carter, John D., (1981). *Psychology and Christianity: Integrative Readings.* Nashville, TN: Abingdon.

Colson, Charles and Pearcy, Nancy. (1999). *How Now Shall We Live?* Wheaton, IL: Tyndale.

Darwin, Charles (1859), *The Origin of Species.* Chapter 14 Recapitulation and Conclusion. Accessed 7/7/2011 online at http://www.literature.org/authors/darwin-charles/the-origin-of-species/chapter-14.html

Faw, Harold W. (1995). *Psychology in Christian Perspective: An Analysis of Key Issues.* Grand Rapids, MI: Baker Books.

Fleck, J. R. & Carter, J. D. (1981). *Psychology and Christianity: Integrative Readings.* Nashville: Abingdon.

Ganz, R. (1993). *PsychoBabble: The Failure of Modern Psychology and the Biblical Alternative.* Wheaton: Crossway.

Jeeves, M. A. (1976). *Psychology and Christianity: The View Both Ways.* Downers Grove: InterVarsity Press.

Johnson, E. L. & Jones, S. L. (2000). Finding One Truth in Four Views. In Johnson, E. L. & Jones, S. L. (Eds.) (2000) *Psychology & Christianity: with Contributions by Gary R. Collins, David G. Myers, David Powlison, Robert C. Roberts.* Downers Grover: InterVarsity.

Myers, David G. (1996). On Professing Psychological Science and Christian Faith. *Journal of Psychology and Christianity, (15),* 143-149.

Myers, David G. and Jeeves, Malcom A. (2003). *New York: Psychology Through the Eyes of Faith.* HarperCollins.

Narramore, Bruce (1985). The Concept of Responsibility in Psychopathology and Psychotherapy. *Journal of Psychology and Christianity, (13),* 91-96.

Rice, Timothy S. (2008). *Homeschool Psych: Preparing Christian Homeschool Students for Psychology 101.* Epworth, GA: Rocking R Ventures.

Slife, B. D. & Whoolery, M. (2006). Are Psychology's Main Methods Biased Against the Worldview of Many Religious People? *Journal of Psychology and Theology, 34(3),* 217-231.

The American Heritage Dictionary of the English Language (4th ed.). (2006). Boston: Houghton Mifflin.

Veith, G. E. (1998). Educational Victory: How Christians Can Reclaim the Culture. *World Magazine, (13)24.*

Watters, W. (1987). Christianity & Mental Health [Electronic version]. *The Humanist,* November/December, 5-11.

Chapter 2 – A Christian Worldview

Aristotle. (ca. 350 BC). *De anima* (J. A. Smith, Trans.). Accessed 7/7/2011 online at http://psychclassics.yorku.ca/Aristotle/De-anima/index.htm.

Blamires, Harry. *Recovering the Christian Mind: Meeting the Challenge of Secularism.* Downers Grove, Illinois: InterVarsity Press, 1988.

Clark, R. E. D. (1953).The Spheres of Revelation and Science. What Are Their Limitations in Relation to Each Other. *Journal of the American Scientific Affiliation (5)*. Accessed 7/7/2011 online at http://www.asa3.org/ASA/PSCF/1953/JASA6-53Clark.html.

Edwards, C. & Noebel. D. (2002). *Thinking Like A Christian.* New York: Broadman & Holman.

Evans, C. S. (1976). Christian perspectives on the sciences of man. *Christian Scholar's Review, (6)*, 97-113.

Evans, C. S. (1989). The Concept of the Self as the Key to Integration. *Journal of Psychology and Christianity, (3)2.*

Foster, J. D. & Ledbetter, M. F. (1987). Christian Anti-psychology and the Scientific Method. *Journal of Psychology and Theology, (15)*, 10-18.

Ham, K. (1987). *The Lie: Evolution.* San Diego: Creation-Life Publishers.

Johnson, E. L. (1993). The Place for the Bible within Psychological Science. *Journal of Psychology and Theology, (20)*, 146-355.

Johnson, E. L. (1997). Christ, the Lord of Psychology. *Journal of Psychology and Theology, (25)*, 11-27.

Johnson, F. R. (1978). The Nature of Human Nature. *Journal of Psychology and Theology, Vol. 6*, 189-199.

Narramore, Bruce (1985). The Concept of Responsibility in Psychopathology and Psychotherapy. *Journal of Psychology and Christianity, (13)*, 91-96.

Rice, Timothy. S. (2007). *The Effect of a Seminar on the Integration of Psychology and a Christian Worldview on the Attitudes of Christian Homeschoolers.* Unpublished Doctoral Dissertation.

Roberts, R. C. (2000). A Christian Psychology Response. In Johnson, E. L., & Jones, S. L. (Eds.) (2000) *Psychology & Christianity: with Contributions by Gary R. Collins, David G. Myers, David Powlison, Robert C. Roberts.* Downers Grover: InterVarsity.

Vitz, P. C. (1977). *Psychology as Religion: The Cult of Self-Worship.* Grand Rapids: Eerdmans.

White, J. (1987). *Putting the Soul Back in Psychology.* Downers Grove, IL: InterVarsity.

Chapter 3 – Psychology's History and Worldview

Boring, E. (1957). *A History of Experimental Psychology (2nd ed.).* New York: Appleton - Century - Crofts.

Cohen, M. (2003). *A Brief Survey of the History of Biblical Psychology.* Accessed 7/7/2011 online at http://www.mattcohn.net/history.html

Fechner (1912). Elements of Psychophysics, Sections VII and XVI, Translated by Herbert Sidney Langfeld in Rand, Benjamin (Ed.)(1912). *The Classical Psychologists*, Boston: Houghton Miffli. Accessed 7//7/2011 online at http://psychclassics.yorku.ca/Fechner/

Lewis, C. S. (1952). *Mere Christianity.* New York: Macmillan.

Lewis, C. S. (1970). *God in the Dock.* Grand Rapids, MI: Eerdmans.

Machan, T. R. (1974) *The Pseudo-Science of B. F. Skinner.* New York: Arlington House Publishers.

Reber, J. S. (2006). Secular Psychology: What's the Problem? *Journal of Psychology and Theology, 34(3)*, 193-204.

Rushdoony, R. J. (1978). *The Mythology of Science.* Nutley: The Craig Press.

Skinner, B. F. (1971). *Beyond Freedom and Dignity.* Harmondsworth: Penguin.

Thompson, B. (2004). *A Christian's Response to Humanism* [Electronic version]. Apologetics Press, Accessed 7/7/2011 online at http://www.apologeticspress.org/rr/reprints/Christians-Response-to-Humanism.pdf.

Titchener, Edward B. (1895). Simple Reactions. *Mind, 4,* 74-81. Accessed 7/7/2011 online at http://psychclassics.yorku.ca/Titchener/reactions.htm.

Titchener, Edward B. (1899). Structural and Functional Psychology. *Philosophical Review, 8,* 290-299.

Titchener, Edward B. (1901). *Experimental Psychology: A Manual of Laboratory Practice.* New York: The Macmillan Co.

Watson, John B. (1913). Psychology as the Behaviorist Views It. *Psychological Review, 20,* 158-177.

Chapter 4 – The Brain and Nervous System

Bernstein, Douglas A. and Nash, Peggy W. (2008). *Essentials of Psychology*. Boston: Houghton Mifflin Company.

Damasio, Hanna; Grabowski, Thomas; Galaburda, Albert M.; and Damsio, Antonio R. (1994). The Return of Phineas Gage: Clues About the Brain from The Skull of a Famous Patient. *Science, News Series, Vol. 264, No. 5162*, 1102-1105.

Faw, Harold W. (1995). *Psychology in Christian Perspective: An Analysis of Key Issues*. Grand Rapids, MI: Baker Books.

Myers, David G. and Jeeves, Malcom A. (2003). *Psychology Through the Eyes of Faith*. New York: HarperCollins.

Chapter 5 – Sensation and Perception

Bernstein, Douglas A. and Nash, Peggy W. (2008). *Essentials of Psychology*. Boston: Houghton Mifflin Company.

Blair-Broeker, Charles T., Ernst, Randal M., and Myers, David G., (2008). *Thinking About Psychology: The Science of Mind and Behavior*. New York: Worth Publishers.

Boring, E. G. (1942) *Sensation and Perception in the History of Experimental Psychology*. New York: Appleton-Century.

Boring, E. G. (1957). *A History of Experimental Psychology (2nd ed.)*. New York: Appleton - Century - Crofts.

Bruner, Jerome S. and Goodman, Cecile C. (1947). Value and Need as Organizing Factors in Perception. *Journal of Abnormal and Social Psychology, 42*, 33-44. Accessed 7/7/2011 online at http://psychclassics.yorku.ca/Bruner/Value/.

Chulder, Eric H. *Neuroscience for Kids*. Accessed 6/7/2011 online at http://faculty.washington.edu/chudler/neurok.html.

Coon, Dennis and Mitterer, John O. (2010). *Introduction to Psychology: Gateways to the Mind and Behavior*. Belmont, CA: Wadsworth.

Coren, S., Ward, Lawrence, M., and Enns, James T. (1999). *Sensation and Perception, 5th ed*. New York: Harcourt Brace College.

Evans, E. F. (1982). Functional Anatomy of the Auditory System. In Barlow, H. B. and Mollon, J. D. (1982). *The Senses*. Melbourne: Cambridge University Press.

Faw, Harold W. (1995). *Psychology in Christian Perspective: An Analysis of Key Issues*. Grand Rapids, MI: Baker Books.

Fechner, Gustav (1912). Elements of Psychophysics, Sections VII and XVI, Translated by Herbert Sidney Langfeld in Rand, Benjamin (Ed.)(1912). *The Classical Psychologists*. Boston: Houghton Miffli. Accessed 7//7/2011 online at http://psychclassics.yorku.ca/Fechner/

James, William. (1890). *The Principles of Psychology*. Accessed 7/7/2100 at http://psychclassics.yorku.ca/James/Principles/index.htm.

Koffka, Kurt (1922). Perception: An Introduction to the Gestalt-theorie. *Psychological Bulletin, Vol. 19*, 531-585. Accessed 7/7/2011 online at http://psychclassics.yorku.ca/Koffka/Perception/perception.htm.

Köhler, Wolfgang. (1959). Gestalt Psychology Today. *American Psychologist, 14*, 727-73.

Koteskey, R. L. (1978). Toward the Development of a Christian Psychology: Sensation and Perception. *Journal of Psychology and Theology. Vol. 6*, 200-209.

Missios, Symeon (2007). Hippocrates, Galen, and Uses of Trepanation in the Ancient Classical World: Galen and the Teaching of Trepanation. *Neurosurgical Focus, Vol. 23(1)*.

Moroney, Stephen K (2000). *The Noetic Effects of Sin. A Historical and Contemporary Exploration of How Sin Affects Our Thinking*. Oxford, England: Lexington Books.

Myers, David G. and Jeeves, Malcom A. (2003). *Psychology Through the Eyes of Faith*. New York: HarperCollins.

U.S. Department of Health and Human Services, National Institutes of Health, National Eye Institute. http://www.nei.nih.gov/.

Wertheimer, Max (1923). Laws of Organization in Perceptual Forms. First published as Untersuchungen zur Lehre von der Gestalt II, in Psycologische Forschung, 4, 301-350. Translation published in Ellis, W. (1938). *A Source Book of Gestalt Psychology* (pp. 71-88). London: Routledge & Kegan Paul. Accessed 7/7/2011 online at http://psychclassics.yorku.ca/Wertheimer/Forms/forms.htm

Chapter 6 – Motivation and Emotion

Bandura, Albert (1977). Self-efficacy: Toward a Unifying Theory of Behavioral Change. *Psychological Review, Vol. 84(2)*, 191-215.

Bard P. (1934) On Emotional Expression after Decortication, With Some Remarks on Certain Theoretical Views, Parts I and II. *Psychological Review Vol. 41*, 309–329 and 424–449

Bargh, J. A. & Ferguson, M. J. (2000). Beyond Behaviorism: On the Automaticity of Higher Mental Processes. *Psychological Bulletin, 126*, 926-945.

Barnard, Larry C. et. al. (2006). An Evolutionary Theory of Human Motivation. *Genetic, Social, and General Psychology Monographs, Vol. 131(2)*, 129-184.

Baumeister, R. F. and Leary, M. R. (1995). The Need to Belong: Desire for Interpersonal Attachment as a Fundamental Human Motivation. *Psychological Bulletin, 117*, 497-529.

Bernstein, Douglas A. and Nash, Peggy W. (2008). *Essentials of Psychology*. Boston: Houghton Mifflin Company.

Cannon W. (1928). *Bodily Changes in Pain, Hunger, Fear and Rage: An Account of Recent Researches into the Function of Emotional Excitement*. Appleton-Century: New York.

Colson, Charles and Nancy Pearcy (1999). *How Now Shall We Live?*, Wheaton, IL: Tyndale.

Ekman, Paul (1970). Universal Facial Expressions of Emotion. *California Mental Health Research Digest, Vol. 8(4)*.

Ekman, Paul (1999). Basic Emotions. In T. Dalgleish and M. Power (Eds.) *Handbook of Cognition and Emotion*. Sussex, U.K.: John Wiley & Sons. Accessed 7/7/2011 online at http://citeseerx.ist.psu.edu/viewdoc/download?doi=10.1.1.123.1143&rep=rep1&type=pdf.

Faw, Harold W. (1995). *Psychology in Christian Perspective: An Analysis of Key Issues*. Grand Rapids, MI: Baker Books.

Festinger, Leon (1954). A Theory of Social Comparison Processes. *Human Relations, 1954, 7*, 117-140.

Holmes TH, and Rahe RH (1967). The Social Readjustment Rating Scale. *Journal of Psychosomatic Research, Vol. 11(2)*, 213–218.

Hull, C. L. (1951). *Essentials of Behavior*. New Haven, CT: Yale University Press.

Irwin, Harvey J. (1993). Belief in the Paranormal: A Review of the Empirical Literature. *The Journal of the American Society for Psychical Research, Vol. 87(1)*.

James, William. (1890). *The Principles of Psychology*. Accessed 7/7/2100 at http://psychclassics.yorku.ca/James/Principles/index.htm

Koteskey, R. I. (1979). Toward the Development of a Christian Psychology: Motivation. *Journal of Psychology and Theology, Vol. 7*.

Lange, Carl G. (1912). The Mechanism of the Emotions. In Benjamin Rand (Ed.) (1912). *The Classical Psychologists*. Boston: Houghton Mifflin. Accessed 7/7/2011 online at http://psychclassics.yorku.ca/Lange/.

Maslow, Abraham H. (1943). A Theory of Human Motivation. *Psychological Review, 50*, 370-396.

Maslow, Abraham H. (1970). *Motivation and Personality*. New York: Harper & Row Publishers, Inc.

McDougall, William (1908). *An Introduction to Social Psychology*. London: Methuen.

Myers, David G. and Jeeves, Malcom A. (2003). *Psychology Through the Eyes of Faith*. New York: HarperCollins.

Plutchik, R, and Conte, H. r. (Eds.) (1997). *Circumplex Models of Personality and Emotions*. Washington, DC: American Psychological Association.

Porter, Brian and VanderVeen, Steve. *Motivation from a Christian Perspective*. Accessed 7/7/2011 online at http://www.cbfa.org/Porter_VanderVeen_Paper.pdf.

Reisenzein, Rainer (1983). The Schachter Theory of Emotion: Two Decades Later. P*sychological Bulletin, Vol. 94(2)*, 239 – 264.

Reiss, Steven (2004), Multifaceted nature of intrinsic motivation: The theory of 16 basic desires. *Review of General Psychology 8 (3)*: 179–193.

Schachter, S. And Singer, J. E. Cognitive, Social, and Physiological Determinants of Emotional State. *Psychological Review, Vol. 69*, 379-399.

Selye, Hans (1950). Stress and the General Adaptation Syndrome. *British Medical Journal*, June 17, 1950.

Taylor, Shelley E. et. al. (2000). Psychological Resources, Positive Illusions, and Health. *American Psychologist, Vol. 55(1)*, 99-109.

Yerkes R. M., and Dodson J. D. (1908). The Relation of Strength of Stimulus to Rapidity of Habit-Formation. *Journal of Comparative Neurology and Psychology 18,* 459–482.

Chapter 7 – Learning and Memory

Abramson, L Y., Seligman, M. E. P., and Teasdale, J. (1978). Learned Helplessness in Humans: Critique and Reformulation. *Psychological Review 87*, 49-74.

Anderson, Craig A. et. al. (2003). The Influence of Media Violence on Youth. *Psychological Science in the Public Interest, Vol. 4(3)*.

Baddeley, Alan D. (1977). *Human Memory: Theory and Practice*. East Sussex, UK: Psychology Press.

Bandura, Albert; Ross, Dorothea; and Ross, Sheila A. (1961). Transmission of Aggressions Through Imitation of Aggressive Models. *Journal of Abnormal and Social Psychology, 63*, 575-582.

Baumrind, Diana, Larzelere, Robert E., and Cowan, Philip A. (2002). Ordinary Physical Punishment: Is it Harmful? *Psychological Bulletin, Vol. 128(4)*, 580-589.

Bolin, E. P. and Goldberg, G. M. (1979). Behavioral Psychology and the Bible: General and Specific Considerations. *Journal of Psychology and Theology, Vol. 7*.

Boring, E. G. (1957). *A History of Experimental Psychology (2nd ed.)*. New York: Appleton - Century - Crofts.

Bufford, R. (1977). God and Behavior Mod: Some Thoughts Concerning the Relationships Between Biblical Principles and Behavior Modification. *Journal of Psychology and Theology, 5*, 13-22.

Coon, Dennis and Mitterer, John O. (2010). *Introduction to Psychology: Gateways to the Mind and Behavior*. Belmont, CA: Wadsworth.

Del Colle, Ralph (1998). The Shape of Pneumatology: Studies in the Doctrine of the Holy Spirit. *Theological Studies, Vol. 59*.

Ebbinghaus, Hermann. (1913). *Memory: A Contribution to Experimental Psychology* (Henry A. Ruger & Clara E. Bussenius, Trans.). (Originally published 1885). Accessed 7/7/2011 online at http://psychclassics.yorku.ca/Ebbinghaus/index.htm.

Faw, Harold W. (1995). *Psychology in Christian Perspective: An Analysis of Key Issues*. Grand Rapids, MI: Baker Books.

Garcia, John et. al. (1955). Conditioned Aversion to Saccharin Resulting from Exposure to Gamma Radiation. *Science, Vol. 22*, 157-158.

James, William. (1890). *The Principles of Psychology*. Accessed 7/7/2100 at http://psychclassics.yorku.ca/James/Principles/index.htm

Loftus, Elizabeth F. (1975). Leading Questions and the Eyewitness Report. *Cognitive Psychology, Vol. 7*, 550-572.

Loftus, Elizabeth F. and Palmer, John C. (1974). Reconstruction of Automobile Destruction: An Example of the Interaction Between Language and Memory. *Journal of Verbal Learning and Verbal Behavior, Vol. 13*, 585-589.

Pavlov, Ivan P. (1927). *Conditioned Reflexes: An Investigation of the Physiological Activity of the Cerebral Cortex* (Translated by G. V. Anrep). Accessed 7/7/2011 online at http://psychclassics.yorku.ca/Pavlov/.

Schauffele, Susan and Baptiste, Ian (2000). Appealing to the Soul; Towards a Judeo-Christian Theory of Learning. *International Journal of Lifelong Education, Vol. 19(5)*, 448-458.

Schwartz, Barry (1978). *Psychology of Learning & Behavior*. New York: W. W. Norton and Company.

Skinner, B. F. (1948). 'Superstition' in the Pigeon. J*ournal of Experimental Psychology, 48*, 168-172.

Skinner, B. F. (1950). Are Theories of Learning Necessary? *Psychological Review, 57*, 193-216.

T.D. Hackenberg: Token Reinforcement: A Review and Analysis. *Journal of the Experimental Analysis of Behavior, 91*, 257-286.

Thorndike, E. L. (1898) Animal Intelligence: An Experimental Study of the Associative Process in Animals. *Psychological Monographs, 2, Whole No. 8.*

Thorndike, E. L. (1907). *The Elements of Psychology*. New York: A. G. Seiler.

Tolman, Edward, C. (1948). Cognitive Maps in Rats and Men. *Psychological Review, 55(4)*, 189-208.

Watson, John B. & Rayner, Rosalie. (1920). Conditioned Emotional Reactions. *Journal of Experimental Psychology, 3*, 1-14.

Watson, John B. (1907). Studying the Mind of Animals. *The World Today, 12,* 421-426

Wixted, J. T. (2004). The Psychology and Neuroscience of Forgetting. *Current Directions in Psychological Science, 55*, 235-269.

Chapter 8 – Human Development

Ainsworth, Mary D. (1993). Attachment as Related to Mother-Infant Interaction. *Advances in Infancy Research, 8,* 1-50.

Ainsworth, Mary D. and Bowlby, John (1991). An Ethological Approach to Personality Development. *American Psychologist, Vol. 46(4),* 333-341.

Baumrind, D. (1966). Effects of Authoritative Parental Control on Child Behavior. *Child Development, 37*, 887-907.

Baumrind, Diana (1971). Current Patterns of Parental authority. *Developmental Psychology, Vol 4(1, Pt.2),* 1-103.

Benson, Janette B. and Haith, Marshall M.(Eds.) (2009). *Social and Emotional Development in Infancy and Early Childhood*. San Diego, CA: Academic Press.

Bretherton, Inge (1992). The Origins of Attachment Theory: John Bowlby and Mary Ainsworth. *Developmental Psychology, Vol 28*, 759-775.

Cattell, R. B. (1941). Some Theoretical Issues in Adult Intelligence Testing. *Psychological Bulletin, 38,* 592.

Chickering, Arthur W. and Reisser, Linda (1993). *Education and Identity*. Hoboken, NJ: Jossey-Bass.

Clouse, B. (1971). Some Developmental Ideas of Jean Piaget. J*ournal of the American Scientific Affiliation, Vol. 23,* 104-108.

Clouse, B. (1973). Psychological Theories of Child Development: Implications for the Christian Family. *Journal of Psychology and Theology, Vol. 1.*

Clouse, B. (1997). "Can Two Walk Together, Except They Be Agreed? Psychology and Theology - A Journey Together or Paths Apart? *Journal of Psychology and Theology, 25,* 38-48.

Colapinto, John (2001). *As Nature Made Him: The Boy Who was Raised as a Girl*. New York: HarperCollins.

Dewey, Russell A. (2007). *The Heritability Index*. Accessed 7/7/2011 online at http://www.psywww.com/intropsych/ch10_development/heritability_index.html

Erikson, Erik H. (1980). *Identity and the Life Cycle*. New York: W. W. Norton & Company.

Faw, Harold W. (1995). *Psychology in Christian Perspective: An Analysis of Key Issues*. Grand Rapids, MI: Baker Books.

Foster, J. D. and Moran, G. T. (1985). Piaget and Parables: The Convergence of Secular and Scriptural Views of Learning. J*ournal of Psychology and Theology. Vol. 13,* Summer 1985.

Galton, Francis. (1865). Hereditary Talent and Character. *Macmillan's Magazine, 12,* 157-166, 318-327.

Gibson, E. J. and Walk, R. D. (1960). The 'Visual Cliff'. *Scientific American Vol. 202*, April, 64-71.

Harlow, Harry F. (1959). Love in Infant Monkeys, *Scientific American Vol. 202(6),* 64-74.

Harlow, Harry F. and Harlow, M. K. (1962). Social Deprivation in Monkeys. *Scientific American 207(5),* 136-46.

Harlow, Harry F. (1958). The Nature of Love. *American Psychologist, 13,* 573-685.

Harlow, Harry F. and Suomi, Stephen J. (1971). Social Recovery by Isolation-Reared Monkeys. *Proceedings of the National Academy of Science of the United States of America 68(7),*1534-1538.

Hedden, Trey and Gabrieli, John D. E. (2004). Insights Into the Ageing Mind: A View From Cognitive Neuroscience. *Nature Reviews Neuroscience 5*, 87-96.

Kail, Robert V. and Cavanaugh, John C. (2010). *Human Development: A Life-Span View*. Belmont, CA: Wadsworth.

Kelly, George A. (1968). Rousseau, Kant, and History. *Journal of the History of Ideas*, Vol. 29(3).

Kohlberg, Lawrence (1981). Essays on Moral Development, Vol. I: The Philosophy of Moral Development. San Francisco, CA: Harper & Row.

Kohlberg, L. (1984). *Essays on Moral Development: Vol II. The Psychology of Moral Devleopment*. San Francisco, CA: Harper & Row.

Kübler-Ross, E. *On Death and Dying*. 1969. New York, NY: Scribner Publishers.

Levinson, D. J.; Darrow, C. N.; Klein, E. B.; and Levinson, M. (1978). *Seasons of a Man's Life*. New York: Random House.

Locke, John (1995). *An Essay Concerning Human Understanding*. New York: Prometheus Books.

Lunzer, E. A. (1960). Some Points of Piagetian Theory in the Light of Experimental Criticism. *Journal of Child Psychology and Psychiatry, Vol. 1(30)*, 191-202.

Martin, C.L., Ruble, D.N., & Szkrybalo, J. (2002). Cognitive Theories of Early Gender Development. *Psychological Bulletin, 128*, 903-933.

McGeown, Kate (2005). What Happened to Romania's Orphans? *BBC News, Romania*. Accessed 7/7/2011 online at http://news.bbc.co.uk/2/hi/europe/4629589.stm.

Morris, H. M. (1988). The Heritage of the Recapitulation Theory [Electronic version]. *Impact, Vol. 183*. Retrieved at http://www.icr.org/article/287/ on July 7, 2011.

Myers, David G. and Jeeves, Malcom A. (2003). *Psychology Through the Eyes of Faith*. New York: HarperCollins.

Paxinos, George and Mai, Jürgen Mai (2004). *The Human Nervous System*. London: Elsevier Academic Press.

Piaget, Jean (1952). *The Origins of Intelligence in Children*. Translated by Margaret Cook. New York: The Norton Library.

Rogers, Chris (2009). What Became of Romania's Neglected Orphans? *BBC News, Romania*. Accessed 7/7/2011 online at http://news.bbc.co.uk/2/hi/europe/8425001.stm.

Ruble, D.N., Martin, C., & Berenbaum, S. (2006). Gender Development. In N. Eisenberg (Ed.) *Handbook of Child Psychology: Vol. 3, Personality and Social Development (6th edition)*. New York: Wiley.

Shaffer, David A. and Kipp, Katherine (2007). *Developmental Psychology: Childhood & Adolescence*. Belmont, CA: Thomson Higher Education.

Sigelman, Carol K. and Rider, Elizabeth A. (2011). *Life-Span Human Development*. Belmont, CA: Wadsworth.

Vygotsky, L. (1978). Interaction Between Learning and Development. *Mind and Society*. Cambridge, MA: Harvard University Press. Accessed 7/7/2011 at http://www.simplypsychology.org/vygotsky78.pdf.

W.C. Crain. (1985). *Theories of Development*. Prentice-Hall. pp. 118-136.

Chapter 9 – Consciousness

Aigner, T. G. and Balster, R. L. (1978). Choice Behavior in Rhesus Monkeys: Cocaine Versus Food. *Science, 201 (4355)*, 534.

American Psychiatric Association: Diagnostic and Statistical Manual of Mental Disorders, Fourth Edition. Washington, DC, American Psychiatric Association, 1994.

Bacaseta, P. E., Carlson, C. R., and Simanton, D. A. (1988). A Controlled Evaluation of Devotional Meditation and Progressive Relaxation. *Journal of Psychology and Theology. Vol. 16*, 362-368.

Bayne, Tim; Cleeremans, Axel; and Wilken, Patrick (2009). *The Oxford Companion to Consciousness*. Oxford: Oxford University Press.

Bernstein, Douglas A. and Nash, Peggy W. (2008). *Essentials of Psychology*. Boston: Houghton Mifflin Company.

Bloom, Paul (2007), Introduction to Psychology: Lecture 17 Transcript. Accessed online on 7/7/2011 at http://oyc.yale.edu/yale/psychology/introduction-to-psychology/content/transcripts/transcript17. html.

Bloom, Paul (2007), Introduction to Psychology: Lecture 2 Transcript. Accessed online on 7/7/2011 at http://oyc.yale.edu/yale/psychology/introduction-to-psychology/content/transcripts/transcript02. html

Braid, James (1850). *Human Hybernation*. London: John Churchilll.

Bube, Richard H. (1977). Pseudo-Science and Pseudo-Theology: (A) Cult and Occult. *Journal of the American Scientific Affiliation. Vol. 29*, 22-28.

Carlson, C., Bacaseta, P, & Simanton, D. (1988). A Controlled Evaluation of Devotional Meditations and Progressive Relaxation. *Journal of Psychology & Theology, (16)*, 362-368.

Chalmers, David J. (1995). Facing Up to the Problem of Consciousness. *Journal of Consciousness Studies. Vol. 2(3)*, 1995, 200-219. Accessed 7//7/2011 online at http://www.imprint.co.uk/chalmers.html.

Cirelli, Chiara and Tononi, Ciulio (2008). Is Sleep Essential? *Public Library of Science Biology Vol. 6(8)*.

Court, John H. (2002). *Hypnosis Healing and the Christian*. Eugene, OR: Wipf & Stock Publishers.

Crick, Francis (1994). *The Astonishing Hypothesis: The Scientific Search For The Soul*. New York: Touchstone.

Dahl, Ronald E. (1999). The Consequences of Insufficient Sleep for Adolescents: Links Between Sleep and Emotional Regulation. *Phi Delta Kappan, Vol. 80(5)*, 354-359.

Faw, Harold W. (1995). *Psychology in Christian Perspective: An Analysis of Key Issues*. Grand Rapids, MI: Baker Books.

Freud, Sigmund (1913). *The Interpretation of Dreams*. Translated by A. A. Brill. Originally published in New York by Macmillan.

Harrub, Brad (2005). *The Human Nervous System: Evidence of Intelligent Design [Part I]*. Montgomery, AL: Apologetics Press. Accessed 7/7/2011online at http://www.apologeticspress.org/apcontent. aspx?category=12&article=1581

Harrub, Brad (2005). *The Human Nervous System: Evidence of Intelligent Design [Part II]*. Montgomery, AL: Apologetics Press. Accessed 7/7/2011online at http://www.apologeticspress.org/apcontent. aspx?category=12&article=1697

Horne, J. A. (1985). Sleep Function, with Particular Reference to Sleep Deprivation. *Annals of Clinical Research,Vol 17(5)*.

http://www.ninds.nih.gov/disorders/brain_basics/understanding_sleep.htm.

Bobgan, Martin and Bobgan, Deidre (1984). *Hypnosis And The Christian*. Minneapolis, MN: Bethany House.

James, William (1902). *The Varieties of Religious Experiences*. Accessed 7/7/2011 online at http://www. gutenberg.org/cache/epub/621/pg621.txt/

James, William. (1904). Does Consciousness Exist? *Journal of Philosophy, Psychology, and Scientific Methods, 1*, 477-491.

Kalat, J. W. (2004). *Biological Psychology*. Belmont, CA: Thompson Wadsworth.

Kales, Anthony and Kales, Joyce D. (1974). Sleep disorders: Recent Findings in the Diagnosis and Treatment of Disturbed Sleep. *The New England Journal of Medicine, Vol 290(9)*, 487-491.

Kales, Anthony; Tan, Tjiauw-Ling; Kollar, Edward J.; Naitoh, Paul; Preston, Terry A.; and Malstom, Edward J. (1970). Sleep Patterns Following 205 Hours of Sleep Deprivation. *Psychosomatic Medicine, Vol. 32(2)*.

Kleitman, N. (1964). The Evolutionary Theory of Sleep and Wakefulness. *Perspectives in Biological Medicine, Vol. 7*, 69-78.

Koteskey, R. L. (1978). Toward the Development of a Christian Psychology: Sensation and Perception. *Journal of Psychology and Theology. Vol. 6*, 200-209.

Mahowald, Mark W. and Schenck, Carlos H. (2005). Insights From Studying Human Sleep Disorders. *Nature, Vol. 437(27)*.

Maquet, P. (2001). The Role of Sleep in Learning and Memory. *Science, Vol. 294*, 1048-1052.

Marin, Helen E. (1979). Meditation: A Requirement. *Journal of the American Scientific Affiliation. Vol. 31*, 96-101.

Martin, George H. (2004). The God Who Reveals Mysteries: Dreams and World Evangelization. *The Southern Baptist Journal of Theology, Vol. 8(1)*.

McNierney, Michael (1992). The Dark Speech of God. *Gnosis, Vol. 22*.

Meddis, R. (1975). On the Function of Sleep. *Animal Behavior, Vol. 23(3)*.

Mesmer, Franz (1980). *Mesmerism: A Translation of the Original Scientific and Medical Writings of F.A. Mesmer / translated and compiled by George Bloch; with an introduction by E.R. Hilgard*. Los Altos, CA: W. Kaufman.

Office of National Drug Control Policy. *The Economic Costs of Drug Abuse in the United States, 1992–2002*. Washington, DC: Executive Office of the President (Publication No. 207303), 2004.

Ospina M. B. et. al. (2007). *Meditation Practices for Health: State of the Research. Evidence Report/ Technology Assessment No. 155. (Prepared by the University of Alberta Evidence-based Practice Center under Contract No. 290-02-0023.) AHRQ Publication No. 07-E010*. Rockville, MD: Agency for Healthcare Research and Quality. June 2007.

Paller, Ken A. and Voss, Joel L. (2004). Memory Reactivation and Consolidation During Sleep. *Learning Memory, Vol 11*, 664-670. Accessed 7/7/2011 online at http://learnmem.cshlp.org/content/11/6/664.full.pdf+html.

Revonsuo, Antti. (2000). The Reinterpretation of Dreams: An Evolutionary Hypothesis of the Function of Dreaming. *Behavioral and Brain Sciences, 23*, 877-901.

Ryle, James (1993). *Hippo in the Garden: A Non-religious Approach to Having a Conversation with God*. Orlando, FL: Creation House.

Stickgold, R., Hobson, J. A., Fosse, R., and Fosse, M. (2001). Sleep, Learning, and Dreams: Off-line Memory Reprocessing. *Science, 294*, 1052-1057.

Stickgold, Robert and Walker, Matthew P. (2005). Sleep and Memory: The Ongoing Debate. *Sleep, Vol. 28(10)*.

Struthers, William H. (2001). Defining Consciousness: Christian and Psychological Perspectives. *Perspectives on Science and Christian Faith, Vol. 53*, 102-106.

U.S. Department of Health and Human Services. (2006). *In Brief: Your Guide to Healthy Sleep*. Bethesda, MD: U.S. Department of Health and Human Services, National Institutes of Health, National Heart, Lung, and Blood Institute. Accessed 7/7/2011 at http://www.nhlbi.nih.gov/health/public/sleep/healthysleepfs.pdf.

U.S. Department of Health and Human Services. (2011). *Understanding Drug Abuse and Addiction*. Bethesda, MD: U.S. Department of Health and Human Services, National Institutes of Health, National Institute on Drug Abuse. Accessed 7/7/2011 at http://www.drugabuse.gov/PDF/InfoFacts/Understanding.pdf.

Chapter 10 – Thinking, Language, and Intelligence

Bates, Elizabeth, Dale, Philip S., & Thal, Donna (1995). Individual Differences and their Implications for Theories of Language Development, in Fletcher, Paul and MacWhinney, Brian (Eds.) *Handbook of Child Language*. Malden, MA: Blackwell. Accessed 7/7/2011 online at http://citeseerx.ist.psu.edu/viewdoc/download?doi=10.1.1.139.3528&rep=rep1&type=pdf.

Binet, Alfred. (1916). New Methods for the Diagnosis of the Intellectual Level of Subnormals. In E. S. Kite (Trans.), *The Development of Intelligence in Children*. Vineland, NJ: Publications of the Training School at Vineland. (Originally published 1905 in L'Année Psychologique, 12, 191-244.)

Bots, Jan (1982). Praying in Two Directions: A Christian Method of Prayerful Decision-making. *Review for Religious, Vol. 41*, 58-64.

Brualdi, A, C. (1996) 'Multiple Intelligences: Gardner's Theory. *ERIC Clearinghouse on Assessment and Evaluation*. Accessed 7/7/2011 at http://www.ericdigests.org/1998-1/multiple.htm. Accessed June 15, 2008.

Cattell, R. B. (1941). SomeTheoretical Issues in Adult Intelligence Testing. *Psychological Bulletin, 38*, 592.

Chomsky, Noam (1995). Language and Nature. *Mind, New Series, Vol. 104(413)*, 1-61.

Cohen, R. J. & Swerdlik, M. E. (2009). *Psychological Testing and Assessment: An introduction to tests and measurement*. New York: McGraw Hill.

Ferrucci, David et. al. (2010). Building Watson: An Overview of the DeepQA Project. *Association for the Advancement of Artificial Intelligence. Fall 2010*, 59. Accessed online 7/11/2011 at http://www.aaai.org/AITopics/articles&columns/Ferrucci-Watson2010.pdf

Galton, Frances (1883). *Inquiries Into Human Faculty and its Development*. Accessed 7/7/2011 online at http://galton.org/books/human-faculty/text/html/index.html.

Galton, Frances (1892). *Hereditary Genius: An Inquiry into its Laws and Consequences*. London: MacMillan and Co. Accessed 7/7/2011 at http://galton.org/books/hereditary-genius/.

Gardner, H. (1993a). *Multiple Intelligences: The Theory in Practice*. NY: Basic Books

Guilford, J.P. (1950). Creativity. *American Psychologist, 5*, 444-454.

Guilford, J.P. (1967). *The Nature of Human Intelligence*. New York: McGraw-Hill

Hoff, Erika (2005). *Language Development*. Belmont, CA: Thomson Wadsworth.

Huitt, W. (1992). Problem Solving and Decision Making: Consideration of Individual Differences Using the Myers-Briggs Type Indicator. *Journal of Psychological Type, 24*, 33-44.

Mayer, R. E. (1992). *Thinking, Problem Solving, Cognition (2nd edition)*. New York: W. H. Freeman and Company.

Myers, David G. (1991). Steering Between the Extremes: On Being a Christian Scholar within Psychology. *Christian Scholar's Review, (20)*, 376-383.

Myers, David G. and Jeeves, Malcom A. (2003). *Psychology Through the Eyes of Faith*. New York: HarperCollins.

Neisser, Ulric et. al. (1996). Report of a Task Force Established by the American Psychological Association. *American Psychologist Vol. 51(2)*.

Spearman, C. (1904). "General Intelligence" Objectively Determined and Measured. *American Journal of Psychology, 15*, 201–293.

Sternberg, Robert (1997). *Thinking Styles*. Boston: Cambridge University Press.

Sternberg, Robert J. (1999). Intelligence as Developing Expertise. *Contemporary Educational Psychology 24*, 359 – 375.

Sternberg, Robert J. (1999). Successful Intelligence: Finding a Balance. T*rends in Cognitive Sciences, Vol. 3(11)*. Accessed 7/7/2011 at http://www.uv.es/~genomica/spa/inves/Sternberg.pdf.

Sternberg, Robert J. and O'Hara, Linda A. (1999). Creativity and Intelligence. In Sternberg, Robert J. (Ed.) (1999). *Handbook of Creativity*. New York: Cambridge University Press.

Sternberg, Robert J., Conway, Barbara E., Ketron, Jerry L., and Bernstein, Morty (1981). People's Conceptions of Intelligence. *Journal of Personality and Social Psychology, Vol 41(1)*, 37-55.

Terman, Lewis M. (1916). *The Measurement of Intelligence*. New York: Houghton Mifflin Company.

Thurstone, L. L. (1934). The Vectors of Mind. *Psychological Review, 41*, 1-32

Todd, James T. and Morris, Edward K. (1983). Misconception and Miseducation: Presentations of Radical Behaviorism in Psychology Textbooks. *The Behavior Analyst, Vol. 6(2)*, 153-160.

Treffert DA, Christensen DD. (2005). Inside the Mind of a Savant. *Scientific American. 293(6)*, 108–113. Accessed 7/11/2011 at http://www.pleasanton.k12.ca.us/avhsweb/emersond/appsych/ch11_development/savant.pdf.

Ulbaek, Ib (1998). The Origin of Language and Cognition. In J. R. Hurford, M. Studdert-Kennedy, and C. Knight (Eds.) *Approaches to the Evolution of Language*. Cambridge University Press.

Vygotsky, L. (1978). Interaction Between Learning and Development. Cambridge, MA: Harvard University Press. Accessed 7/7/2011 at http://www.simplypsychology.org/vygotsky78.pdf.

Wechsler, David (1958). *The Measurement and Appraisal of Adult Intelligence*. Baltimore, MD: Williams & Witkins

Chapter 11 -- Personality

Adler, A. (1956). *The Individual Psychology of Alfred Adler*. H. L. Ansbacher and R. R. Ansbacher (Eds.). New York: Harper Torchbooks.

Allport, Floyd H. & Allport, Gordon W. (1921). Personality traits: Their classificiation and measurement. *Journal of Abnormal and Social Psychology, 16, 6-40*.

Allport, Gordon W. (1927). Concepts of Trait and Personality. *Psychological Bulletin, 24*, 284-293.

Bandura, Albert, Ross, Dorothea, & Ross, Sheila A. (1961). Transmission of Aggressions Through Imitation of Aggressive models. *Journal of Abnormal and Social Psychology, 63*, 575-582.

Bess, Tammy L., Harvey, Robert J., and Swartz, and Swartz, Dana (2003). *Hierarchical Confirmatory Factor Analysis of the Myers-Briggs Type Indicator*. Paper presented at the 2003 Annual Conference of the Society for Industrial and Organizational Psychology, Orlando. Accessed 7/7/2011 online at http://harvey.psyc.vt.edu/Documents/BessHarveySwartzSIOP2003.pdf.

Cattell, R. B. (1943). The Description of Personality: Basic Traits Resolved Into Clusters. *Journal of Abnormal and Social Psychology, 38*, 476-506.

Cattell, R. B. (1949). *Description and Measurement of Personality*. New York: World Book

Collins, G. R. (1967). Wanted: A Christian Theory of Personality. *Journal of the American Scientific Affiliation. Vol. 19*. Accessed 7/7/2011 online at http://www.asa3.org/ASA/PSCF/1967/JASA6-67Collins.html.

Eysenck, H. J. (1991). Dimensions of Personality: 16, 5 or 3?—Criteria for a Taxonomic Paradigm. *Personality and Individual Differences 12*, 773–790.

Faw, Harold W. (1995). *Psychology in Christian Perspective: An Analysis of Key Issues*. Grand Rapids, MI: Baker Books.

Hall, Calvin S. and Lindzey, Gardner, (1959). *The Nature of Personality Theory. Theories of Personality*. Hoboken, NJ: John Wiley & Son.

Hans Eysenck, (1967). *The Biological Basis of Personality*. Springfield, IL: Thomas.

James, William. (1890). *The Principles of Psychology*. Accessed 7/7/2100 online at http://psychclassics.yorku.ca/James/Principles/index.htm.

Kelly, George A. (1963). *A Theory of Personality: The Psychology of Personal Constructs*. New Yorl: W. W. Norton & Co.

Lindzey, Gardner and Hall, Calvin S. (Eds) (1965). *Theories of Personality: Primary Sources and Research*. Oxford, England: John Wiley & Sons.

Maslow, Abraham H. (1970). *Motivation and Personality*. New York: Harper & Row Publishers, Inc.

McKinley, J. C. and Hathaway, S. R. (1944). The Minnesota Multiphasic Personality Inventory. V. Hysteria, Hypomania and Psychopathic Deviate. *Journal of Applied Psychology, Vol 28(2)*.

Meyer, Gregory J. and Kurtz, John E. (2006). Advancing Personality Assessment Terminology: Time to Retire "Objective" and "Projective" As Personality Test Descriptors. *Journal of Personality Assessment, Vol. 87(3)*, 223-225.

Myers, David G. and Jeeves, Malcom A. (2003). *Psychology Through the Eyes of Faith*. New York: HarperCollins.

Schultz, Duane P. and Schultz, Sydney E. (2005). *Theories of Personality*. Belmont, CA: Thomson Wadsworth.

Chapter 12 – Abnormal Psychology

American Psychiatric Association (1994). *Diagnostic and Statistical Manual of Mental Disorders, Fourth Edition*. Washington, DC, American Psychiatric Association.

Bloom, Paul (2007), *Introduction to Psychology: Lecture 19 Transcript*. Accessed online on 7/7/2011 at http://oyc.yale.edu/yale/psychology/introduction-to-psychology/content/transcripts/transcript19.html.

Boylan, Michael (2005). Hippocrates (c.450 – c.380 BCE). *Internet Encyclopedia of Philosophy*. Accessed 7/7/2011 online at http://www.iep.utm.edu/hippocra/

Faw, Harold W. (1995). *Psychology in Christian Perspective: An Analysis of Key Issues*. Grand Rapids, MI: Baker Books.

Freud, Sigmund. (1910). The Origin and Development of Psychoanalysis. *American Journal of Psychology, 21*, 181-218.

Grob, Gerald N. (1991). Origins of DMS-I: A Study in Appearance and Reality. *The American Journal of Psychiatry, Vol. 148(4)*.

Johnson, E. L. (1987). Sin, Weakness, and Psychopathology. *Journal of Psychology and Theology, (15)*, 218-226.

Johnson, E. L. and Jones, Stanton L. In Johnson, E. L. & Jones, S. L. (Eds.) (2000). *Psychology & Christianity: with Contributions by Gary R. Collins, David G. Myers, David Powlison, Robert C. Roberts*. Downers Grover: InterVarsity.

Myers, David G. (2000). A Levels-of-Explanation View. In Johnson, E. L., & Jones, S. L. (Eds.) (2000). *Psychology & Christianity: with Contributions by Gary R. Collins, David G. Myers, David Powlison, Robert C. Roberts*. Downers Grover: InterVarsity.

Myers, David G. and Jeeves, Malcom A. (2003). *Psychology Through the Eyes of Faith*. New York: HarperCollins.

Nicol, W. D. (1956). General Paralysis of the Insane. *British Journal of Venereal Disease Vol 23(9)*.

Porter, Roy. (1983). The Rage of Party: A Glorious Revolution in English Psychiatry? *Medical History, 27*, 35-50.

Presbyterian Church USA. (2008). *Comfort My People: A Policy Statement on Serious Mental Illness with Study Guide*. Accessed 7/7/2011 online at http://oga.pcusa.org/publications/serious-mental-illness2008.pdf.

Rosenhan, David L. (1973). On Being Sane in Insane Places. *Science, Vol. 179*, 250-258.

Seeman, M. V. (2009). The Changing Role of Mother of the Mentally Ill: From Schizophrenogenic Mother to Multigenerational Caregiver. *Psychiatry, Vol. 72(3)*, 284-94.

Szasz, Thomas S. (1960). *The Myth of Mental illness*. American Psychologist, 15, 113-118.

U.S. Department of Health and Human Services (1999). *Mental Health: A Report of the Surgeon General*. Rockville, MD: U.S. Department of Health and Human Services, Substance Abuse and Mental Health Services Administration, Center for Mental Health Services, National Institutes of Health.

Walsh, J.J. (1910). Asylums and Care for the Insane. In *The Catholic Encyclopedia*. New York: Robert Appleton Company. Retrieved July 6, 2011 from New Advent: http://www.newadvent.org/cathen/08038b.htm

Watson, John B. (1916) Behavior and the Concept of Mental Disease. *Journal of Philosophy, Psychology, and Scientific Methods, 13*, 589-597. Accessed 7/7/2011 at http://psychclassics.yorku.ca/Watson/mental.htm.

Westendorp, F. (1974). The Value of Freud's Illusion. In Fleck, J. & Carter, J. (Eds.), *Psychology and Christianity: Integrative Readings*. Nashville: Abingdon.

Chapter 13 – Treatment

Adams, J. E. (1972). *Competent to Counsel*. Philadelphia: Presbyterian and Reformed Publishing Company.

Adams, J. E. (1972). *The Big Umbrella: And Other Essays on Christian Counseling*. Grand Rapids: Baker.

Adams, J. E. (1979). *A Theology of Christian Counseling*. Grand Rapids: Zondervan.

Bobgan, M. and Bobgan, D. (1977). *The End of Christian Psychology*. Santa Barbara: EastGate Publishers.

Bobgan, M. and Bobgan, D. (1996). *Competent to Minister: The Biblical Care of Souls*. Santa Barbara, CA: EastGate Publishers.

Bufford, R. (1989). Demonic Influence and Mental Disorders. *Journal of Psychology and Theology. Vol. 8, 35-48*.

Carter, J. D. and Narramore B. (1979). *The Integration of Psychology and Theology*. Grand Rapids, MI: Zondervan.

Carter, J. D. (1975). Adams' Theory of Nouthetic Counseling. In Fleck, J. R., & Carter, J. D. (Eds.), (1981). *Psychology and Christianity: Integrative Readings*. Nashville: Abingdon.

Dain, Norman. (1975). *From Colonial America to Bicentenial America: Two Centuries of Vicissitudes in the Institutional Care of Mental Patients*. Presented before the Section on Psychiatry and the Section on Historical Medicine of the New York Academy of Medicine December 17, 1975. Accessed 7/7/2011 at http://www.ncbi.nlm.nih.gov/pmc/articles/PMC1807273/pdf/bullnyacadmed00156-0025.pdf

Eysenck, H.J. (1952), The Effects of Psychotherapy: An Evaluation. *Journal of Consulting Psychology, Vol. 16*.

Faw, Harold W. (1995). *Psychology in Christian Perspective: An Analysis of Key Issues*. Grand Rapids, MI: Baker Books.

Freeman, Walter (1950). Psychosurgery. *Journal of the National Medical Association. Vol. 42(4)*.

Freud, Sigmund. (1910). The Origin and Development of Psychoanalysis. *American Journal of Psychology, 21, 181-218.*

Hubble, Mark A., Duncan, Barry L., and Miller Scott D. (1999). *The Heart and Soul of Change: What Works in Therapy*. American Psychological Association.

Jones, S. L., & Butman, R. E. (1991). *Modern Psychotherapies: A Comprehensive Christian Appraisal*. Downers Grove: InterVarsity Press.

L'Abate, Luciano (1998). *Family Psychopathology: The Relational Roots of Dysfunctional Behavior*. New York: The Guilford Press.

Matzat, D. (1996). The Intrusion of Psychology into Christian Theology. *Issues, Etc. Journal, (1)9*.

McMinn, Mark R. and Campbell, Clark D. (2007). *Integrative Psychotherapy: Toward a Comprehensive Christian Approach*. Downers Grove, IL: Intervarsity Press.

Miller-McLemore, Bonnie J. (2003). Thinking About Children; Christian Faith and Popular Psychology. Excerpted from *Let the Children Come: Reimagining Childhood from a Christian Perspective*. San Francisco: Jossey-Bass. Accessed 7/7/2011 at http://discoverarchive.vanderbilt.edu/bitstream/handle/1803/3270/Psych&Child_Ch2_FamMin.pdf?sequence=1.

Myers, David G. and Jeeves, Malcom A. (2003).*Psychology Through the Eyes of Faith*. New York: HarperCollins.

Powlison, D. (2000). A Biblical Counseling Response. In Johnson, E. L., & Jones, S. L. (Eds.) (2000) *Psychology & Christianity: with Contributions by Gary R. Collins, David G. Myers, David Powlison, Robert C. Roberts*. Downers Grover: InterVarsity.

Rogers, Carl R. (1946). Significant Aspects of Client-centered Therapy. *American Psychologist, 1*, 415-422

Sharf, R.S. (2004). *Theories of Psychotherapy and Counseling: Concepts and Cases (3d ed.)*. Pacific Grove, CA: Brooks/Cole—Thomson Learning.

Chapter 14 – Social Psychology

Ajzen, Icek and Fishbein, Martin (1977). Attitude – Behavior Relations: A Theoretical Analysis and Review of Empirical Research. *Psychological Bulletin, Vol. 84(5)*.

Allport, Gordon (1979). *The Nature of Prejudice*. Cambridge, MA: Addison-Wesley.

Asch, Solomon E. (1955). Opinions and Social Pressure. *Scientific American, Vol 193(5)*.

Asch, Solomon E. (1956). Studies of Independence and Conformity: A Minority of One Against a Unanimous Majority. *Psychological Monographs, Vol 70(9)*.

Banuazizi, Ali and Movahedi, Siamak. (1975). Interpersonal Dynamics in a Simulated Prison. A Methodological Analysis. *American Psychologist Vol. 30(2)*.

Beck, J. & Banks, J. (1992). Christian Anti-psychology Sentiment: Hints of an Historical Analogue. *Journal of Psychology and Theology, (20)*, 3-10.

Bernstein, Douglas A. and Nash, Peggy W. (2008). *Essentials of Psychology*. Boston: Houghton Mifflin Company.

Bloom, Paul (2007). I*ntroduction to Psychology: Lecture 15 Transcript*. Accessed online on 7/7/2011 at http://oyc.yale.edu/yale/psychology/introduction-to-psychology/content/transcripts/transcript15.html

Darley, John M. and Batson, C. Daniel (1973). From Jerusalem to Jericho: A study of situational and dispositional variables in helping behavior. *Journal of Personality and Social Psychology, Vol 27(1)*.

Dueck, A. (1989). On Living in Athens: Models of Relating Psychology, Church and Culture. *Journal of Psychology and Christianity, Vol. 8(1)*, 5-18.

Dykstra, Michelle L., et al. (1995). Integrating Across the Psychology Curriculum: A Content Review Approach. *Journal of Psychology and Theology (23)*, 277-88.

Esser, James K. (1998). Alive and Well After 25 Years: A Review of Groupthink Research. *Organizational Behavior and Human Decision Process. Vol. 73(3)*.

Faw, Harold W. (1995). P*sychology in Christian Perspective: An Analysis of Key Issues*. Grand Rapids, MI: Baker Books.

Festinger, L. (1954). A Theory of Social Comparison Processes. *Human Relations, 7(2)*, 117-140.

Festinger, L. (1957). *A Theory of Cognitive Dissonance*. Standford, CA: Stanford University Press.

Fishbein, M. & Ajzen, I. (1975). *Belief, Attitude, Intention, and Behavior: An Introduction to Theory and Research*. Reading: Addison-Wesley.

Forsyth, D. R. (2009). *Group Dynamics (5th ed.)*. Pacific Grove, CA: Brooks/Cole.

Gansberg, Martin (1964). Thirty-eight Who Saw Murder Didn't Call the Police. *New York Times. March 27, 1964.*

Hafer, C.L. & Bègue, L. (2005). Experimental Research on Just-world Theory: Problems, Developments, and Future Challenges. *Psychological Bulletin, 131.*

Haney, C. and Zimbardo, P. (1976). Social Roles and Role playing: Observations from the Stanford Prison Study, in E. Hollander and R. Hunt (eds,) *Current Perspectives in Social Psychology*, New York: Oxford University Press.

Haney, Craig, Banks, Curtis, and Zimbardo, Philip (1973). Interpersonal Dynamics in a Simulated Prison. *International Journal of Criminology and Penology. Vol. 1.*

Hayduk, Leslie A. (1978). Personal space: An Evaluative and Orienting Overview. *Psychological Bulletin, Vol 85(1).*

Imhof, Maragrete (1998). What Makes a Good Listener? Listening Behavior in Instructional Settings. *International Journal of Listening, v12 p81-105.*

Milgram, Stanley (1963). Behavioral Study of Obedience. *The Journal of Abnormal and Social Psychology, Vol 67(4).*

Myers, David G. (1996). On Professing Psychological Science and Christian Faith. J*ournal of Psychology and Christianity, 15*, 143-149.

Myers, David G. (2008). *Social Psychology*. New York: McGraw Hill.

Petty, Richard E., Wegener, Duane T., and Fabrigar, Leandre R. (1997). Attitudes and Attitude Change. *Annual Review Psychology, 48.*

Rubin, Z., & Peplau, L. A. (1975). Who Believes in a Just World? *Journal of Social Issues, 31(3)*, 65-90. Reprinted (1977) in Reflections, XII(1).

Schaeffer, F. A. (1976). *How Should We Then Live: The Rise and Decline of Western Thought and Culture.* Old Tappan: Revell.

Shannon, Claude E. (1948). A Mathematical Theory of Communication. *Bell System Technical Journal: 27,* 379–423 and 623–656.

Sherif, Muzafer, Harvey, O. J., White, B. Jack, Hood, William R., & Sherif, Carolyn W. (1961). Intergroup Conflict and Cooperation: The Robbers Cave Experiment. Accessed online at http://psychclassics. yorku.ca/Sherif/chap7.htm.

Veitch, Russell and Piccione, Anthony (1978). The Role of Attitude Similarity in the Attribution Process. *Social Psychology Vol 41(2).*

Weiner, Bernard (1972). Attribution Theory, Achievement Motivation, and the Educational Process. *Review of Educational Research. Vol. 42, No. 2.*

Wyer, Robert S. and Srull, Thomas K. (1986). Human Cognition in its Social Context. *Psychological Review, Vol 93(3).*

Chapter 15 – Research Methods

Clark, R. E. D. (1953). The Spheres of Revelation and Science. What Are Their Limitations in Relation to Each Other. *Journal of the American Scientific Affiliation, Vol. 5.* Accessed at http://www.asa3.org/ASA/PSCF/1953/JASA6-53Clark.html on 7/05/11.

Cohen, R. J. & Swerdlik, M. E. (2009). *Psychological Testing and Assessment: An Introduction to Tests and Measurement*. New York: McGraw Hill.

Leedy, P. D. & Ormrod, J. E. (2009). *Practical Research: Planning and Design*. Columbus: Pearson.

Sanderson, W. A. (1978). Christian Empiricism as an Integrating Perspective in Psychology and Theology. *Christian Scholar's Review, (8)*, 32-41.

CPSIA information can be obtained
at www.ICGtesting.com
Printed in the USA
FSHW011718200719
60177FS